Excel® 2007 Data Analysis For Dummies®

Cheat Sheet

S0-AHH-540

Excel Database Functions

Excel provides a set of handy-to-use database functions for making statistical calculations using information from lists, as described in Chapter 8:

Function	Description
DAVERAGE	Calculates arithmetic mean
DCOUNT	Counts the number of cells with values
DCOUNTA	Counts the number of cells that aren't empty
DGET	Returns a value from a database list
DMAX	Finds the largest value in a list
DMIN	Finds the smallest value in a list
DPRODUCT	Calculates the product of values matching criteria
DSTDEV	Calculates the standard deviation of a sample
DSTDEVP	Calculates the standard deviation of a population
DSUM	Calculates the sum of values matching criteria
DVAR	Calculates the variance of a sample
DVARP	Calculates the variance of a population

All these database functions use a standard three-argument syntax. For example, the DAVERAGE function looks like this:

`=DAVERAGE(database, field, criteria)`

where *database* is a range reference to the Excel list that holds the value you want to examine, *field* tells Excel which column in the database to examine, and *criteria* is a range reference that identifies the fields and values used to define your selection criteria. The *field* argument can be a cell reference holding the field name, the field name enclosed in quotation marks, or a number that identifies the column (1 for the first column, 2 for the second column, and so on).

Quick Statistical Measures

To perform some other statistical calculation of the selected range list, right-click the status bar. When you do, Excel displays a pop-up menu that includes several statistical measures that you can make on the selected range.

Statistical Measures Option	What It Does
None	Tells Excel that you don't want it to calculate and then show a statistic on the status bar
Average	Finds the meaning of values in selected range
Count	Tallies the cells that hold labels, values, or formulas. Use this when you want to count the number of cells that aren't empty
Numerical Count	Tallies the number of cells in a selected range that hold values or formulas
Maximum	Finds the largest value in the selected range
Minimum	Finds the smallest value in the selected range
Sum	Adds the values in the selected range

Using Boolean Expressions

To construct a Boolean expression, such as when you filter criteria, use a comparison operator and then a value used in the comparison: (>5, for example).

Comparison Operator	What It Means
=	Equals
>	Greater than
>=	Greater than or equal to
<	Less than
<=	Less than or equal to
<>	Not equal to

For Dummies: Bestselling Book Series for Beginners

Excel® 2007 Data Analysis For Dummies®

Key Statistics Terms

average: Typically, an average is the arithmetic mean for a set of values. Excel supplies several average functions.

chi-square: Use chi-squares to compare observed values with expected values, returning the level of significance, or probability (also called a *p-value*). A p-value helps you to assess whether differences between the observed and expected values represent chance.

cross-tabulation: This is an analysis technique that summarizes data in two or more ways. Summarizing sales information both by customer and product is a cross-tabulation.

descriptive statistics: Descriptive statistics just describe the values in a set. For example, if you sum a set of values, that sum is a descriptive statistic. Finding the biggest value or the smallest value in a set of numbers is also a descriptive statistic.

exponential smoothing: Exponential smoothing calculates the moving average but weights the values included in the moving average calculations so that more recent values have a bigger effect.

inferential statistics: Inferential statistics are based on the very useful, intuitively obvious idea that if you look at a sample of values from a population and if the sample is representative and large enough, you can draw conclusions about the population based on characteristics of the sample.

kurtosis: This is a measure of the tails in a distribution of values.

median: The median is the middle value in a set of values. Half of the values fall below the median, and half of the values fall above the median.

mode: Mode is the most common value in a set.

moving average: A moving average is calculated using only a specified set of values, such as an average based on just the last three values.

normal distribution: Also known as a Gaussian distribution, normal distribution is the infamous bell curve.

p-value: A p-value is the level of significance, or probability.

regression analysis: Regression analysis involves plotting pairs of independent and dependent variables in an XY chart and then finding a linear or exponential equation that best describes the plotted data.

skewness: This is a measure of the symmetry of a distribution of values.

standard deviation: A standard deviation describes dispersion about the data set's mean. You can kind of think of a standard deviation as an *average* deviation from the mean.

variance: A variance describes dispersion about the data set's mean. The variance is the square of the standard deviation; the standard deviation is the square root of the variance.

z-value: This is the distance between a value and the mean in terms of standard deviations.

For Dummies: Bestselling Book Series for Beginners

Microsoft® Office

Excel® 2007
Data Analysis
FOR
DUMMIES®

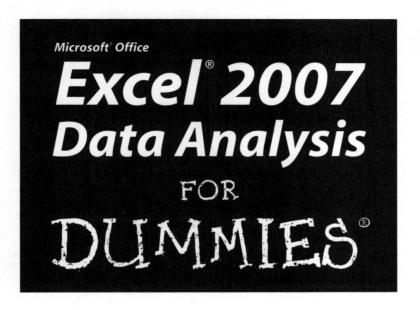

Microsoft® Office

Excel® 2007
Data Analysis
FOR
DUMMIES®

by Stephen L. Nelson

Wiley Publishing, Inc.

Excel® 2007 Data Analysis For Dummies®

Published by
Wiley Publishing, Inc.
111 River Street
Hoboken, NJ 07030-5774
www.wiley.com

For general information on our other products and services, please contact our Customer Care Department within the U.S. at 800-762-2974, outside the U.S. at 317-572-3993, or fax 317-572-4002.

For technical support, please visit www.wiley.com/techsupport.

Wiley also publishes its books in a variety of electronic formats. Some content that appears in print may not be available in electronic books.

Library of Congress Control Number: 2006939598

ISBN: 978-0-470-04599-2

Manufactured in the United States of America

10 9 8 7 6 5 4 3 2 1

WILEY

About the Author

Stephen L. Nelson is the author of more than two dozen best-selling books, including *Quicken For Dummies* and *QuickBooks For Dummies* (Wiley Publishing, Inc.). In fact, Nelson's books have sold more than 4,000,000 copies in English and have been translated into more than ten other languages.

Nelson is a certified public accountant and a member of both the Washington Society of CPAs and the American Institute of CPAs. He holds a Bachelor of Science in Accounting, magna cum laude, from Central Washington University, and a Masters in Business Administration in Finance from the University of Washington (where, curiously, he was the youngest person ever to graduate from the program), and a Master of Science in Taxation from Golden Gate University.

Nelson's work experience includes stints as a book publisher and packager, as the chief financial officer, treasurer, and controller of a high-technology manufacturer, and as a senior consultant with one of the Big Five public accounting firms.

Nelson lives in the foothills east of Redmond, Washington with his wife, two daughters, and an indeterminate number of mice.

Author's Acknowledgments

The curious thing about writing a book is this: Although an author's name appears on the cover, it's always really a team project. Take the case of this book, for example. Truth be told, the book was really the idea of Andy Cummings, the publisher of *For Dummies* technology books, and Bob Woerner, my long-suffering acquisitions editor. I wrote the manuscript, and then a lot of folks at Wiley expended a lot of effort into turning my rough manuscript into a polished book. Nicole Sholly, project editor, Virginia Sanders, copy editor, Michael Talley, technical editor, and a host of page layout technicians, proofreaders, and graphic artists are just some of the people who helped this book come to life.

Publisher's Acknowledgments

We're proud of this book; please send us your comments through our online registration form located at www.dummies.com/register/.

Some of the people who helped bring this book to market include the following:

Acquisitions, Editorial, and Media Development

Project Editor: Nicole Sholly

Senior Acquisitions Editor: Bob Woerner

Copy Editor: Virginia Sanders

Technical Editor: Michael Talley

Editorial Manager: Kevin Kirschner

Media Development Specialists: Angela Denny, Kate Jenkins, Steven Kudirka, Kit Malone

Media Project Supervisors: Laura Moss, Laura Atkinson

Media Development Manager: Laura VanWinkle

Editorial Assistant: Amanda Foxworth

Sr. Editorial Assistant: Cherie Case

Cartoons: Rich Tennant (www.the5thwave.com)

Composition Services

Project Coordinator: Erin Smith

Layout and Graphics: Claudia Bell, Stephanie D. Jumper, Rashell Smith

Proofreaders: Laura Albert, Techbooks

Indexer: Techbooks

Anniversary Logo Design: Richard Pacifico

Special Help: Andy Hollandbeck

Publishing and Editorial for Technology Dummies

    Richard Swadley, Vice President and Executive Group Publisher

    Andy Cummings, Vice President and Publisher

    Mary Bednarek, Executive Acquisitions Director

    Mary C. Corder, Editorial Director

Publishing for Consumer Dummies

    Diane Graves Steele, Vice President and Publisher

    Joyce Pepple, Acquisitions Director

Composition Services

    Gerry Fahey, Vice President of Production Services

    Debbie Stailey, Director of Composition Services

Contents at a Glance

Table of Contents

Introduction

So here's a funny deal: You know how to use Excel. You know how to create simple workbooks and how to print stuff. And you can even, with just a little bit of fiddling, create cool-looking charts.

But I bet that you sometimes wish that you could do more with Excel. You sometimes wish, I wager, that you could use Excel to really gain insights into the information, the data, that you work with in your job.

Using Excel for data analysis is what this book is all about. This book assumes that you want to use Excel to learn new stuff, discover new secrets, and gain new insights into the information that you're already working with in Excel — or the information stored electronically in some other format, such as in your accounting system.

About This Book

This book isn't meant to be read cover to cover like a Dan Brown page-turner. Rather, it's organized into tiny, no-sweat descriptions of how to do the things that must be done. Hop around and read the chapters that interest you.

If you're the sort of person who, perhaps because of a compulsive bent, needs to read a book cover to cover, that's fine. I recommend that you delve in to the chapters on inferential statistics, however, only if you've taken at least a couple of college-level statistics classes. But that caveat aside, feel free. After all, maybe *Lost* is a rerun tonight.

What You Can Safely Ignore

This book provides a lot of information. That's the nature of a how-to reference. So I want to tell you that it's pretty darn safe for you to blow off some chunks of the book.

For example, in many places throughout the book I provide step-by-step descriptions of the task. When I do so, I always start each step with a bold-faced description of what the step entails. Underneath that bold-faced step description, I provide detailed information about what happens after you perform that action. Sometimes I also offer help with the mechanics of the step, like this:

1. **Press Enter.**

   Find the key that's labeled *Enter*. Extend your index finger so that it rests ever so gently on the Enter key. Then, in one sure, fluid motion, press the key by using your index finger. Then release the key.

Okay, that's kind of an extreme example. I never actually go into that much detail. My editor won't let me. But you get the idea. If you know how to press Enter, you can just do that and not read further. If you need help — say with the finger-depression part or the finding-the-right-key part — you can read the nitty-gritty details.

You can also skip the paragraphs flagged with the Technical Stuff icon. These icons flag information that's sort of tangential, sort of esoteric, or sort of questionable in value . . . at least for the average reader. If you're really interested in digging into the meat of the subject being discussed, go ahead and read 'em. If you're really just trying to get through your work so that you can get home and watch TV with your kids, skip 'em.

I might as well also say that you don't have to read the information provided in the paragraphs marked with a Tip icon, either. I assume that you want to know an easier way to do something. But if you like to do things the hard way because that improves your character and makes you tougher, go ahead and skip the Tip icons.

What You Shouldn't Ignore (Unless You're a Masochist)

By the way, don't skip the Warning icons. They're the text flagged with a picture of a 19th century bomb. They describe some things that you really shouldn't do.

Out of respect for you, I don't put stuff in these paragraphs such as, "Don't smoke." I figure that you're an adult. You get to make your own lifestyle decisions.

I reserve these warnings for more urgent and immediate dangers — things that you can but shouldn't do. For example: "Don't smoke while filling your car with gasoline."

Three Foolish Assumptions

I assume just three things about you:

1. You have a PC with Microsoft Excel 2007 installed.
2. You know the basics of working with your PC and Microsoft Windows.
3. You know the basics of working with Excel 2007, including how to start and stop Excel, how to save and open Excel workbooks, and how to enter text and values and formulas into worksheet cells.

How This Book Is Organized

This book is organized into five parts:

Part 1: Where's the Beef?

In Part I, I discuss how you get data into Excel workbooks so that you can begin to analyze it. This is important stuff, but fortunately most of it is pretty straightforward. If you're new to data analysis and not all that fluent yet in working with Excel, you definitely want to begin in Part I.

Part 11: PivotTables and PivotCharts

In the second part of this book, I cover what are perhaps the most powerful data analysis tools that Excel provides: its cross-tabulation capabilities using the PivotTable and PivotChart commands.

No kidding, I don't think any Excel data analysis skill is more useful than knowing how to create pivot tables and pivot charts. If I could, I would give you some sort of guarantee that the time you spent reading how to use these tools is always worth the investment you make. Unfortunately, after consultation with my attorney, I find that this is impossible to do.

Part III: Advanced Tools

In Part III, I discuss some of the more sophisticated tools that Excel supplies for doing data analysis. Some of these tools are always available in Excel, such as the statistical functions. (I use a couple of chapters to cover these.) Some of the tools come in the form of Excel add-ins, such as the Data Analysis and the Solver add-ins.

I don't think that these tools are going to be of interest to most readers of this book. But if you already know how to do all the basic stuff and you have some good statistical and quantitative methods, training, or experience, you ought to peruse these chapters. Some really useful whistles and bells are available to advanced users of Excel. And it would be a shame if you didn't at least know what they are and the basic steps that you need to take to use them.

Part IV: The Part of Tens

In my mind, perhaps the most clever element that Dan Gookin, the author of the original and first Dummies book, _DOS For Dummies,_ came up with is the part with chapters that just list information in David Letterman-ish fashion. These chapters let us authors list useful tidbits, tips, and factoids for you.

Excel 2007 Data Analysis For Dummies includes three such chapters. In the first, I provide some basic facts most everybody should know about statistics and statistical analysis. In the second, I suggest ten tips for successfully and effectively analyzing data in Excel. Finally, in the third chapter, I try to make some useful suggestions about how you can visually analyze information and visually present data analysis results.

The Part of Tens chapters aren't technical. They aren't complicated. They're very basic. You should be able to skim the information provided in these chapters and come away with at least a few nuggets of useful information.

Part V: Appendix

The appendix contains a handy glossary of terms you should understand when working with data in general and Excel specifically. From _kurtosis_ to _histograms,_ these sometimes baffling terms are defined here.

Special Icons

Like other *For Dummies* books, this book uses icons, or little margin pictures, to flag things that don't quite fit into the flow of the chapter discussion. Here are the icons that I use:

Technical Stuff: This icon points out some dirty technical details that you might want to skip.

Tip: This icon points out a shortcut to make your life easier or more fulfilling.

Remember: This icon points out things that you should, well, remember.

Warning: This icon is a friendly but forceful reminder not to do something . . . or else.

Where to Next?

If you're just getting started with Excel data analysis, flip the page and start reading the first chapter.

If you have a bit of skill with Excel or you have a special problem or question, use the Table of Contents or the index to find out where I cover a topic and then turn to that page.

Good luck! Have fun!

Part I
Where's the Beef?

The 5th Wave   By Rich Tennant

"I started running 'what if' scenarios on my spreadsheet, like, 'What if I were sick of this dirtwad job and funneled some of the company's money into an off—shore account?'"

In this part . . .

In Part I, I talk about how you get data into Excel workbooks so that you can begin to analyze it. This is
important stuff, but fortunately, most of it is pretty
straightforward. Read here to discover what makes an
Excel table, how to get data from external sources, and
how to clean your data.

Chapter 1

Introducing Excel Tables

*F*irst things first. I need to start my discussion of using Excel for data analysis by introducing Excel tables, or what Excel used to call *lists*. Why? Because, except in the simplest of situations, when you want to analyze data with Excel, you want that data stored in a table. In this chapter, I discuss what defines an Excel table; how to build, analyze, and sort a table; and why using filters to create a subtable is useful.

What Is a Table and Why Do I Care?

A table is, well, a list. This definition sounds simplistic, I guess. But take a look at the simple table shown in Figure 1-1. This table shows the items that you might shop for at a grocery store on the way home from work.

As I mention in the introduction of this book, many of the Excel workbooks that you see in the figures of this book are available in a compressed Zip file available at the Dummies Web site. You can download this Zip file from www. dummies.com/go/e2007dafd.

Commonly, tables include more information than Figure 1-1 shows. For example, take a look at the table shown in Figure 1-2. In column A, for example, the table names the store where you might purchase the item. In column C, this expanded table gives the quantity of some item that you need. In column D, this table provides a rough estimate of the price.

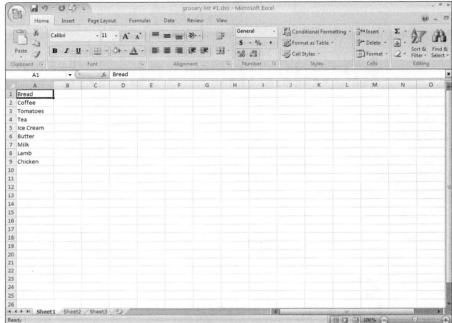

Figure 1-1:
A table: Start out with the basics.

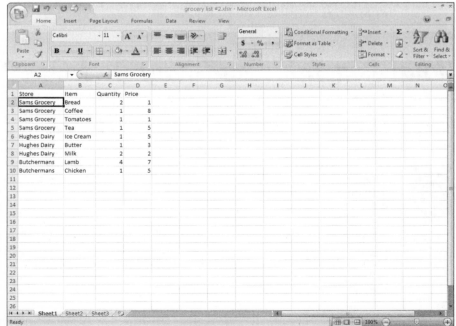

Figure 1-2:
A grocery list for the more serious shopper . . . like me.

Something to understand about Excel tables

An Excel table is a *flat-file database*. That flat-file-ish-ness means that there's only one table in the database. And the flat-file-ish-ness also means that each record stores every bit of information about an item.

In comparison, popular desktop database applications such as Microsoft Access are *relational databases*. A relational database stores information more efficiently. And the most striking way in which this efficiency appears is that you don't see lots of duplicated or redundant information in a relational database. In a relational database, for example, you might not see

Sams Grocery appearing in cells A2, A3, A4, and A5. A relational database might eliminate this redundancy by having a separate table of grocery stores.

This point might seem a bit esoteric; however, you might find it handy when you want to grab data from a relational database (where the information is efficiently stored in separate tables) and then combine all this data into a super-sized flat-file database in the form of an Excel list. In Chapter 2, I discuss how to grab data from external databases.

An Excel table usually looks more like the list shown in Figure 1-2. Typically, the table enumerates rather detailed descriptions of numerous items. But a table in Excel, after you strip away all the details, essentially resembles the expanded grocery-shopping list shown in Figure 1-2.

Let me make a handful of observations about the table shown in Figure 1-2. First, each column shows a particular sort of information. In the parlance of database design, each *column* represents a field. Each *field* stores the same sort of information. Column A, for example, shows the store where some item can be purchased. (You might also say that this is the Store field.) Each piece of information shown in column A — the Store field — names a store: Sams Grocery, Hughes Dairy, and Butchermans.

The first row in the Excel worksheet provides field names. For example, in Figure 1-2, row 1 names the four fields that make up the list: Store, Item, Quantity, and Price. You always use the first row, called the *header row,* of an Excel list to name, or identify, the fields in the list.

Starting in row 2, each row represents a record, or item, in the table. A *record* is a collection of related fields. For example, the record in row 2 in Figure 1-2 shows that at Sams Grocery, you plan to buy two loaves of bread for a price of $1 each. (Bear with me if these sample prices are wildly off; I usually don't do the shopping in my household.)

Row 3 shows or describes another item, coffee, also at Sams Grocery, for $8. In the same way, the other rows of the super-sized grocery list show items that you will buy. For each item, the table identifies the store, the item, the quantity, and the price.

Building Tables

You build a table that you want to later analyze by using Excel in one of two ways:

- ✔ Export the table from a database.
- ✔ Manually enter items into an Excel workbook.

Exporting from a database

The usual way to create a table to use in Excel is to export information from a database. Exporting information from a database isn't tricky. However, you need to reflect a bit on the fact that the information stored in your database is probably organized into many separate tables that need to be combined into a large flat-file database or table.

In Chapter 2, I describe the process of exporting data from the database and then importing this data into Excel so it can be analyzed. Hop over to that chapter for more on creating a table by exporting and then importing.

Even if you plan to create your tables by exporting data from a database, however, read on through the next paragraphs of this chapter. Understanding the nuts and bolts of building a table makes exporting database information to a table and later using that information easier.

Building a table the hard way

The other common way to create an Excel table (besides exporting from a relational database) is to do it manually. For example, you can create a table in the same way that I create the grocery list shown in Figure 1-2. You first enter field names into the first row of the worksheet and then enter individual records, or items, into the subsequent rows of the worksheet. When a table isn't too big, this method is very workable. This is the way, obviously, that I created the table shown in Figure 1-2.

Building a table the semi-hard way

To create a table manually, what you typically want to do is enter the field names into row 1, select those field names and the empty cells of row 2, and then choose Insert⇨Table. Why? The Table command tells Excel, right from the get-go, that you're building a table. But let me show you how this process works.

Manually adding records into a table

To manually create a list by using the Table command, follow these steps:

1. **Identify the fields in your list.**

   To identify the fields in your list, enter the field names into row 1 in a blank Excel workbook. For example, Figure 1-3 shows a workbook fragment. Cells A1, B1, C1, and D1 hold field names for a simple grocery list.

2. **Select the Excel table.**

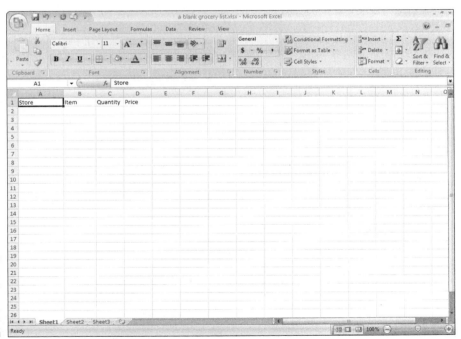

Figure 1-3:
The start of something important.

The Excel table must include the row of the field names and at least one other row. This row might be blank or it might contain data. In Figure 1-3, for example, you can select an Excel list by dragging the mouse from cell A1 to cell D2.

3. **Choose Insert⇨Table to tell Excel that you want to get all official right from the start.**

   If Excel can't figure out which row holds your field names, Excel displays the dialog box shown in Figure 1-4. Essentially, this dialog box just lets you confirm that the first row in your range selection holds the field names. To accept Excel's guess about your table, click OK. Excel re-displays the worksheet set up as a table, as shown in Figure 1-5.

Figure 1-4: Excel tries to figure out what you're doing.

Figure 1-5: Enter your table rows into nicely colored rows.

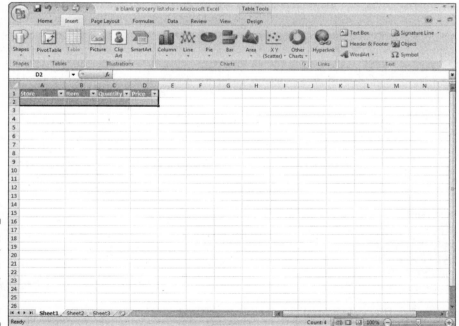

4. **Describe each record.**

To enter a new record into your table, fill in the next empty row. For example, use the Store text box to identify the store where you purchase each item. Use the — oh, wait a minute here. You don't need me to tell you that the store name goes into the Store column, do you? You can figure that out. Likewise, you already know what bits of information go into the Item, Quantity, and Price column, too, don't you? Okay. Sorry.

5. **Store your record in the table.**

Click the Tab or Enter button when you finish describing some record or item that goes onto the shopping list. Excel adds another row to the table so that you can add another item. Excel shows you which rows and columns are part of the table by using color.

Previous versions of Excel included a Data⇨Form command, which was another way to enter records into an Excel table. When you chose the Data⇨Form command, Excel displayed a cute, little, largely useless dialog box that collected the bits of record information and then entered them into the table.

Some table-building tools

Excel includes an AutoFill feature, which is particularly relevant for table building. Here's how AutoFill works: Enter a label into a cell in a column where it's already been entered before, and Excel guesses that you're entering the same thing again. For example, if you enter the label **Sams Grocery** in cell A2 and then begin to type **Sams Grocery** in cell A3, Excel guesses that you're entering **Sams Grocery** again and finishes typing the label for you. All you need to do to accept Excel's guess is press Enter. Check it out in Figure 1-6.

Excel also provides a Fill command that you can use to fill a range of cells — including the contents of a column in an Excel table — with a label or value. To fill a range of cells with the value that you've already entered in another cell, you drag the Fill Handle down the column. The Fill Handle is the small plus sign (+) that appears when you place the mouse cursor over the lower-right corner of the active cell. In Figure 1-7, I use the Fill Handle to enter **Sams Grocery** into the range A5:A12.

Analyzing Table Information

Excel provides several handy, easy-to-use tools for analyzing the information that you store in a table. Some of these tools are so easy and straightforward that they provide a good starting point.

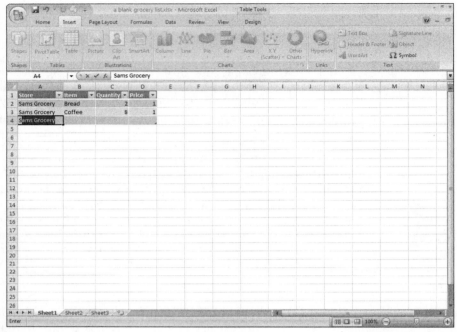

Figure 1-6:
A little
workbook
fragment,
compliments
of AutoFill.

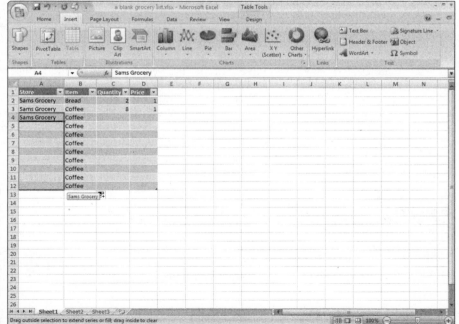

Figure 1-7:
Another
little
workbook
fragment,
compliments
of the Fill
Handle.

Simple statistics

Look again at the simple grocery list table that I mention earlier in the section, "What Is a Table and Why Do I Care?" See Figure 1-8 for this grocery list as I use this information to demonstrate some of the quick-and-dirty statistical tools that Excel provides.

One of the slickest and quickest tools that Excel provides is the ability to effortlessly calculate the sum, average, count, minimum, and maximum of values in a selected range. For example, if you select the range C2 to C10 in Figure 1-8, Excel calculates an average, counts the values, and even sums the quantities, displaying this useful information in the status bar. In Figure 1-8, note the information on the status bar (the lower edge of the workbook):

```
Average: 1.555555556    Count: 9    Sum: 14
```

This indicates that the average order quantity is (roughly) 1.5, that you're shopping for 9 different items, and that the grocery list includes 14 items: Two loaves of bread, one can of coffee, one tomato, one box of tea, and so on.

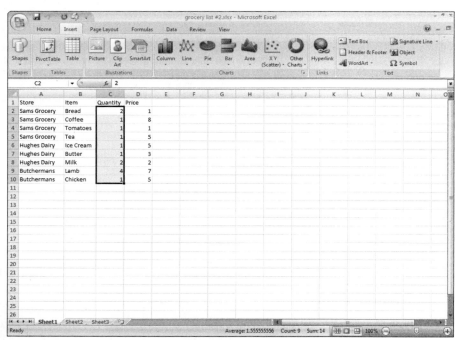

Figure 1-8: Start at the beginning.

The big question here, of course, is whether, with 9 different products but a total count of 14 items, you'll be able to go through the express checkout line. But that information is irrelevant to our discussion. (You, however, might want to acquire another book I'm planning, *Grocery Shopping For Dummies*.)

You aren't limited, however, to simply calculating averages, counting entries, and summing values in your list. You can also calculate other statistical measures.

To perform some other statistical calculation of the selected range list, right-click the status bar. When you do, Excel displays a pop-up Status Bar Configuration menu. Near the bottom of that menu bar, Excel provides six statistical measures that you can add to or remove from the Status Bar: Average, Count, Count Numerical, Maximum, Minimum, and Sum. In Table 1-1, I describe each of these statistical measures briefly, but you can probably guess what they do. Note that if a statistical measure is displayed on the Status Bar, Excel places a check mark in front of the measure on the Status Bar Confirmation menu. To remove the statistical measure, select the measure.

Table 1-1	Quick Statistical Measures Available on the Status Bar
Option	*What It Does*
Count	Tallies the cells that hold labels, values, or formulas. In other words, use this statistical measure when you want to count the number of cells that are *not* empty.
Count Numerical	Tallies the number of cells in a selected range that hold values or formulas.
Maximum	Finds the largest value in the selected range.
Minimum	Finds the smallest value in the selected range.
Sum	Adds up the values in the selected range.

No kidding, these simple statistical measures are often all you need to gain wonderful insights into data that you collect and store in an Excel table. By using the example of a simple, artificial grocery list, the power of these quick statistical measures doesn't seem all that earthshaking. But with real data, these measures often produce wonderful insights.

In my own work as a writer, for example, I first noticed the slowdown in the computer book publishing industry that followed the dot.com meltdown when the total number of books that one of the larger distributors sold — information that appeared in an Excel table — began dropping. Sometimes, simply adding, counting, or averaging the values in a table gives extremely useful insights.

Sorting table records

After you place information in an Excel table, you'll find it very easy to sort the records. You can use the Sort A to Z button, the Sort Z to A button, or the Sort dialog box.

Using the Sort buttons

To sort table information by using a Sort buttons, click in the column you want to use for your sorting. For example, to sort a grocery list like the one shown in Figure 1-8 by the store, click a cell in the Store column.

After you select the column you want to use for your sorting, click the Sort A to Z button to sort table records in ascending, A-to-Z order using the selected column's information. Alternatively, click the Sort Z to A button to sort table records in descending, Z-to-A order using the selected column's information.

Using the Sort dialog box

When you can't sort table information exactly the way you want by using the Sort A to Z and Sort Z to A buttons, use the Sort dialog box.

To use the Sort dialog box, follow these steps:

1. **Click a cell inside the table.**

2. **Choose the Data⇨Sort command.**

    Excel displays the Sort dialog box, as shown in Figure 1-9.

Figure 1-9:
Set sort parameters here.

3. **Select the first sort key.**

   Use the Sort By drop-down list to select the field that you want to use for sorting. Next, choose what you want to use for sorting: values, cell colors, font colors, or icons. Probably, you're going to sort by values, in which case, you'll also need to indicate whether you want records arranged in ascending or descending order by selecting either the ascending A to Z or descending Z to A entry from the Order box. Ascending order, predictably, alphabetizes labels and arranges values in smallest-value-to-largest-value order. Descending order arranges labels in reverse alphabetical order and values in largest-value-to-smallest-value order. If you sort by color or icons, you need to tell Excel how it should sort the colors by using the options that the Order box provides.

   Typically, you want the key to work in ascending or descending order. However, you might want to sort records by using a chronological sequence, such as Sunday, Monday, Tuesday, and so on, or January, February, March, and so forth. To use one of these other sorting options, select the custom list option from the Order box and then choose one of these other ordering methods from the dialog box that Excel displays.

4. **(Optional) Specify any secondary keys.**

   If you want to sort records that have the same primary key with a secondary key, click the Add Level button and then use the next row of choices from the Then By drop-down lists to specify which secondary keys you want to use. If you add a level that you later decide you don't want or need, click the sort level and then click the Delete Level button. You can also duplicate the selected level by clicking Copy Level. Finally, if you do create multiple sorting keys, you can move the selected sort level up or down in significance by clicking the Move Up or Move Down buttons.

   Note: The Sort dialog box also provides a My Data Has Headers check box that enables you to indicate whether the worksheet range selection includes the row and field names. If you've already told Excel that a worksheet range is a table, however, this check box is disabled.

5. **(Really optional) Fiddle-faddle with the sorting rules.**

   If you click the Options button in the Sort dialog box, Excel displays the Sort Options dialog box, shown in Figure 1-10. Make choices here to further specify how the first key sort order works.

Figure 1-10:
Sorting out your sorting options.

For a start, the Sort Options dialog box enables you to indicate whether case sensitivity (uppercase versus lowercase) should be considered.

You can also use the Sort Options dialog box to tell Excel that it should sort rows instead of columns or columns instead of rows. You make this specification by using either Orientation radio button: Sort Top to Bottom or Sort Left to Right. Click OK when you've sorted out your sorting options.

6. Click OK.

Excel then sorts your list.

Using AutoFilter on a table

Excel provides an AutoFilter command that's pretty cool. When you use AutoFilter, you produce a new table that includes a subset of the records from your original table. For example, in the case of a grocery list table, you could use AutoFilter to create a subset that shows only those items that you'll purchase at Butchermans or a subset table that shows only those items that cost more than, say, $2.

To use AutoFilter on a table, take these steps:

1. Select your table.

Select your table by clicking one of its cells. By the way, if you haven't yet turned the worksheet range holding the table data into an "official" Excel table, select the table and then choose the Insert⇨Table command.

2. (Perhaps unnecessary) Choose the AutoFilter command.

When you tell Excel that a particular worksheet range represents a table, Excel turns the header row, or row of field names, into drop-down lists. Figure 1-11 shows this. If your table doesn't include these drop-down lists, add them by choosing Data⇨Filter. Excel turns the header row, or row of field names, into drop-down lists.

3. Use the drop-down lists to filter the list.

Each of the drop-down lists that now make up the header row can be used to filter the list.

Drop-down list boxes appear when you turn on AutoFiltering.

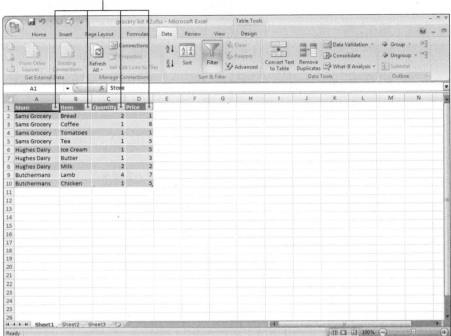

To filter the list by using the contents of some field, select (or open) the drop-down list for that field. For example, in the case of the little workbook shown in Figure 1-11, you might choose to filter the grocery list so that it shows only those items that you'll purchase at Sams Grocery. To do this, click the Store drop-down list down-arrow button. When you do, Excel displays a menu of table sorting and filtering options. To see just those records that describe items you've purchased at Sams Grocery, select Sams Grocery. Figure 1-12 shows the filtered list with just the Sams Grocery items visible.

If your eyes work better than mine do, you might even be able to see a little picture of a funnel on the Store column's drop-down list button. This icon tells you the table is filtered using the Store columns data.

To unfilter the table, open the Store drop-down list and choose Select All.

If you're filtering a table using the table menu, you can also sort the table's records by using table menu commands. Sort A to Z sorts the records (filtered or not) in ascending order. Sort Z to A sorts the records (again, filtered or not) in descending order. Sort by Color lets you sort according to cell colors.

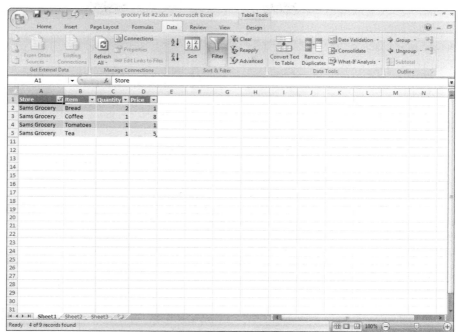

Figure 1-12:
Sams and
Sams alone.

Undoing a filter

To remove an AutoFilter, display the table menu by clicking a drop-down list's button. Then choose the Clear Filter command from the table menu.

Turning off filter

The Data➪Filter command is actually a toggle switch. When filtering is turned on, Excel turns the header row of the table into a row of drop-down lists. When you turn off filtering, Excel removes the drop-down list functionality. To turn off filtering and remove the Filter drop-down lists, simply choose Data➪Filter.

Using the custom AutoFilter

You can also construct a custom AutoFilter. To do this, select the Text Filter command from the table menu and choose one of its text filtering options. No matter which text filtering option you pick, Excel displays the Custom AutoFilter dialog box, as shown in Figure 1-13. This dialog box enables you to specify with great precision what records you want to appear on your filtered list.

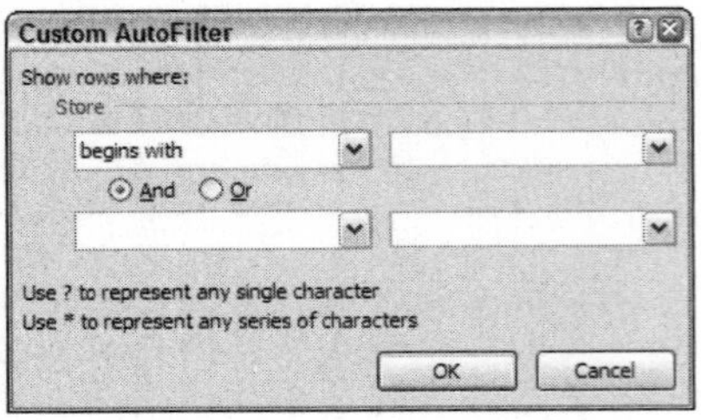

Figure 1-13:
The Custom
AutoFilter
dialog box.

To create a custom AutoFilter, take the following steps:

1. **Turn on the Excel Filters.**

   As I mention earlier in this section, filtering is probably already on because you've created a table. However, if filtering isn't turned on, select the table and then choose Data⇨Filter.

2. **Select the field that you want to use for your custom AutoFilter.**

   To indicate which field you want to use, open the filtering drop-down list for that field to display the table menu, select Text Filters, and then select a filtering option. When you do this, Excel displays the Custom AutoFilter dialog box. (Refer to Figure 1-13.)

3. **Describe the AutoFilter operation.**

   To describe your AutoFilter, you need to identify (or confirm) the filtering operation and the filter criteria. Use the left-side set of drop-down lists to select a filtering option. For example, in Figure 1-15, the filtering option selected in the first Custom AutoFilter set of dialog boxes is Begins With. If you open this drop-down list, you'll see that Excel provides a series of filtering options:

   - Begins With
   - Equals
   - Does Not Equal
   - Is Greater Than or Equal To
   - Is Less Than
   - Is Less Than or Equal To
   - Begins With
   - Does Not Begin With
   - Ends With
   - Does Not End With
   - Contains
   - Does Not Contain

The key thing to be aware of is that you want to pick a filtering operation that, in conjunction with your filtering criteria, enables you to identify the records that you want to appear in your filtered list. Note that Excel initially fills in the filtering option that matches the command you selected on the Text Filter submenu, but you can change this initial filtering selection to something else.

In practice, you won't want to use precise filtering criteria. Why? Well, because your list data will probably be pretty dirty. For example, the names of stores might not match perfectly because of misspellings. For this reason, you'll find filtering operations based on Begins With or Contains and filtering criteria that use fragments of field names or ranges of values most valuable.

4. Describe the AutoFilter filtering criteria.

After you pick the filtering option, you describe the filtering criteria by using the right-hand drop-down list. For example, if you want to filter records that equal *Sams Grocery* or, more practically, that begin with the word *Sams*, you enter **Sams** into the right-hand box. Figure 1-14 shows this custom AutoFilter criterion.

You can use more than one AutoFilter criterion. If you want to use two custom AutoFilter criteria, you need to indicate whether the criteria are both applied together or are applied independently. You select either the And or Or radio button to make this specification.

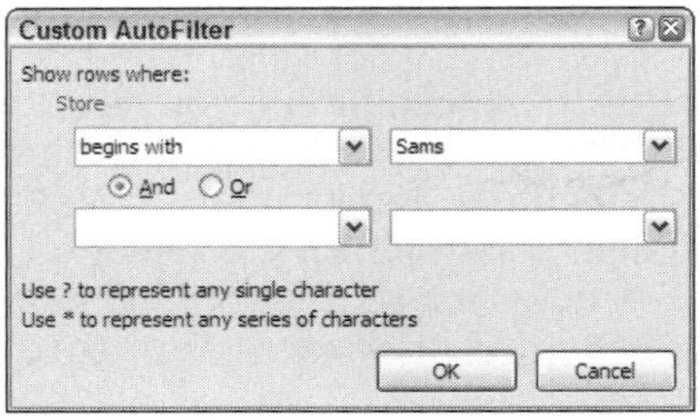

Figure 1-14:
Setting up a custom AutoFilter.

5. **Click OK.**

Excel then filters your table according to your custom AutoFilter.

Filtering a filtered table

You can filter a filtered table. What this often means is that if you want to build a highly filtered table, you will find your work easiest if you just apply several sets of filters.

If you want to filter the grocery list to show only the most expensive items that you purchase at Sams Grocery, for example, you might first filter the table to show items from Sams Grocery only. Then, working with this filtered table, you would further filter the table to show the most expensive items or only those items with the price exceeding some specified amount.

The idea of filtering a filtered table seems, perhaps, esoteric. But applying several sets of filters often reduces a very large and nearly incomprehensible table to a smaller subset of data that provides just the information that you need.

Building on the earlier section "Using the custom AutoFilter," I want to make this important point: Although the Custom AutoFilter dialog box does enable you to filter a list based on two criteria, sometimes filtering operations apply to the same field. And if you need to apply more than two filtering operations to the same field, the only way to easily do this is to filter a filtered table.

Using advanced filtering

Most of the time, you'll be able to filter table records in the ways that you need by using the Data➪Filter command or that unnamed table menu of filtering options. However, in some cases, you might want to exert more control over the way filtering works. When this is the case, you can use the Excel advanced filters.

Writing Boolean expressions

Before you can begin to use the Excel advanced filters, you need to know how to construct Boolean logic expressions. For example, if you want to filter the grocery list table so that it shows only those items that cost more than $1 or those items with an extended price of more than $5, you need to know how to write a Boolean logic, or algebraic, expression that describes the condition in which the price exceeds $1 or the extended price exceeds or equals $5.

See Figure 1-15 for an example of how you specify these Boolean logic expressions in Excel. In Figure 1-15, the range A13:B14 describes two criteria: one in which price exceeds $1, and one in which the extended price equals or exceeds $5. The way this works, as you may guess, is that you need to use the first row of the range to name the fields that you use in your expression. After you do this, you use the rows beneath the field names to specify what logical comparison needs to be made using the field.

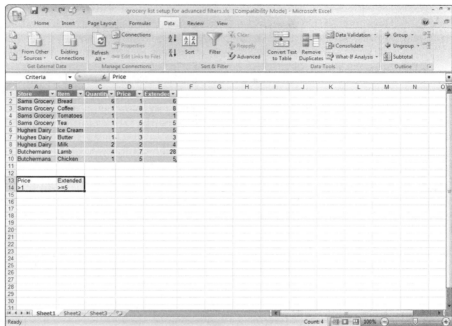

Figure 1-15:
A table set
up for
advanced
filters.

To construct a Boolean expression, you use a comparison operator from Table 1-2 and then a value used in the comparison.

Table 1-2	Boolean Logic
Operator	*What It Does*
=	Equals
<	Is less than
<=	Is less than or equal to
>	Is greater than
>=	Is greater than or equal to
<>	Is not equal to

In Figure 1-15, for example, the Boolean expression in cell A14 (>1), checks to see whether a value is greater than 1, and the Boolean expression in cell B14 (>=5) checks to see whether the value is greater than or equal to 5. Any record that meets *both* of these tests gets included by the filtering operation.

Here's an important point: Any record in the table that meets the criteria in *any* one of the criteria rows gets included in the filtered table. Accordingly, if you want to include records for items that *either* cost more than $1 apiece *or* that totaled at least $5 in shopping expense (after multiplying the quantity times the unit price), you use two rows — one for each criterion. Figure 1-16 shows how you would create a worksheet that does this.

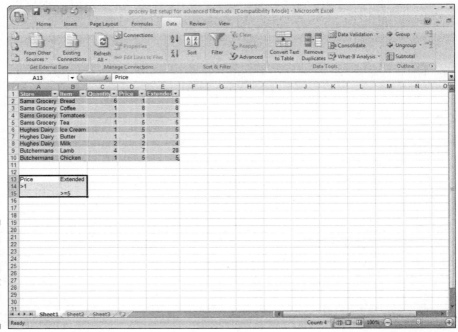

Figure 1-16:
A work-sheet with items that meet both criteria.

Running an advanced filter operation

After you set up a table for an advanced filter and the criteria range — what I did in Figure 1-17 — you're ready to run the advanced filter operation. To do so, take these steps:

1. **Select the table.**

   To select the table, drag the mouse from the top-left corner of the list to the lower-right corner. You can also select an Excel table by selecting the cell in the top-left corner, holding down the Shift key, pressing the End key, pressing the right arrow, pressing the End key, and pressing the down arrow. This technique selects the Excel table range using the arrow keys.

2. **Choose Data⇨Advanced Filter.**

   Excel displays the Advanced Filter dialog box, as shown in Figure 1-17.

Figure 1-17:
Set up an
advanced
filter here.

3. **Tell Excel where to place the filtered table.**

   Use either Action radio button to specify whether you want the table filtered in place or copied to some new location. You can either filter the table in place (meaning Excel just hides the records in the table that don't meet the filtering criteria), or you can copy the records that meet the filtering criteria to a new location.

4. **Verify the list range.**

   The worksheet range shown in the List Range text box — $A$1:$E$10 in Figure 1-17 — should correctly identify the list. If your text box doesn't show the correct worksheet range, however, enter it. (Remember how I said earlier in the chapter that Excel used to call these tables "lists"? Hence the name of this box.)

5. **Provide the criteria range.**

   Make an entry in the Criteria Range text box to identify the worksheet range holding the advanced filter criteria. In Figure 1-17, the criteria range is $A$13:$B$15.

6. **(Optional) If you're copying the filtering results, provide the destination.**

   If you tell Excel to copy the filter results to some new location, use the Copy To text box to identify this location.

7. **Click OK.**

   Excel filters your list . . . I mean table.

And that's that. Not too bad, eh? Advanced filtering is pretty straightforward. All you really do is write some Boolean logic expressions and then tell Excel to filter your table using those expressions.

Chapter 2

Grabbing Data from External Sources

*I*n many cases, the data that you want to analyze with Excel resides in an external database or in a database application, such as a corporate accounting system. Thus, often your very first step and very first true challenge are to get that data into an Excel workbook and in the form of an Excel table.

You can use two basic approaches to grab the external data that you want to analyze. You can export data from another program and then import that data into Excel, or you can query a database directly from Excel. I describe both approaches in this chapter.

Getting Data the Export-Import Way

You can usually easily export data from popular database programs and accounting systems. Excel is the dominant data analysis tool available to business. Because of this, most database programs and most management information systems export data in a format that makes it simple to import the data into Excel later.

Exporting: The first step

Your first step when grabbing data from one of these external sources, assuming that you want to later import the data, is to first use the other application program — such as an accounting program — to export the to-be-analyzed data to a file.

You have two basic approaches available for exporting data from another application: direct exporting and exporting to a text file.

Direct exporting

Direct exporting is available in many accounting programs because accountants love to use Excel to analyze data. For example, the most popular small business accounting program in the world is QuickBooks from Intuit. When you produce an accounting report in QuickBooks, the report document window includes a button labeled *Excel* or *Export*. Click this button, and QuickBooks displays the Export Report dialog box, as shown in Figure 2-1.

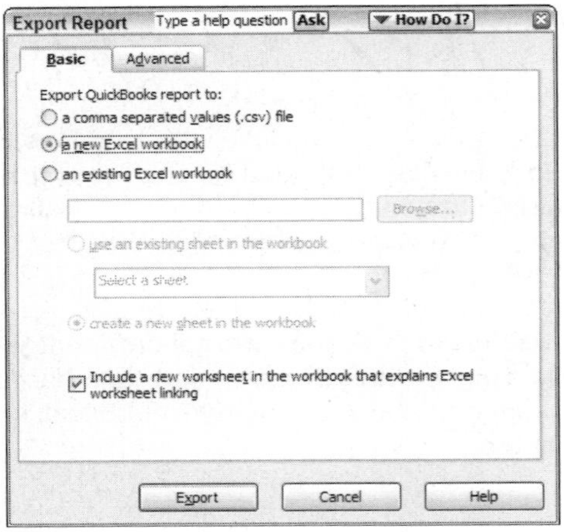

Figure 2-1:
Begin
exporting
here.

The Export Report dialog box provides radio buttons with which you indicate whether you want to send the report to a comma-separated-values file, to a new Excel spreadsheet, or to an existing Excel spreadsheet. To send (*export*) the report to an existing Excel spreadsheet, you need to identify that workbook by entering the workbook pathname and filename into the text box provided. Or, click the Browse button and use the Open Microsoft Excel File dialog box that appears (as shown in Figure 2-2) to identify the folder and workbook file.

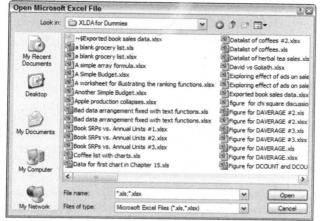

Figure 2-2:
Find the file
to be
exported
here.

In Figure 2-3, you can see how the QuickBooks report looks after it has been
directly exported to Excel.

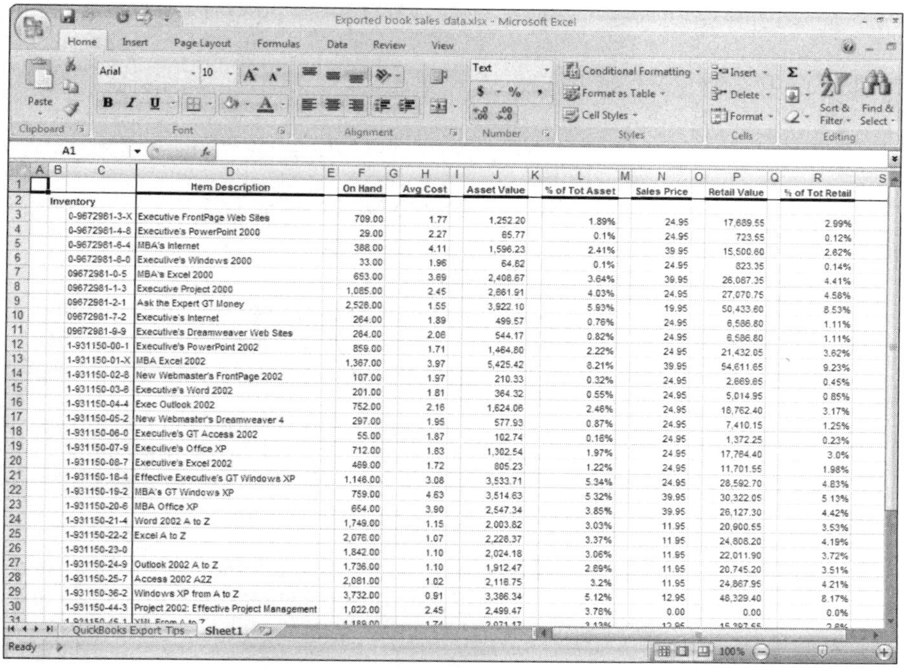

Figure 2-3:
A
QuickBooks
report that
has been
directly
exported to
Excel.

In this example using QuickBooks, the Export Report dialog box also includes an Advanced tab. Click this tab, and QuickBooks displays options which you can use to control how the exported report looks. For example, you get to pick which fonts, colors, spacing, and row height that you want. You also get to turn on and turn off Excel features in the newly created workbook, including AutoFit, Gridline, and so on.

Okay, obviously, you might not want to export from QuickBooks. You might have other applications that you want to export data from. You can export data directly from a database program like Microsoft Access, for example. But the key thing that you need to know — and the reason that I discuss in detail how QuickBooks works — is that applications that store and collect data often provide a convenient way for you to export information to Excel. Predictably, some application programs work differently, but usually, the process is little more than clicking a button labeled *Excel* (as is the case in QuickBooks) or choosing a command labeled something like *Export* or *Export to Excel*.

Therefore, when exporting data from some other program, your first step is to do a little bit of digging and research to see whether there's a way to easily and automatically export data to Excel. This fact-finding shouldn't take much time if you use the online Help system.

Versions of Microsoft Access up through and including Access 2003 include an Export command on the File menu, and Access 2007 includes an Export command on its Microsoft Office menu. Choose the Export command to export an Access table, report, or query to Excel. Just choose the appropriate command and then use the dialog box that Access displays to specify where the exported information should be placed.

Exporting to a text file

When you need to export data first to a text file because the other application won't automatically export your data to an Excel workbook, you need to go to a little more effort. Fortunately, the process is still pretty darn straightforward.

When you work with applications that won't automatically create an Excel workbook, you just create a text version of a report that shows the data that you want to analyze. For example, to analyze sales of items that your firm makes, you first create a report that shows this.

The trick is that you send the report to a text file rather than sending this report to a printer. This way, the report gets stored on disk as text rather than printed. Later, Excel can easily import these text files.

See how this works in more concrete terms by following how the process works in QuickBooks. Suppose, for the sake of illustration, that you really did want to print a list of items that you sell. The first step is to produce a report that shows this list. In QuickBooks, you produce this report by choosing the appropriate command from the Reports menu. Figure 2-4 shows such a report.

Type	Date	Num	Memo	Name	Item	Qty	Sales Price	Amount	Balance
Castle Rock Coffee House									
Invoice	07/26/2006	4	Red Mugs	Castle Rock Coffe...	Red mugs	100	5.00	500.00	500.00
Invoice	07/26/2006	4	Rainbow Mu...	Castle Rock Coffe...	Rainbow...	100	2.75	275.00	775.00
Invoice	07/26/2006	4	Yellow Mugs	Castle Rock Coffe...	Yellow ...	100	2.45	245.00	1,020.00
Invoice	08/25/2007	6	Blue Mugs	Castle Rock Coffe...	Blue mugs	50	5.00	250.00	1,270.00
Invoice	08/25/2007	6	Yellow Mugs	Castle Rock Coffe...	Yellow ...	25	3.25	81.25	1,351.25
Invoice	08/25/2007	6	Preferred Cu...	Castle Rock Coffe...	Discount		-25.0%	-82.81	1,268.44
Invoice	10/31/2007	2	Red Mugs	Castle Rock Coffe...	Red mugs	250	3.25	812.50	2,080.94
Credit Memo	10/31/2007	3	Red Mugs	Castle Rock Coffe...	Red mugs	-27	3.25	-87.75	1,993.19
Invoice	11/26/2007	5	Red Mugs	Castle Rock Coffe...	Red mugs	100	5.00	500.00	2,493.19
Invoice	11/26/2007	5	Rainbow Mu...	Castle Rock Coffe...	Rainbow...	100	2.75	275.00	2,768.19
Invoice	11/26/2007	5	Yellow Mugs	Castle Rock Coffe...	Yellow ...	100	2.45	245.00	3,013.19
Total Castle Rock Coffee House								3,013.19	3,013.19
Rainy Day Collectibles									
Sales Receipt	07/26/2007	1	Red Mugs	Rainy Day Collectib...	Red mugs	2,500	3.50	8,750.00	8,750.00
Invoice	10/31/2007	7	Redesign of...	Rainy Day Collectib...	Design	5	150.00	750.00	9,500.00
Invoice	10/31/2007	7	Design meet...	Rainy Day Collectib...	Design	4	150.00	600.00	10,100.00
Invoice	10/31/2007	7	Studio proto...	Rainy Day Collectib...	Design	4	150.00	600.00	10,700.00
Invoice	10/31/2007	7	Studio proto...	Rainy Day Collectib...	Design	8	150.00	1,200.00	11,900.00
Invoice	10/31/2007	7	Review new...	Rainy Day Collectib...	Design	2	150.00	300.00	12,200.00
Credit Memo	10/31/2007	8		Rainy Day Collectib...	Design	-10	75.00	-750.00	11,450.00
Total Rainy Day Collectibles								11,450.00	11,450.00
TOTAL								14,463.19	14,463.19

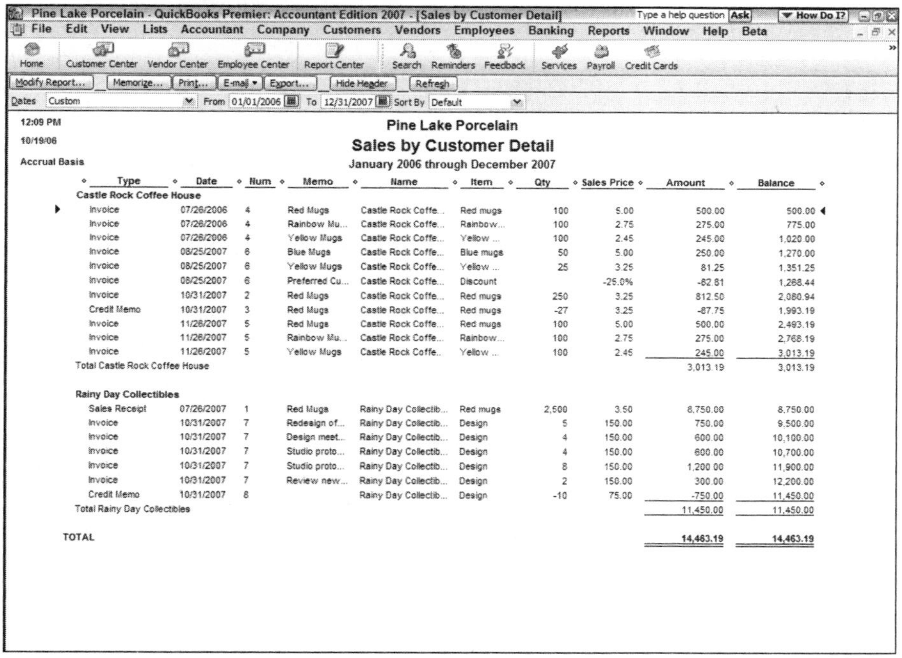

Figure 2-4: Begin to export a text file from a QuickBooks report.

The next step is to print this report to a text file. In QuickBooks, you click the Print button or choose File➪Print Report. Using either approach, QuickBooks displays the Print Reports dialog box, as shown in Figure 2-5.

TIP

Pay attention to the Print To radio buttons shown near the top of the Settings tab. QuickBooks, like many other programs, gives you the option of printing your report either to a printer or to a file.

If you want to later import the information on the report, you should print the report to a file. In the case of QuickBooks, this means that you select the File radio button. (Refer to Figure 2-5.)

Print Reports   Type a help question [Ask]   ▼ How Do I?   ☒

| Settings | Margins |

Print to:
⦿ Printer: Auto Brother HL-5140 series (Copy 1) o... ✓   [Options...]
○ File: ASCII text file ✓

Note: To install additional printers or to change port assignments, use the Windows Control Panel.

Orientation:
○ Portrait
⦿ Landscape

Page Range:
⦿ All
○ Pages:
   From: 1   To: 9999

Page Breaks:
☑ Smart page breaks (widow/orphan control)
☐ Page break after each major grouping

☐ Fit report to 1 page(s) wide

Number of copies: 1
☑ Collate

☐ Print in color (color printers only)

[Print] [Cancel] [Help] [Preview]

Figure 2-5:
Print a
QuickBooks
report here.

The other thing that you need to do — if you're given a choice — is to use a delimiter. In Figure 2-5, the File drop-down list shows ASCII text file as the type of file that QuickBooks will print. Often, though, applications — including QuickBooks — let you print delimited text files.

Delimited text files use standard characters, called *delimiters,* to separate fields of information in the report. You can still import a straight ASCII text file, but importing a delimited text file is easier. Therefore, if your other program gives you the option of creating delimited text files, do so. In QuickBooks, you can create both comma-delimited files and tab-delimited files.

In QuickBooks, you indicate that you want a delimited text file by choosing Comma Delimited File or Tab Delimited File from the File drop-down list of the Print Reports dialog box.

To print the report as a file, you simply click the Print button of the Print Reports dialog box. Typically, the application (QuickBooks, in this example) prompts you for a pathname, like in the Create Disk File dialog box shown in Figure 2-6. The *pathname* includes both the drive and folder location of the text file as well as the name of the file. You provide this information, and then the application produces the text file . . . or hopefully, the delimited text file. And that's that.

Importing: The second step (if necessary)

When you don't or can't export directly to Excel, you need to take the second step of importing the ASCII text file that you created with the other program. (To read more about exporting to a text file, see the preceding section.)

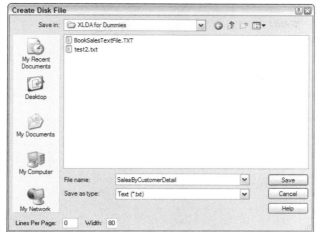

Figure 2-6:
The Create
Disk File
dialog box.

To import the ASCII text file, first open the text file itself from within Excel. When you open the text file, Excel starts the Text Import Wizard. This wizard walks you through the steps to describe how information in a text file should be formatted and rearranged as it's placed in an Excel workbook.

One minor wrinkle in this importing business is that the process works differently depending on whether you're importing straight (ASCII) text or delimited text.

Importing straight text

Here are the steps that you take to import a straight text file:

1. **Open the text file by choosing Open from the Microsoft Office menu or by choosing the Data tab's Get External Data from Text command.**

   Excel displays the Open dialog box, shown in Figure 2-7, if you choose the Open command. Excel displays a nearly identical Import Text File dialog box if you choose the Data tab's Get External Data from Text command.

2. **Choose Text Files from the Files of Type drop-down list.**

3. **Use the Look In drop-down list to identify the folder in which you placed the exported text file.**

   You should see the text file listed in the Open dialog box.

4. **To open the text file, double-click its icon.**

   Excel starts the Text Import Wizard, as shown in Figure 2-8.

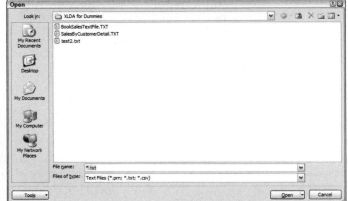

Figure 2-7:
Open the
text file that
you want to
import.

Figure 2-8:
Step 1 of the
Text Import
Wizard.

5. **Select the Fixed Width radio button.**

   This tells Excel that the fields in the text file are arranged in evenly spaced columns.

6. **In the Start Import at Row text box, identify the row in the ASCII text file that should be the first row of the spreadsheet.**

   In general, ASCII text files use the first several rows of the file to show report header information. For this reason, you typically won't want to start importing at row 1; you'll want to start importing at row 10 or 20 or 5.

Don't get too tense about this business of telling the Text Import Wizard which row is the first one that should be imported. If you import too many rows, you can easily delete the extraneous rows later in Excel.

You can preview the to-be-imported report shown on the bottom section of the Text Import Wizard dialog box.

7. **Click Next.**

Excel displays the second step dialog box of the Text Import Wizard, as shown in Figure 2-9. You use this second Text Import Wizard dialog box to break the rows of the text files into columns.

You might not need to do much work identifying where rows should be broken into columns. Excel, after looking carefully at the data in the to-be-imported text file, suggests where columns should be broken and draws vertical lines at the breaks.

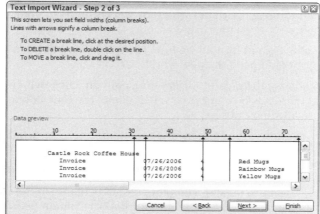

Figure 2-9:
Step 2 of the
Text Import
Wizard.

8. **In the Data Preview section of the second wizard dialog box, review the text breaks and amend them as needed.**

   • If they're incorrect, drag the break lines to a new location.

   • To remove a break, double-click the break line.

   • To create or add a new break, click at the point where you want the break to occur.

9. **Click Next.**

Excel displays the third step dialog box of the Text Import Wizard, as shown in Figure 2-10.

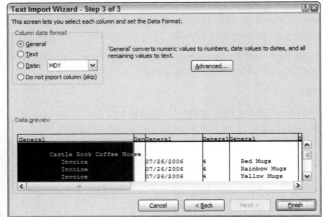

10. (Optional) Choose the data format for the columns in your new workbook.

You can pick default formatting from the third Text Import Wizard dialog box for the columns of the new workbook.

- To choose the default format for a column, click that column in the Data Preview box and then select one of the four Column Data Format radio buttons.

- If you choose the Date format radio button as the default for a column, use the Date drop-down list to choose a Date format.

11. (Optional) Identify any columns that Excel should not import.

If you don't want to import a column, select a column in the Data Preview box and then select the Do Not Import Column (Skip) radio button.

12. (Optional) Nit-pick how the data appears in the text file.

You can click the Advanced button (on the third Text Import Wizard dialog box) to display the Advanced Text Import Settings dialog box, as shown in Figure 2-11. The Advanced Text Import Settings dialog box provides text boxes that you can use to specify in more detail or with more precision how the data in the text file is arranged.

- Choose what symbol is used to separate whole numbers from decimal values by using the Decimal Separator drop-down list.

- Choose what symbol is used to separate thousands by using the Thousands Separator drop-down list.

Click OK after you make choices here; you return to the third wizard dialog box.

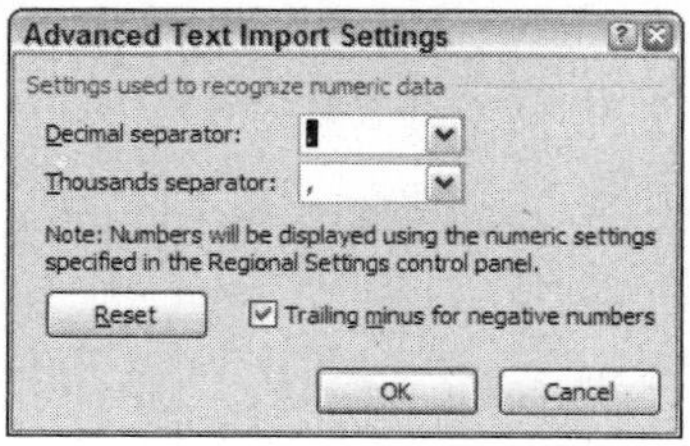

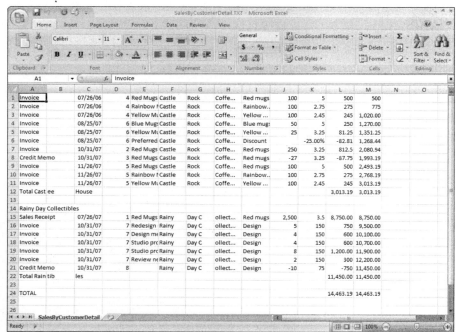

Figure 2-11:
The
Advanced
Text Import
Settings
dialog box.

13. Click Finish.

Excel imports the text file according to your specifications and places it into a new Excel workbook, as shown in Figure 2-12. The data probably won't be perfectly laid out. Still, when you have very large data sets, you'll find importing a tremendous timesaver. In general, you won't find it terribly difficult to clean up the new workbook. You only need to delete a few rows or perhaps columns or maybe do a bit of additional formatting or row and column resizing.

Figure 2-12:
The
imported
text file in
an Excel
workbook.

Importing delimited text files

Here are the steps that you take to import a delimited text file:

1. **Choose the Microsoft Office menu's Open command or click the Data tab's Get External Data from Text button.**

   Excel displays the Open dialog box (refer to Figure 2-7) or the Import Text File dialog box (which is nearly identical to Figure 2-7).

2. **Choose Text Files from the Files of Type drop-down list.**

3. **Use the Look In drop-down list to identify the folder in which you placed the exported text file.**

   You should see the text file listed in the Open dialog box.

4. **To open the text file, double-click its icon.**

   Excel starts the Text Import Wizard, as shown in Figure 2-13.

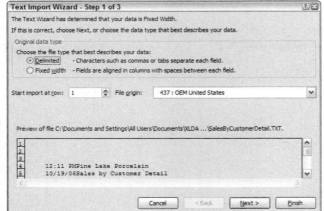

Figure 2-13:
The first
Text Import
Wizard
dialog box.

5. **Select the Delimited radio button.**

   This tells Excel that the fields in the text file are separated by (one or more) delimiters.

6. **In the Start Import at Row text box, identify the point in the delimited text file that should be the first row of the spreadsheet.**

   In general, ASCII text files use the first several rows of the file to show report header information. For this reason, you typically want to start importing at row 10 or 20 or 5.

Don't get too tense about this business of telling the Text Import Wizard which row is the first one that should be imported. You can easily delete the extraneous rows later in Excel.

You can preview the to-be-imported report shown on the bottom section of the Text Import Wizard dialog box.

7. Click Next.

Excel displays the second dialog box of the Text Import Wizard, as shown in Figure 2-14. You use this second Text Import Wizard dialog box to identify the character or characters used as the delimiter to break the text into columns. For example, if the file that's being imported is a tab-delimited file, select the Tab check box in the Delimiters area.

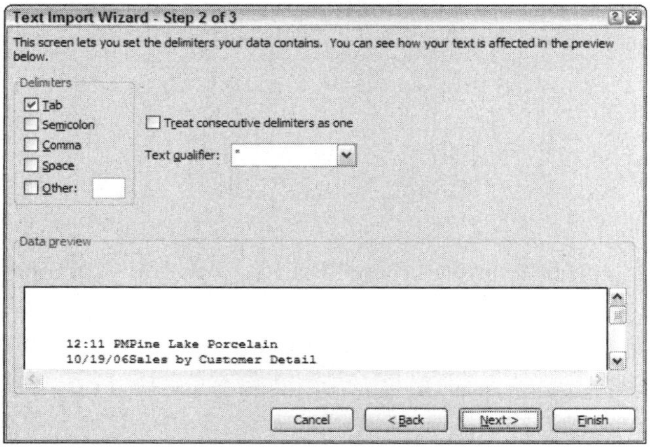

Figure 2-14:
The second Text Import Wizard dialog box.

8. Click Next.

The third Text Import Wizard dialog box appears, as shown in Figure 2-15.

9. (Optional) Choose the data format for the columns in your new workbook:

- To choose the default format for a column, click that column in the Data Preview box and then select one of the Column Data Format radio buttons.

- To use the Date format as the default for a column, select the Date radio button and use the Date drop-down list to choose a Date format.

The Data Preview box on the second Text Import Wizard dialog box shows how the file will look after it's imported based on the delimiters that you identified. Experiment a bit to make sure that you import the data in a clean format.

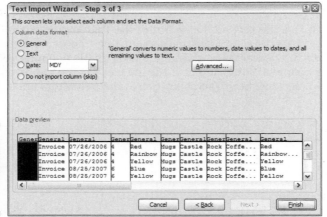

Figure 2-15:
The third
Text Import
Wizard
dialog box.

10. **(Optional) Identify any columns that Excel should skip importing.**

   If you don't want to import a column, select the column and then select the Do Not Import Column (Skip) radio button.

11. **(Optional) Nit-pick how the data appears in the text file.**

   Click the Advanced command button of the third Text Import Wizard dialog box to display the Advanced Text Import Settings dialog box. (Refer to Figure 2-11.) Here, you can specify in more detail how the data in the text file is arranged.

   Click OK to return to the third Text Import Wizard dialog box.

12. **Click Finish.**

   Excel imports the delimited text file according to your specifications. As for a straight text file, the data probably won't be perfectly laid out. But you won't find it difficult to clean up the new workbook. A few deletions, a little resizing, and pretty soon the workbook will look the way you want.

Querying External Databases and Web Page Tables

Another approach to collecting data that you want to analyze is to extract data from a Web page or from an external database. Excel 2007 provides three very neat ways to grab this sort of external data:

- ✔ You can perform a Web query, which means that you can grab data from a table stored in a Web page.
- ✔ You can import tables stored in common databases, such as Microsoft Access.
- ✔ You can use Microsoft Query to first query a database and then place the query results into an Excel workbook.

All three approaches for grabbing external data are described in the paragraphs that follow.

The difference between importing information that you want to analyze by using the Open command or Get External Data from Text command (read the preceding sections of the chapter) and importing information by using the Get External Data from Web or Get External Data from Access commands (read the following paragraphs) is somewhat subtle. In general, however, these latter two commands enable you to grab data directly from some external source without first massaging the data so that it's more recognizable.

Running a Web query

One of the neatest ways to grab external data is through a Web query. As you know if you've wasted any time surfing the Web, Internet Web sites provide huge volumes of interesting data. Often, you'd like to grab this data and analyze it in some way. Unfortunately, in the past, you haven't had an easy way to get the data from a Web page into Excel.

With the Excel Web Query tool, as long as the data that you want to grab or analyze is stored in something that looks like a table — that is, in something that uses rows and columns to organize the information — you can grab the information and place it into an Excel workbook.

To perform a Web query, follow these steps:

1. **Choose the Microsoft Office menu's New command to open a blank workbook.**

   You need to place query results into a blank worksheet. Therefore, your first step might need to be to open a workbook with a blank worksheet.

   If you need to insert a blank worksheet into an existing workbook, click the Insert Worksheet button. This button appears on the bottom edge of the worksheet next to the sheet tabs: Sheet1, Sheet2, Sheet3, and so on.

2. **Tell Excel that you want to run a Web query by choosing the Data tab's Get External Data from Web command.**

   Excel displays the New Web Query dialog box, as shown in Figure 2-16.

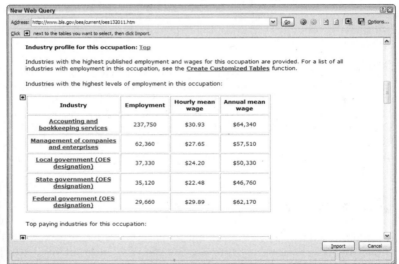

Figure 2-16: The New Web Query dialog box.

3. **Open the Web page containing the table that you want to extract data from by entering its URL into the Address field.**

   In Figure 2-16, I show a page from the United States Bureau of Labor Statistics. The Bureau of Labor Statistics Web site provides tons of tabular information, so if you want to play along, go ahead and visit the Web site at www.bls.gov and poke around until you find a page that shows a table.

4. **Identify the table by clicking the small yellow arrow button next to the table.**

Excel places this small yellow right-arrow button next to any tables that it sees in the open Web page. All you need to do is to click one of the buttons to grab the data that the arrow points to.

Excel replaces the yellow arrow button with a green check button.

5. **Verify that the green check button marks the table that you want to import and then import the table data by clicking the Import button.**

   Excel displays the Import Data dialog box, as shown in Figure 2-17.

Figure 2-17:
The Import
Data dialog
box.

6. **In the Import Data dialog box, tell Excel where to place the imported Web data.**

   Select the Existing Worksheet radio button to place the table data into the existing, open, empty worksheet. Alternatively, select the New Worksheet radio button to have Excel place the table data into a newly inserted blank sheet.

7. **Click OK.**

   Excel places the table data into the specified location. But I should tell you that sometimes grabbing the table data might take a few moments. Excel goes to some work to grab and arrange the table information. Figure 2-18 shows worksheet data retrieved from a Web page table.

Web query operations don't always work smoothly. In this case, you might want to revisit the Web page that displays the table and verify that you clicked the correct select button. The select button, again, is the small yellow button with the arrow that points to the table data.

Importing a database table

Another powerful method for retrieving data from an external data source, such as a database, is to retrieve the information directly from one of a database's tables. In relational databases, as in Excel, information gets stored in tables.

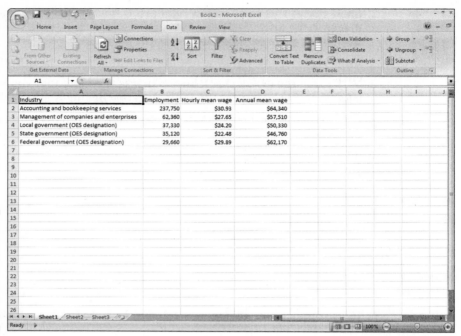

Figure 2-18:
Imported
worksheet
data from a
Web page
table. You
rock, man.

To import data from a database table, follow these steps:

1. **Choose the Data tab's Get External Data from Access command.**

   Excel displays the Select Data Source dialog box, as shown in Figure 2-19.

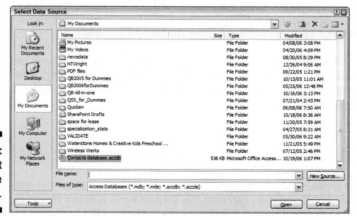

Figure 2-19:
The Select
Data Source
dialog box.

2. **Identify the database that you want to query by using the Look In drop-down list to identify the folder that stores the database from which you will grab information.**

3. **After you see the database listed in the Select Data Source dialog box, click it and then click Open.**

   If Excel displays the Select Table dialog box, continue to Step 4.

   If Excel doesn't display the Select Table dialog box but instead displays the Import Data dialog box (see Figure 2-20), skip ahead to Step 5.

4. **If Excel displays the Select Data Source dialog box, select the table that you want to retrieve information from by clicking it; then click OK.**

   Excel displays the Import Data dialog box, as shown in Figure 2-20.

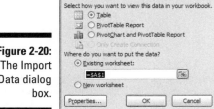

Figure 2-20:
The Import
Data dialog
box.

5. **Select either the Existing Worksheet radio button or the New Worksheet radio button to tell Excel where to place the information retrieved from the table.**

   If you want to place the data in an existing worksheet, use the Existing Worksheet text box to specify the top-left cell that should be filled with data. In other words, specify the first cell into which data should be placed.

6. **Click OK.**

   Excel retrieves information from the table and places it at the specified worksheet location. Figure 2-21 shows an Excel worksheet with data retrieved from a database table in the manner just described.

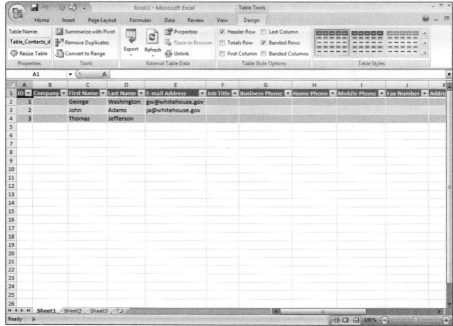

Figure 2-21:
An Excel
worksheet
with
imported
data.

Querying an external database

Excel provides one other powerful method for retrieving information from external databases. You aren't limited to simply grabbing all the information from a specified table. You can, alternatively, query a database. By querying a database, you retrieve only information from a table that matches your criteria. You can also use a query to combine information from two or more tables. Therefore, use a query to massage and filter the data before it's actually placed in your Excel workbook.

Querying is often the best approach when you want to combine data before importing it and when you need to filter the data before importing it. For example, if you were querying a very large database or very large table — one with hundreds of thousands of records — you would need to run a query in order to reduce the amount of information actually imported into Excel.

To run a database query and import query results, follow these steps:

1. **From the Data tab, choose From Other Sources⇨From Microsoft Query.**

Excel displays the Choose Data Source dialog box, as shown in Figure 2-22.

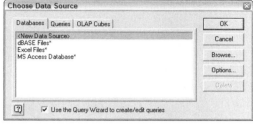

Figure 2-22:
The Choose
Data Source
dialog box.

2. **Using the Databases tab, identify the type of database that you want to query.**

   For example, to query a Microsoft Access database, click the MS Access Database entry.

   You can query the results of a query by clicking the Queries tab and then selecting one of the items listed there.

   You can also query an OLAP cube and grab information from that. If you want to query a query or an OLAP cube, consult with the database administrator. The database administrator can tell you what query or OLAP cube you want to grab data from.

3. **Select the database.**

   Excel displays the Select Database dialog box, as shown in Figure 2-23. Use this dialog box to identify both the location and the name of the database that you want to query.

Figure 2-23:
The Select
Database
dialog box.

4. **Select the database that you want to query from the directories list and then click OK.**

Excel displays the Query Wizard - Choose Columns dialog box, as shown in Figure 2-24.

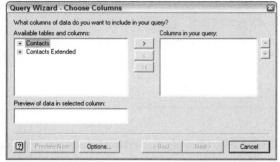

Figure 2-24:
The Query
Wizard -
Choose
Columns
dialog box.

You use the Query Wizard - Choose Columns dialog box to pick which tables and which table fields you want to appear in your query results. In the Available Tables and Columns box, Excel lists tables and fields. Initially, this list shows only tables, but you can see the fields within a table by clicking the + symbol next to the table.

5. **When you see a field that you want as a column in your Excel list, click its field and then click the right-facing arrow button that points to the Columns in Your Query list box.**

To add all the fields in a table to your list, click the table name and then click the right-facing arrow button that points to the Columns in Your Query list box.

To remove a field, select the field in the Columns in Your Query list box and then click the left-facing arrow button that points to the Available Tables and Columns list box.

This all sounds very complicated, but it really isn't. Essentially, all you do is to identify the columns of information that you want in your Excel list. Figure 2-25 shows how the Query Wizard - Choose Columns dialog box looks if you want to build a data list that includes the contact's first and last name, e-mail address, job title, business phone, home phone, and so on.

6. **After you identify which columns you want in your query, click the Next button to filter the query data as needed.**

Excel displays the Query Wizard - Filter Data dialog box, as shown in Figure 2-26.

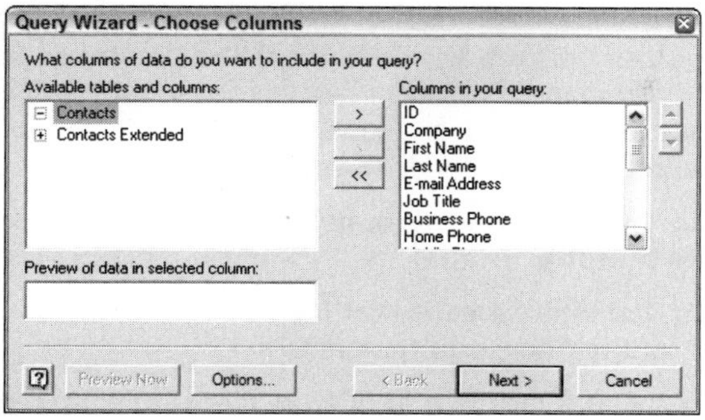

Figure 2-25:
The Query
Wizard -
Choose
Columns
dialog box
query
information
is defined.

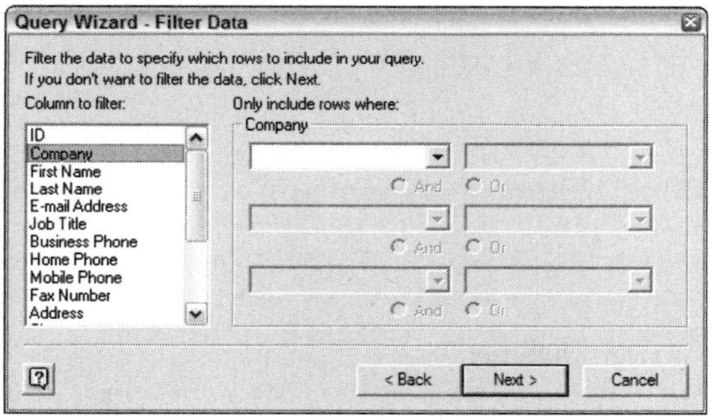

Figure 2-26:
The Query
Wizard -
Filter Data
dialog box.

You can filter the data returned as part of your query by using the Only Include Rows Where text boxes. For example, to include only rows in which the company name is *Acme Corporation,* click the Company field in the Column to Filter list box. Then select the Contains filtering operation from the first drop-down list and enter or select the value **Acme Corporation** into the second drop-down list; see how this looks in Figure 2-27.

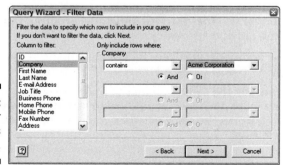

Figure 2-27:
Add filter
descriptions
here.

The Query Wizard - Filter Data dialog box performs the same sorts of filtering that you can perform with the AutoFilter command and the Advanced Filter command. Because I discuss these tools in Chapter 1, I won't repeat that discussion here. However, note that you can perform quite sophisticated filtering as part of your query.

7. **(Optional) Filter your data based on multiple filters by selecting the And or Or radio buttons.**

   - *And:* Using *And* filters means that for a row to be included, it must meet each of the filter requirements.

   - *Or:* Using *Or* filters means that if a row meets any filtered condition, the row is included.

8. **Click Next.**

   Excel displays the Query Wizard - Sort Order dialog box, as shown in Figure 2-28.

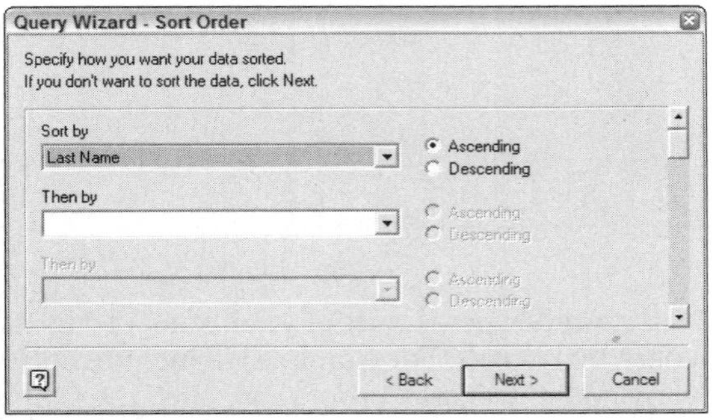

Figure 2-28: The Query Wizard - Sort Order dialog box.

9. **Choose a sort order for the query result data from the Query Wizard - Sort Order dialog box.**

   Select the field or column that you want to use for sorting from the Sort By drop-down list. By selecting either the Ascending or Descending radio button, choose whether the field should be arranged in an ascending or descending order, respectively.

   You can also use additional sort keys by selecting fields in the first and second Then By drop-down lists.

   You sort query results the same way that you sort rows in an Excel table. If you have more questions about how to sort rows, refer to Chapter 1. Sorting works the same whether you're talking about query results or rows in a list.

10. **Click Next.**

    Excel displays the Query Wizard - Finish dialog box, as shown in Figure 2-29.

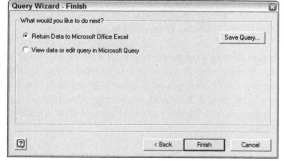

Figure 2-29:
The Query
Wizard -
Finish dialog
box.

11. **In the Query Wizard - Finish dialog box, specify where Excel should place the query results.**

    This dialog box provides radio buttons, from which you choose where you want to place your query result data: in Excel, in a Microsoft Query window that you can then review, or in an OLAP cube. Typically (and this is what I assume here in this book), you simply want to return the data to Microsoft Excel and place the data in a workbook. To make this choice, select the Return Data to Microsoft Office Excel radio button.

12. **Click the Finish button.**

    After you click the Finish button to complete the Query Wizard, Excel displays the Import Data dialog box; refer to Figure 2-20.

13. **In the Import Data dialog box, choose the worksheet location for the query result data.**

    Use this dialog box to specify where query result data should be placed.

    • To place the query result data in an existing worksheet, select the Existing Worksheet radio button. Then identify the cell in the top-left corner of the worksheet range and enter this in the Existing Worksheet text box.

    • Alternatively, to place the data into a new worksheet, select the New Worksheet radio button.

14. **Click OK.**

    Excel places the data at the location that you chose.

It's Sometimes a Raw Deal

By using the instructions that I describe in this chapter to retrieve data from some external source, you can probably get the data rather quickly into an Excel workbook. But it's possible that you've also found that the data is pretty raw. And so you are saying to yourself (or at least if I were in your shoes, I would be saying this), "Wow, this stuff is pretty raw."

But don't worry: You are where you need to be. It's okay for your information to be raw at this point. In Chapter 3, I discuss how you clean up the workbook by eliminating rows and columns and information that's not part of your data. I also cover how you scrub and rearrange the actual data in your workbook so that it appears in a format and structure that's useful to you in your upcoming analysis.

The bottom line is this: Don't worry that your data seems pretty raw right now. Getting your data into a workbook accomplishes an important step. All you need to do now is spend a little time on your housekeeping. Read through the next chapter for the lowdown on how to do that.

By the way, if the process of importing data from some external source has resulted in very clean and pristine data — and this might be the case if you've grabbed data from a well-designed database or with help from the corporate database administrator — that's great. You can jump right into the data analysis techniques that I start describing in Chapter 4.

Chapter 3

Scrub-a-Dub-Dub: Cleaning Data

*Y*ou will greatly benefit from exploring the techniques often necessary for cleaning up and rearranging workbook data. You know why? Because almost always the data that you start with — especially data that you import from other programs — will be pretty disorganized and dirty. Getting your data into a clean form makes it easier to work with and analyze the data.

Editing Your Imported Workbook

I start this discussion with some basic workbook editing techniques. If you take a look at the workbook shown in Figure 3-1, you see that the data, although neatly formatted, doesn't appear as an Excel table. The workbook shown in Figure 3-1, for example, includes blank columns and rows. The workbook also uses some columns that are inadequately sized. The width for column I, for example, is too small to display the values stored there. (That's why those #s appear.)

You will often encounter situations like this. The workbook shown in Figure 3-1, for example, has actually been imported from QuickBooks. You can use several workbook-editing techniques to clean up a workbook. In the following sections, I give you a rundown of the most useful ones.

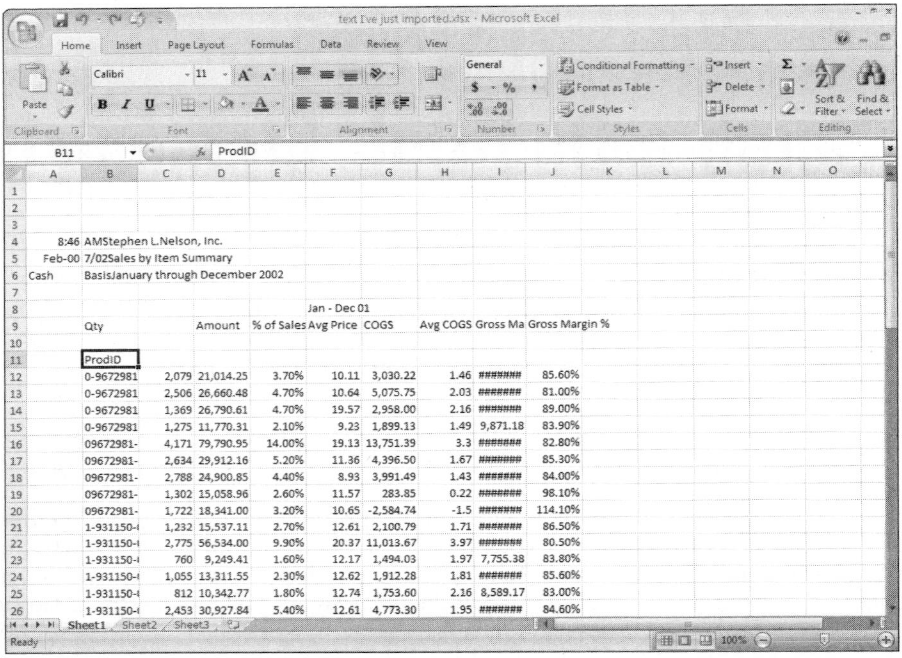

Figure 3-1:
This
worksheet
needs to
clean up
its act.

Delete unnecessary columns

To delete unnecessary columns (these might be blank columns or columns that store data that you don't need), click the column letter to select the column. Then choose the Home tab's Delete command.

You can select multiple columns for multiple deletions by holding down the Ctrl key and then individually clicking column letters.

Delete unnecessary rows

To delete unnecessary rows, you follow the same steps that you do to delete unnecessary columns. Just click the row number and then choose the Home tab's Delete command. To delete multiple rows, hold down the Ctrl key and then select the row numbers for each of the rows that you want to delete. After making your selections, choose the Home tab's Delete command.

Resize columns

To resize (enlarge the width of) a column so that its contents clearly show, double-click the column letter box's right corner or click AutoFit Column Width on the Format button's drop-down (Home tab). For example, in Figure 3-2, column H is too narrow to displays its values. Excel displays several pound signs (########) in the cells in column H to indicate the column is too narrow to adequately display its values.

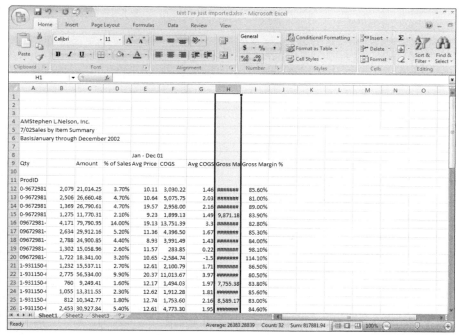

Figure 3-2: Column H needs to gain a little weight.

Just double-click the column letter label, and Excel resizes the column so that it's wide enough to display the values or labels stored in that column. Check out Figure 3-3 to see how Excel has resized the width of column H to display its values.

You can also resize a column by selecting it and then choosing the Home tab's Format➪Width command. When Excel displays the Column Width dialog box, as shown in Figure 3-4, you can enter a larger value into the Column Width text box and then click OK. The value that you enter is the number of characters that can fit in a column.

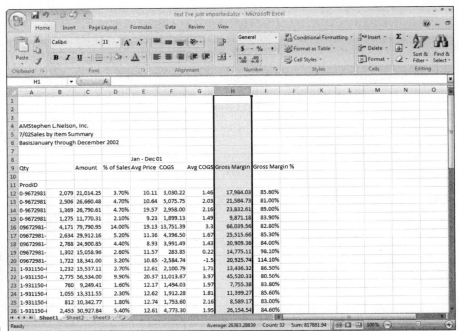

Figure 3-3:
Ah . . . now
you can see
the data.

Figure 3-4:
Set column
width here.

For you manually inclined fiddlers, you can also resize a column by clicking
and dragging the left corner of the column letter label box. You can resize the
column to any width by dragging this border.

Resize rows

You can resize rows like you resize columns. Just select the row number label
and then choose the Home tab's Format➪Height command. When Excel displays the Row Height dialog box, as shown in Figure 3-5, you can enter a
larger value into the Row Height text box.

Row height is measured in points. (A point equals ½₂ of an inch.)

Figure 3-5:
Set row
height here.

Erase unneeded cell contents

To erase the contents of a range that contains unneeded data, select the worksheet range and then choose the Home tab's Clear⇨Clear All command. Excel erases both the contents of the cells in the selected range and any formatting assigned to those cells.

Format numeric values

To change the formatting of values in a workbook that you want to analyze, first select the range of what you want to reformat. Then choose the Home tab's Number command. When Excel displays the Format Cells dialog box, as shown in Figure 3-6, choose from its tabs to change the formatting of the selected range. For example, use choices from the Number tab to assign numeric formatting to values in the selected range. You use options from the Alignment tab to change the way the text and values are positioned in the cell, from the Font tab to choose the font used for values and labels in the selected range, and from the Border tab to assign cell border borders to the selected range.

The buttons and boxes that appear just above the Number command button provide for several, convenient, one-click formatting options. For example, you can click the command button marked with the currency symbol to format the selected range using the accounting format.

Copying worksheet data

To copy worksheet data, first select the data that you want to duplicate. You can copy a single cell or range of cells. Choose the Home tab's Copy command and then select the range into which you want to place the copied data. Remember: You can select a single cell or a range of cells. Then choose the Home tab's Paste command.

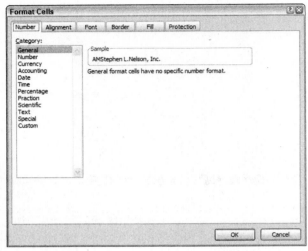

Figure 3-6:
Format
numeric
values here.

You can also copy worksheet ranges by dragging the mouse. To do this, select the worksheet range that you want to copy. Then hold down the Ctrl key and drag the range border.

Moving worksheet data

To move worksheet data to some new location, select the range that stores the data. Choose the Home tab's Cut command and click the cell in the upper-left corner of the range into which you want to move the worksheet data. Then choose the Home tab's Paste command.

You can also move worksheet ranges by dragging the mouse. To do this, select the worksheet range that you want to copy and then drag the range border.

Replacing data in fields

One of the most common commands that I find myself using to clean up a list is the Home tab's Find & Select command. To use this command, first select the column with the data that you want to clean by clicking that column's letter. Next choose Find & Select⇨Replace so that Excel displays the Find and Replace dialog box, as shown in Figure 3-7.

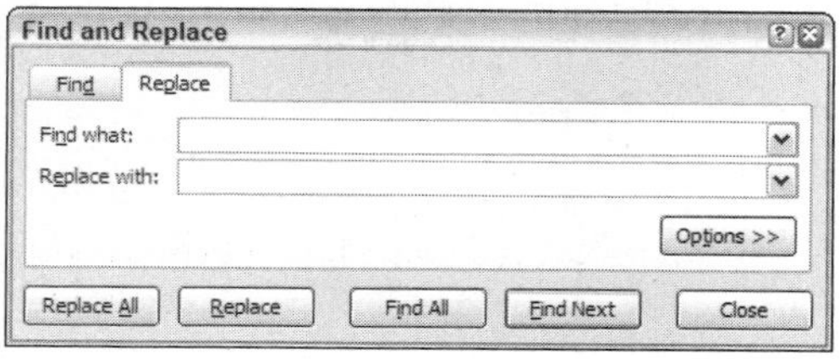

Figure 3-7: Keep data in its place with the Find and Replace dialog box.

Enter the incorrect text that you want to find in the Find What text box and then enter the correct text in the Replace With text box. Then click the Replace All button to fix the incorrect text.

Cleaning Data with Text Functions

One of the common problems with data that you import is that your text labels aren't quite right. For example, you might find yourself with the city, state, and Zip code information that's part of an address stored in a single cell rather than in three separate cells. Or, you might find that same information stored in three separate cells when you want the data stored in a single cell. You might also find that pieces of information that you want stored as labels instead are stored as values and vice versa.

What's the big deal, Steve?

Just to give you a quick idea of what I mean here, take a look at Figures 3-8 and 3-9. Okay, this is fake data, sure. But the examples show a common situation. The list information shown in Figure 3-8 uses unnecessarily lengthy product names, goofs up some customer names by appending store numbers to customer names, and then puts all of the city and state information into one field. Yuk.

In Figure 3-9, see how I rearrange this information so that it's much more easily sorted and filtered. For example, the PRODUCT2 field abbreviates the product name by changing *Big Bob's Guide to* to just *BBgt*. The store names are essentially edited down to just the first word in the store name — an easy change that enables you to see sales for Bean's Tackle, Mac's Shack, and Steve's Charters. The ADDRESS information is split into two fields: CITY and STATE.

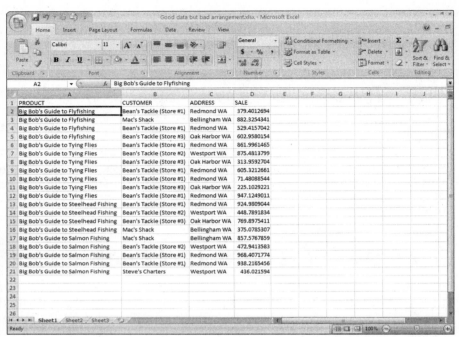

Figure 3-8:
Good worksheet data; tough to analyze.

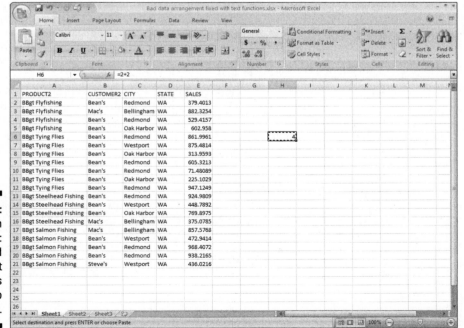

Figure 3-9:
Much better: Rearranged worksheet data that's easy to analyze.

Here's one other important point about Figure 3-9: The rearrangement shown in Figure 3-9 makes it possible to cross-tabulate the data using a pivot table (something I talk more about in Chapter 4).

The answer to some of your problems

All the editing performed in Figure 3-9 is performed using text functions, so here, I discuss these babies.

You can grab a Zip file from the Dummies Web site that includes most of the Excel workbooks shown in the pages of this book. I mention this because if you're really curious about how text functions are used in Figure 3-9, you can grab the actual workbook and check out the formulas. The Zip file is available at www.dummies.com/go/e2007dafd.

Excel provides two dozen text functions that enable you to manipulate text strings in ways to easily rearrange and manipulate the data that you import into an Excel workbook. In the following paragraphs, I explain how to use the primary text functions.

If you've just read the word *function* and you're scratching your head, you might want to review the contents of the Appendix.

By the way, I skip discussions of three text functions that I don't think you'll have occasion to use for scrubbing data: BAHTEXT (rewrites values using Thai characters); CHAR (returns the character represented by an American National Standards Institute [ANSI] code number); and CODE (returns the ANSI code represented by character). To get descriptions of these other text functions, choose Insert⇨Function, select the Text entry from the Or Select A Category box, and then scroll through the list of text functions that Excel displays in the Select a Function box until you see the function that you have a question for — most likely, the function that I incorrectly assume you don't need information about.

The CLEAN function

Using the CLEAN function removes nonprintable characters text. For example, if the text labels shown in a column are using crazy nonprintable characters that end up showing as solid blocks or goofy symbols, you can use the CLEAN function to clean up this text. The cleaned-up text can be stored in another column. You can then work with the cleaned text column.

The CLEAN function uses the following syntax:

```
CLEAN(text)
```

The text argument is the text string or a reference to the cell holding the text string that you want to clean. For example, to clean the text stored in Cell A1, use the following syntax:

CLEAN(A1)

The CONCATENATE function

The CONCATENATE function combines, or joins chunks of text into a single text string. The CONCATENATE function uses the following syntax:

```
CONCATENATE(text1,text2,text3,...)
```

The *text1*, *text2*, *text3*, and so on arguments are the chunks of text that you want to combine into a single string. For example, if the city, state, and Zip code were stored in fields named city, state, and zip, you could create a single text string that stores this information by using the following syntax:

```
CONCATENATE(city,state,zip)
```

If city were Redmond, state were WA, and zip were 98052, this function returns this text string:

```
RedmondWA98052
```

The smashed together nature of the concatenated city, state, and Zip code information isn't a typographical mistake, by the way. To concatenate this information but include spaces, you need to include spaces as function arguments. For example, the following syntax:

```
CONCATENATE("Redmond", " ","WA", " ","98052")
```

returns the text string

```
Redmond WA 98052
```

The EXACT function

The EXACT function compares two text strings. If the two text strings are exactly the same, the EXACT function returns the logical value for true, which is 1. If the two text strings differ in any way, the EXACT function returns the logical value for false, which is 0. The EXACT function is case-sensitive. For example, *Redmond* spelled with a capital *R* differs from *redmond* spelled with a lowercase *r.*

The EXACT function uses the following syntax:

```
EXACT(text1,text2)
```

The `text1` and `text2` arguments are the text strings that you want to compare. For example, to check whether the two strings `"Redmond"` and `"redmond"` are the same, use the following formula:

```
EXACT("Redmond","redmond")
```

This function returns the logical value for false, 0, because these two text strings don't match exactly. One begins with an uppercase *R* and the other begins with a lowercase *r.*

The FIND function

The FIND function finds the starting character position of one text string within another text string. For example, if you want to know at what position within a text string the two-letter state abbreviation WA starts, you could use the FIND function.

The FIND function uses the following syntax:

```
FIND(find_text,within_text,start_num)
```

The `find_text` argument is the text that you're looking for. The `within_text` argument identifies where or what you're searching. The `start_num` argument tells Excel at what point within the string it should begin its search. For example, to find at what point the two-letter state abbreviation WA begins in the string Redmond WA 98052, use the following formula:

```
FIND("WA","Redmond WA 98052",1)
```

The function returns the value 9 because WA begins at the ninth position (because spaces are counted).

The `start_num` function argument is optional. If you omit this argument, Excel begins searching at the very beginning of the string.

The FIXED function

The FIXED function rounds a value to specified precision and then converts the rounded value to text. The function uses the following syntax:

```
FIXED(number,decimals,no_commas)
```

The *number* argument supplies the value that you want to round and convert to text. The optional *decimals* argument tells Excel how many places to the right of the decimal point that you want to round. The optional *no_commas* argument needs to be either 1 (if you want commas) or 0 (if you don't want commas) in the returned text.

For example, to round to a whole number and convert to text the value 1234.56789, use the following formula:

```
FIXED(1234.56789,0,1)
```

The function returns the text 1,235.

The LEFT function

The LEFT function returns a specified number of characters from the left end of a text string. The function uses the following syntax:

```
LEFT(text,num_chars)
```

The *text* argument either supplies the text string or references the cell holding the text string. The optional *num_chars* argument tells Excel how many characters to grab.

For example, to grab the leftmost seven characters from the text string Redmond WA, use the following formula:

```
LEFT("Redmond WA",7)
```

The function returns the text Redmond.

The LEN function

The LEN function counts the number of characters in a text string. The function uses the following syntax:

```
LEN(text)
```

The *text* argument either supplies the text string that you want to measure or references the cell holding the text string. For example, to measure the length of the text string in cell I81, use the following formula:

```
LEN(I81)
```

If cell I81 holds the text string Semper fidelis, the function returns the value 14. Spaces are counted as characters, too.

The LOWER function

The LOWER function returns an all-lowercase version of a text string. The function uses the following syntax:

```
LOWER(text)
```

The *text* argument either supplies the text string that you want to convert or references the cell holding the text string. For example, to convert the text string PROFESSIONAL to professional, use the following formula:

```
LOWER("PROFESSIONAL")
```

The function returns professional.

The MID function

The MID function returns a chunk of text in the middle of text string. The function uses the following syntax:

```
MID(text,start_num,num_char)
```

The *text* argument either supplies the text string from which you grab some text fragment or it references the cell holding the text string. The *start_num* argument tells Excel where the text fragment starts that you want to grab. The *num_char* argument tells Excel how long the text fragment is. For example, to grab the text fragment tac from the text string tic tac toe, use the following formula:

```
=MID("tic tac toe",5,3)
```

The function returns tac.

The PROPER function

The PROPER function capitalizes the first letter in every word in a text string. The function uses the following syntax:

```
PROPER(text)
```

The *text* argument either supplies the text string or references the cell holding the text string. For example, to capitalize the initial letters in the text string ambassador kennedy, use the following formula:

```
PROPER("ambassador kennedy")
```

The function returns the text string Ambassador Kennedy.

The REPLACE function

The REPLACE function replaces a portion of a text string. The function uses the following syntax:

```
REPLACE(old_text,start_num,num_chars,new_text)
```

The *old_text* argument, which is case-sensitive, either supplies the text string from which you grab some text fragment or it references the cell holding the text string. The *start_num* argument, which is the starting position, tells Excel where the text starts that you want to replace. The *num_chars* argument tells Excel the length of the text fragment (how many characters) that you want to replace. The *new_text* argument, also case-sensitive, tells Excel what new text you want to use to replace the old text. For example, to replace the name Chamberlain with the name Churchill in the text string Mr. Chamberlain, use the following formula:

```
REPLACE("Mr. Chamberlain",5,11,"Churchill")
```

The function returns the text string Mr. Churchill.

The REPT function

The REPT function repeats a text string. The function uses the following syntax:

```
REPT(text,number_times)
```

The *text* argument either supplies the text string or references the cell holding the text string. The *number_times* argument tells Excel how many times you want to repeat the text. For example, the following formula:

```
REPT("Walla",2")
```

returns the text string WallaWalla.

The RIGHT function

The RIGHT function returns a specified number of characters from the right end of a text string. The function uses the following syntax:

```
RIGHT(text,num_chars)
```

The *text* argument either supplies the text string that you want to manipulate or references the cell holding the text string. The *num_chars* argument tells Excel how many characters to grab.

For example, to grab the rightmost two characters from the text string Redmond WA, use the following formula:

```
RIGHT("Redmond WA",2)
```

The function returns the text WA.

The SEARCH function

The SEARCH function calculates the starting position of a text fragment within a text string. The function uses the following syntax:

```
SEARCH(find_text,within_text,start_num)
```

The *find_text* argument tells Excel what text fragment you're looking for. The *within_text* argument tells Excel what text string that you want to search. The *start_num* argument tells Excel where to start its search. The *start_num* argument is optional. If you leave it blank, Excel starts the search at beginning of the *within_text* string.

For example, to identify the position at which the text fragment Churchill starts in the text string Mr. Churchill, use the following formula:

```
SEARCH("Churchill","Mr. Churchill",1)
```

The function returns the value 5.

The SUBSTITUTE function

The SUBSTITUTE function replaces occurrences of text in a text string. The function uses the following syntax:

```
SUBSTITUTE(text,old_text,new_text,instances)
```

The `text` argument tells Excel what text string you want to edit by replacing some text fragment. The `old_text` argument identifies the to-be-replaced text fragment. The `new_text` supplies the new replacement text.

As an example of how the SUBSTITUTE function works, suppose that you need to replace the word `Governor` with the word `President` in the text string `Governor Bush`.

```
SUBSTITUTE("Governor Bush","Governor","President")
```

The function returns the text string `President Bush`.

The `instances` argument is optional, but you can use it to tell Excel for which instance of `old_text` you want to make the substitution. For example, the function

```
SUBSTITUTE("Governor Governor Bush","Governor","President",1)
```

returns the text string `President Governor Bush`.

The function

```
SUBSTITUTE("Governor Governor Bush","Governor","President",2)
```

returns the text string `Governor President Bush`.

If you leave the instances argument blank, Excel replaces each occurrence of the `old_text` with the `new_text`. For example, the function

```
SUBSTITUTE("Governor Governor Bush","Governor","President")
```

returns the text string `President President Bush`.

The T function

The T function returns its argument if the argument is text. If the argument isn't text, the function returns nothing. The function uses the following syntax:

```
T(value)
```

For example, the formula T(123) returns nothing because 123 is a value. The formula T("Seattle") returns Seattle because Seattle is a text string.

The TEXT function

The TEXT function formats a value and then returns the value as text. The function uses the following syntax:

```
TEXT(value,format_text)
```

The value argument is the value that you want formatted and returned as text. The *format_text* argument is a text string that shows the currency symbol and placement, commas, and decimal places that you want. For example, the formula

```
=TEXT(1234.5678,"$##,###.00")
```

returns the text $1,234.57.

Note that the function rounds the value.

The TRIM function

The TRIM function removes extra spaces from the right end of a text string. The function uses the following syntax:

```
TRIM(text)
```

The *text* argument is the text string or, more likely, a reference to the cell holding the text string.

The UPPER function

The UPPER function returns an all-uppercase version of a text string. The function uses the following syntax:

```
UPPER(text)
```

The *text* argument either supplies the text string that you want to convert or it references the cell holding the text string. For example, to convert the text string professional to PROFESSIONAL, you can use the following formula:

```
UPPER("professional")
```

The function returns the text string PROFESSIONAL.

The VALUE function

The VALUE function converts a text string that looks like a value to a value. The function uses the following syntax:

```
VALUE(text)
```

The *text* argument either supplies the text string that you want to convert or it references the cell holding the text string. For example, to convert the text string $123,456.78 — assume that this isn't a value but a text string — you can use the following formula:

```
VALUE("$123,456.78")
```

The function returns the value 123456.78.

Converting text function formulas to text

You might need to know how to convert a formula — such as a formula that uses a text function — to the label or value that it returns. For example, suppose you find yourself with a worksheet full of text-function-based formulas because you used the text functions to clean up the list data. And now you want to just work with labels and values.

You can convert formulas to the labels and values that they return by selecting the worksheet range that holds the formulas, choosing the Home tab's Copy command, and then choosing the Home tab's Paste⇨Paste Values command without deselecting the currently selected range. Note that to get to the Paste submenu, you need to click the lower half of the Paste command button.

Using Validation to Keep Data Clean

One useful command related to this business of keeping your data clean is the Data Validation command. Use this command to describe what information can be entered into a cell. The command also enables you to supply messages that give data input information and error messages that attempt to help someone correct data entry errors.

To use Data Validation, follow these steps:

1. **Select the worksheet range where the to-be-validated data will go.**

   You can do this by dragging your mouse or by using the navigation keys.

2. **Choose the Data tab's Data Validation command to tell Excel that you want to set up data validation for the selected range.**

   Excel displays the Data Validation dialog box, as shown in Figure 3-10.

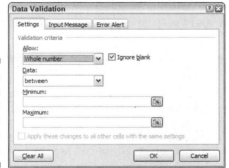

Figure 3-10:
Keep data clean with the Data Validation dialog box.

3. **On the Settings tab of the Data Validation dialog box, use the Validation Criteria text boxes to describe what is valid data.**

   Use choices from the Allow drop-down list box, for example, to supply what types of information can go into the range: whole numbers, decimal numbers, values from the list, valid dates, valid times, text of a particular length, and so on.

   Use choices from the Data drop-down list box to further define your validation criteria. The Data drop-down list box provides several comparisons that can be made as part of the validation: between, not between, equal to, not equal to, greater than, and so on.

Refine the validation criteria, if necessary, using any of the other drop-down list boxes available. *Note:* The other validation criteria options depend on what you enter into the Allow and Data drop-down list boxes. For example, as shown in Figure 3-11, if you indicate that you want to allow only whole numbers between a particular range of minimum and maximum values, Excel provides Minimum and Maximum text boxes for you to enter or define the range. However, if you select other entries from the Allow or Data drop-down list boxes, you see other text boxes appearing on the Settings tab. In other words, Excel customizes the Settings tab depending on the kind of validation criteria that you define.

4. **Fine-tune the validation.**

After you describe the validation criteria, either select or deselect (clear) the Ignore Blank check box to indicate whether blank cells are allowed.

5. **(Optional) Consider expanding the scope of the data validation.**

Select the Apply These Changes to All Other Cells with the Same Settings check box to indicate whether the validation criteria should be expanded to other similar cells.

Click the Clear All button, and Excel clears (removes) the validation criteria.

6. **Provide an input message from the Input Message tab of the Data Validation dialog box.**

The Input Message tab, as shown in Figure 3-11, enables you to tell Excel to display a small message when a cell with specified data validation is selected. To create the input message, you enter a title for the message into the Title text box and message text into the Input Message text box. Make sure that the Show Input Message When Cell Is Selected check box is selected. Look at Figure 3-12 to see how the Input Message entered in Figure 3-11 looks on the workbook.

Figure 3-11: Create a data entry instruction message.

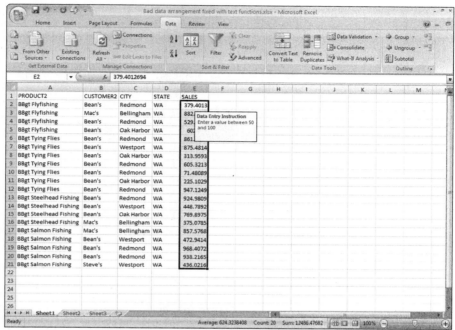

Figure 3-12:
A data entry
instruction
message is
helpful.

7. **Provide an error message from the Error Alert tab of the Data Validation dialog box. (See Figure 3-13.)**

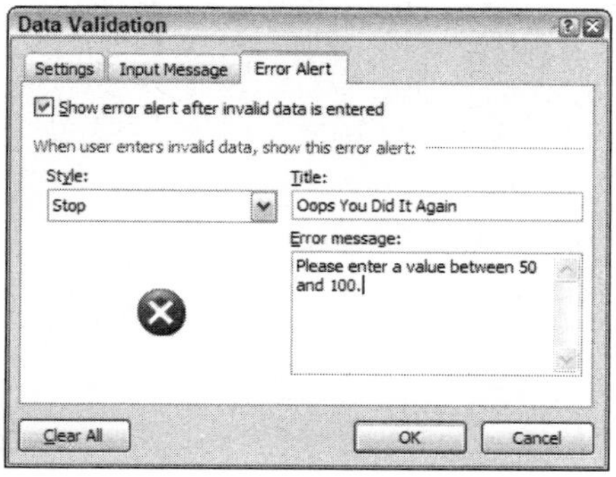

Figure 3-13:
Create an
annoying
data entry
error
message.

You can also supply an error message that Excel displays when someone attempts to enter invalid data. To create an error message, first verify that the Show Error Alert After Invalid Data Is Entered check box is selected. Then use the Style drop-down list box to select what Excel should do when it encounters invalid data: Stop the data entry on the user without the incorrect data entry, or simply display an informational message after the data has been entered.

Just like creating an input message, enter the error message title into the Title text box. Then enter the full text of the error message into the Error Message text box. In Figure 3-13, you can see a completed Error Alert tab. Check out Figure 3-14 for how the error message appears after a user enters invalid data.

Figure 3-14:
Britney
would be
proud.

Oops You Did It Again

Please enter a value between 50 and 100.

Retry   Cancel   Help

Was this information helpful?

Curious about the options in the Style drop-down list box (as shown in Figure 3-13)? The style of the error alert determines what command buttons the error message presents when someone attempts to enter bad data. If the error style is Stop, the error message box displays Retry and Cancel command buttons. If the error style is Warning, the error message box displays Yes, No, and Cancel command buttons. If the error style is Informational, the error message box displays OK and Cancel command buttons.

Part II

PivotTables and PivotCharts

In this part . . .

In this part of the book, I discuss the most powerful data analysis tool that Excel provides — its cross-tabulation capability, which is available through the PivotTable and PivotChart command. Discover here how to unlock the power of this tool as I cover how to create pivot tables and charts, customize pivot charts, and build pivot table formulas.

Chapter 4

Working with PivotTables

*P*erhaps the most powerful analytical tool that Excel provides is the PivotTable command, with which you can cross-tabulate data stored in Excel lists. A cross-tabulation summarizes information in two (or more) ways: for example, sales by product and state, or sales by product and month.

Cross-tabulations, performed by pivot tables in Excel, are a basic and very interesting analytical technique that can be tremendously helpful when you're looking at data that your business or life depends on. Excel's cross-tabulations are neater than you might at first expect. For one thing, they aren't static: You can cross-tabulate data and then re-cross-tabulate and re-cross-tabulate it again simply by dragging buttons. What's more, as your underlying data changes, you can update your cross-tabulations simply by clicking a button.

Looking at Data from Many Angles

Cross-tabulations are important, powerful tools. Here's a quick example: Assume that in some future century that you're the plenipotentiary of the Freedonian Confederation and in charge of security for a distant galaxy. (Rough directions? Head toward Alpha Centauri for about 50 million light years and then hang a left. It'll be the second galaxy on your right.)

Unfortunately, in recent weeks, you're increasingly concerned about military conflicts with the other major political-military organizations in your corner of the universe. Accordingly, assume for a moment that a list maintained by the Confederation tracks space trooper movements in your galaxy. Assume that the list stores the following information: troop movement data, enemy name, and type of troop spaceships involved. Also assume that it's your job to maintain this list and use it for analysis that you then report to appropriate parties.

With this sort of information, you could create cross-tabulations that show the following information:

- ✔ **Enemy activity over time:** One interesting cross-tabulation is to look at the troop movements by specific enemy by month over a two- or five-year period of time. You might see that some enemies were gearing up their activity or that other enemies were dampening down their activity. All this information would presumably be useful to you while you assess security threats and brief Freedonian Confederation intelligence officers and diplomats on which enemies are doing what.

- ✔ **Troop movements by spaceship type:** Another interesting cross-tabulation would be to look at which spaceships your (potential) enemies are using to move troops. This insight might be useful to you to understand both the intent and seriousness of threats. As your long experience with the Uglinites (one of your antagonists) might tell you, for example, if you know that Jabbergloop troop carriers are largely defensive, you might not need to worry about troop movements that use these ships. On the other hand, if you notice a large increase in troop movements via the new photon-turbine fighter-bomber, well, that's significant.

Pretty powerful stuff, right? With a rich data set stored in an Excel table, cross-tabulations can give you remarkable insights that you would probably otherwise miss. And these cross-tabulations are what pivot tables do.

Getting Ready to Pivot

To create a pivot table, your first step is to create the Excel table that you want to cross-tabulate. Figure 4-1 shows an example Excel table that you might want a pivot table based on. In this list, I show sales of herbal teas by month and state. Pretend that this is an imaginary business that you own and operate. Further pretend that you set it up in a list because you want to gain insights into your business's sales activities.

Note: You can find this Herbal Teas Excel Data list of herbal tea sales Workbook, available in the Zip file of sample Excel workbooks related to this book, at the *For Dummies* Web site (www.dummies.com/go/e2007dafd). You might want to download this list in order to follow along with the discussion here.

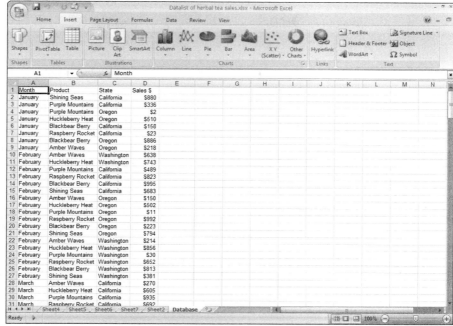

Running the PivotTable Wizard

You create a pivot table — Excel calls a cross-tabulation a *pivot table* — by
using the PivotTable command. To run the PivotTable command, take the following steps:

1. Click the Insert tab's PivotTable command button.

Excel displays the Create PivotTable dialog box, as shown in Figure 4-2.

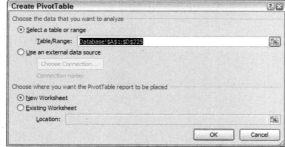

2. **Select the radio button that indicates where the data you want to analyze is stored.**

   If the to-be-analyzed data is in an Excel table or worksheet range, for example, select the Table/Range radio button. I demonstrate this approach here. And if you're just starting out, you ought to use this approach because it's the easiest.

   If the data is in an external data source, select the Use an External Data Source radio button. I don't demonstrate this approach here because I'm assuming in order to keep things simple and straightforward that you've already grabbed any external data and placed that data into a worksheet list. (If you haven't done that and need help doing so, skip back to Chapter 2.)

   If the data is actually stored in a bunch of different worksheet ranges, simply separate each worksheet range with a comma. (This approach is more complicated, so you probably don't want to use it until you're comfortable working with pivot tables.)

   If you have data that's scattered around in a bunch of different locations in a worksheet or even in different workbooks, pivot tables are a great way to consolidate that data.

3. **Tell Excel where the to-be-analyzed data is stored.**

   If you're grabbing data from a single Excel table, enter the list range into the Table/Range text box. You can do so in two ways.

   • You can type the range coordinates: For example, if the range is cell A1 to cell D225, type **$A$1:$D$225**.

   • Alternatively, you can click the button at the right end of the Table/Range text box. Excel collapses the Create PivotTable dialog box, as shown in Figure 4-3.

   Now use the mouse or the navigation keys to select the worksheet range that holds the data that you want to pivot. After you select the worksheet range, click the button at the end of the Range text box again. Excel redisplays the Create PivotTable dialog box. (Refer to Figure 4-2.)

Figure 4-3:
The collapsed Create PivotTable dialog box.

4. **After you identify the data that you want to analyze in a pivot table, click OK.**

   Excel displays the new workbook with the partially constructed pivot table in it, as shown in Figure 4-4.

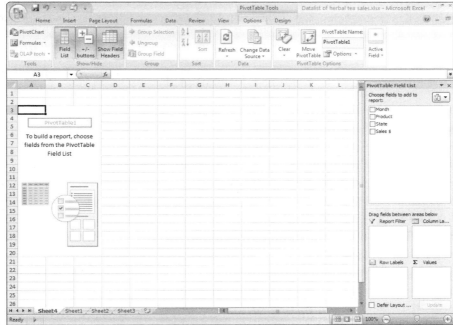

Figure 4-4:
Create an empty pivot table; then tell Excel what to cross-tabulate.

5. **Select the Row field.**

   You need to decide first which field from the list that you want to summarize by using rows in the pivot table. After you decide this, you drag the field from the PivotTable Field List box (on the right side of Figure 4-4) to the Row Labels box (beneath the PivotTable Field List). For example, if you want to use rows that show product, you drag the Product field to the Row Labels box.

   Using the example data from Figure 4-1, after you do this, the partially constructed Excel pivot table looks like the one shown in Figure 4-5.

6. **Select the Column field.**

   Just like you did for the Row field, indicate what list information you want stored in the columns of your cross-tabulation. After you make this choice, drag the field item from the PivotTable Field List to the box marked Column Labels. Figure 4-6 shows the way the partially constructed pivot table looks now, using columns to show states.

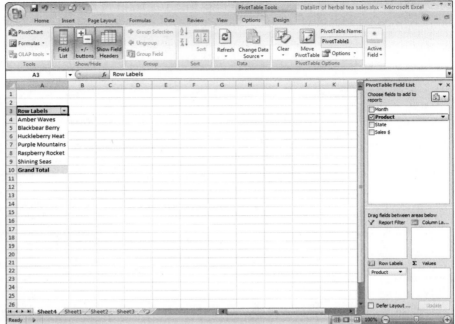

Figure 4-5:
Your cross-
tabulation
after you
select the
rows.

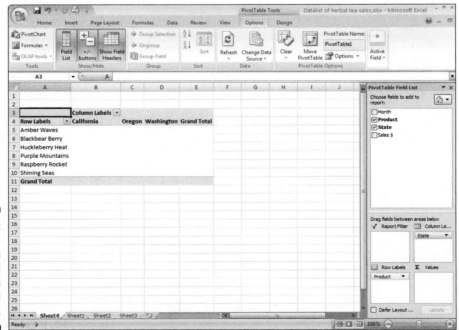

Figure 4-6:
Your cross-
tabulation
after you
select rows
and
columns.

7. Select the data item that you want.

After you choose the rows and columns for your cross-tabulation, you indicate what piece of data you want cross-tabulated in the pivot table. For example, to cross-tabulate sales revenue, drag the sales item from the PivotTable Field List to the Values box. Figure 4-7 shows the completed pivot table after I select the row fields, column fields, and data items.

Note that the pivot table cross-tabulates information from the Excel table shown in Figure 4-1. Each row in the pivot table shows sales by product. Each column in the pivot table shows sales by state. You can use column E to see grand totals of product sales by product item. You can use row 11 to see grand totals of sales by state.

Another quick note about the data item that you cross-tabulate: If you select a numeric data item — such as sales revenue — Excel cross-tabulates by summing the data item values. That's what you see in Figure 4-7. If you select a textual data item, Excel cross-tabulates by counting the number of data items.

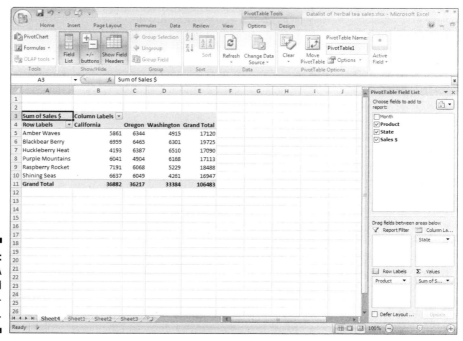

Figure 4-7:
Tah dah! A
completed
cross-
tabulation.

Although you can use pivot tables for more than what this simple example illustrates, this basic configuration is very valuable. With a table that reports the items you sell, to whom you sell, and the geographic locations where you sell, a cross-tabulation enables you to see exactly how much of each product you sell, exactly how much each customer buys, and exactly where you sell the most. Valuable information, indeed.

Fooling Around with Your Pivot Table

After you construct your pivot table, you can further analyze your data with some cool tools that Excel provides for manipulating information in a pivot table.

Pivoting and re-pivoting

The thing that gives the pivot table its name is that you can continue cross-tabulating the data in the pivot table. For example, take the data shown in Figure 4-7: By swapping the row items and column items (you do this merely by swapping the State and Product buttons), you can flip-flop the organization of the pivot table. Figure 4-8 shows the same information as Figure 4-7; the difference is that now the state sales appear in rows and the product sales appear in columns.

Note: The observant ones in the audience will notice that some of the worksheet now appears to the right of the portion viewable in the Excel workbook window in Figure 4-8. You'd need to scroll to see the rest of this information.

Another nifty thing about pivot tables is that they don't restrict you to using just two items to cross-tabulate data. For example, in both the pivot tables shown in Figures 4-7 and 4-8, I use only a single row item and a single column item. You're not limited to this, however: You can also further cross-tabulate the herbal tea data by also looking at sales by month *and* state. For example, if you drag the month data item to the Row Labels, Excel creates the pivot table shown in Figure 4-9. This pivot table enables you to view sales information for all the months, as shown in Figure 4-9, or just one of the months.

Filtering pivot table data

And here's another cool thing you can do: filtering. To filter sales by month, drag the Month PivotTable field to the Report Filter box. Excel re-cross-tabulates the PivotTable as shown in Figure 4-10. To see sales of herbal teas by state for only a specific month — say, January — you would click the down-arrow button that looks like it's in cell B1. When Excel displays a drop-down list box, select the month you want to see. Figure 4-11 shows sales for just the month of January. (Check out cell B1 again.)

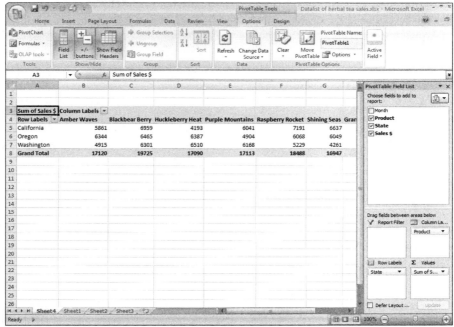

Figure 4-8:
Change
your focus
with a re-
pivoted
pivot table.

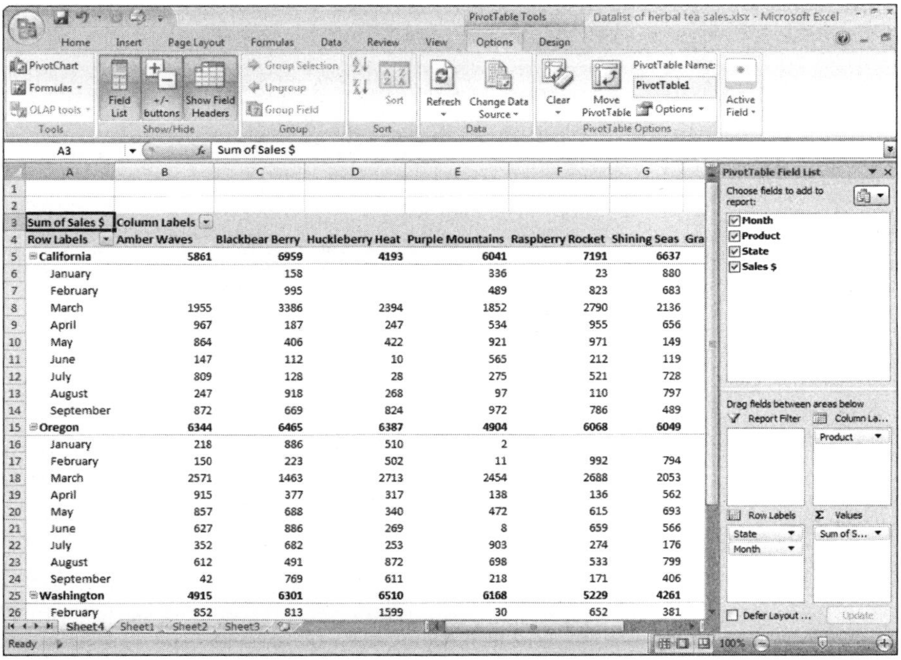

Figure 4-9:
Use multiple
PivotTable
fields for
rows.

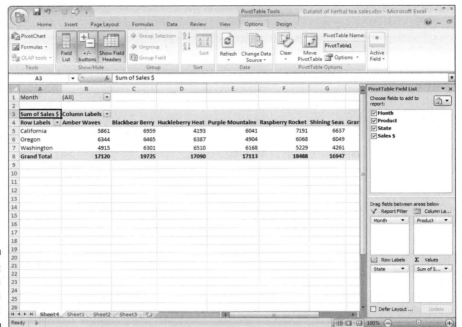

Figure 4-10:
You can
filter page
fields.

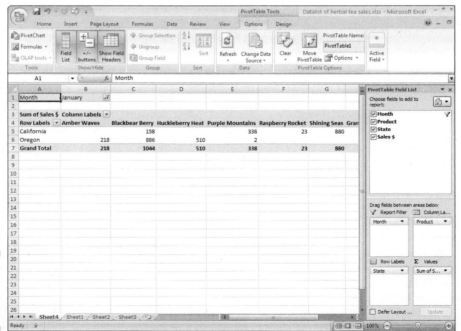

Figure 4-11:
Filtered
pivot table
information.

To remove an item from the pivot table, simply drag the item's button back to the PivotTable Field List. Also, as I mention earlier, to use more than one row item, drag the first item that you want to use to the Row Labels box and then also drag the second item that you also want to use to Row Labels Here.

Drag the row items from the PivotTable Field List. Do the same for columns: Drag each column item that you want from the PivotTable Field List Here to the Column Labels box.

Check out Figure 4-12 to see how the pivot table looks when I also use Month as a column item. Based on the data in Figure 4-1, this pivot table is very wide when I use both State and Month items for columns. For this reason, only a portion of the pivot table that uses both Month and State column items shows in Figure 4-12.

Sometimes having multiple row items and multiple column items makes sense. Sometimes it doesn't. But the beauty of a pivot table is that you can easily cross-tabulate and re-cross-tabulate your data simply by dragging those little item buttons. Accordingly, try viewing your data from different frames of reference. Try viewing your data at different levels of granularity. Spend some time looking at the different cross-tabulations that the PivotTable command enables you to create. Through careful, thoughtful viewing of these cross-tabulations, you can most likely gain insights into your data.

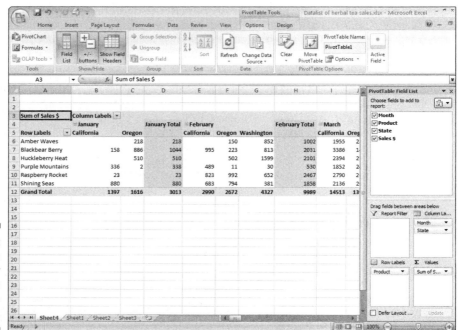

Figure 4-12: Slice data however you want in a cross-tabulation.

You can remove and redisplay the PivotTable Field List. To hide — perhaps to show a large portion of the pivot table — right-click PivotTable and choose the Hide Field List command. To show a previously hidden field list, right-click the PivotTable again and this time choose the Show Field List command. Predictably, whether the PivotTable shortcut menu displays the Show Field List command or the Hide Field List command depends on whether the field list shows or not. And, yes, this is the sort of insightful commentary you can count on me to supply.

Refreshing pivot table data

In many circumstances, the data in your Excel list changes and grows over time. This doesn't mean, fortunately, that you need to go to the work of re-creating your pivot table. If you update the data in your underlying Excel table, you can tell Excel to update the pivot table information.

You have four methods for telling Excel to refresh the pivot table:

- ✔ Click the PivotTable Tools Options tab's Refresh command. Note that the Refresh command button is visible in Figure 4-12, shown earlier.

- ✔ Choose the Refresh Data command from the shortcut menu that Excel displays when you right-click a pivot table.

- ✔ Tell Excel to automatically refresh the pivot table whenever the pivot table is opened. To do this, click the PivotTable tool, choose the Options command, and then after Excel displays the PivotTable Options dialog box, select the Refresh Data on Opening the File check box, located on the Data tab.

- ✔ Tell Excel to refresh the pivot table when opening the file. To do this, click the Options command on the PivotTable Tools Options tab, and then after Excel displays the PivotTable Options dialog box, click the Data tab and select the Refresh Data When Opening File check box.

You can point to any Ribbon command button and see its name in a pop-up ScreenTip. Use this technique when you don't know which command is which.

Sorting pivot table data

You can sort pivot table data in the same basic way that you sort an Excel list. Say that you want to sort the pivot table information shown in Figure 4-13 by product in descending order of sales to see a list that highlights the best products.

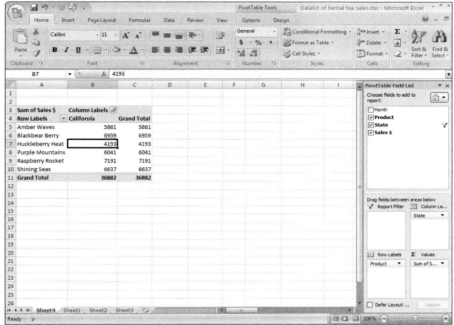

Figure 4-13:
A pivot table before you sort on California herbal sales.

To sort pivot table data in this way, right-click a cell in the column that holds the *sort key.* For example, in the case of the pivot table shown in Figure 4-13, and assuming that you want to sort by sales, you click a cell in the worksheet range C5:C10. Then, when Excel displays the shortcuts menu, choose either the Sort A to Z or the Sort Z to A command. Excel sorts the PivotTable data, as shown in Figure 4-14.

You can also exercise more control over the sorting of pivot table data. To do this, follow these steps:

1. **Choose Data tab's Sort command.**

   Excel displays the Sort dialog box shown in Figure 4-15.

2. **Select your sorting method.**

   You can select the Ascending (A to Z) By option to sort by the selected PivotTable field in ascending order. Or you can select the Descending (Z to A) By option to sort by the selected PivotTable field in descending order. Or you can select the Manual sort option, which lets you choose your own, wildly random sort order.

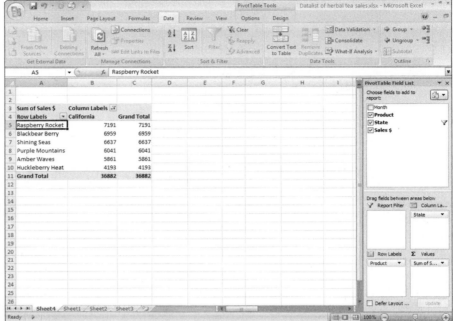

Figure 4-14:
A pivot table
after you
sort on
California
herbal tea
sales.

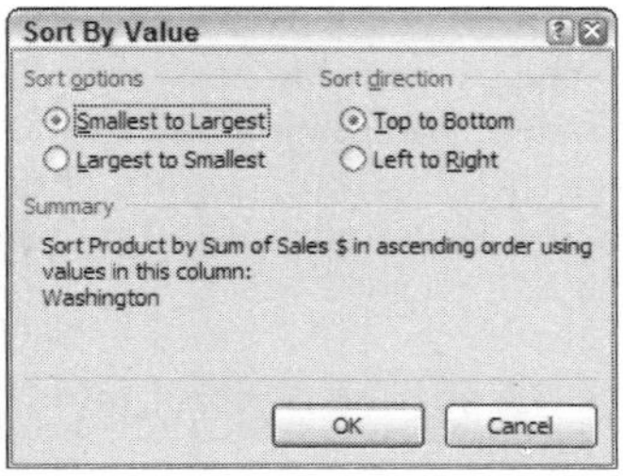

Figure 4-15:
The Sort
dialog box.

Pseudo-sorting

You can manually organize the items in your pivot table, too. You might want to do this so the order of rows or columns matches the way that you want to present information or the order in which you want to review information.

To change the order of items in your pivot table, right-click the pivot table row or column that you want to move. From the shortcut menu that Excel displays, choose the Move command. You should see a list of submenu commands: Move [X] to Beginning, Move [X] Up, Move [X] Down, and so forth. (Just so you know, [X] will be the name of the field you clicked.) Use these commands to rearrange the order of items in the pivot table. For example, you can move a product down in this list. Or you can move a state up in this list.

Grouping and ungrouping data items

You can group rows and columns in your pivot table. You might want to group columns or rows when you need to segregate data in a way that isn't explicitly supported by your Excel table.

In this chapter's running example, suppose that I combine Oregon and Washington. I want to see sales data for California, Oregon, and Washington by salesperson. I have one salesperson who handles California and another who handles Oregon and Washington. I want to combine (group) Oregon and Washington sales in my pivot table so that I can compare the two salespersons. The California sales (remember that California is covered by one salesperson) appear in one column, and Oregon and Washington sales appear either individually or together in another column.

To create a grouping, select the items that you want to group, right-click the pivot table, and then choose Group from the shortcut menu that appears.

Excel creates a new grouping, which it names in numerical order starting with Group1. As shown in Figure 4-16, Excel still displays detailed individual information about Oregon and Washington in the pivot table. However, the pivot table also groups the Oregon and Washington information into a new category: Group1.

You can rename the group by clicking the cell with the Group1 label and then typing the replacement label.

To ungroup previously grouped data, right-click the cell with the group name (probably Group1 unless you changed it) to again display the shortcut menu and then choose Ungroup. Excel removes the grouping from your pivot table.

Important point: You don't automatically get group subtotals. You get them when you filter the pivot table to show just that group. (I describe filtering earlier, in the section "Filtering pivot table data.") You also get group subtotals, however, when you collapse the details within a group. To collapse the detail within a group, right-click the cell labeled with the group name (probably Group1), and choose Expand/Collapse⇨Collapse from the shortcut menu that appears. Figure 4-17 shows a collapsed group. To expand a previously collapsed group, right-click the cell with the group name again and choose Expand/Collapse⇨Expand from the shortcut menu that appears. Or just double-click the group name.

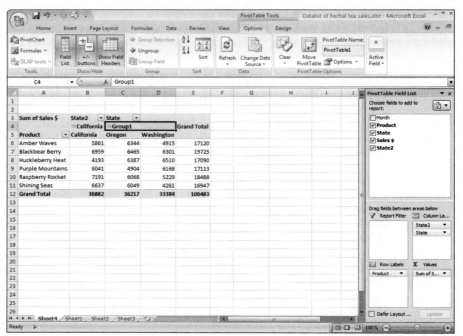

Figure 4-16:
Group data
in a pivot
table.

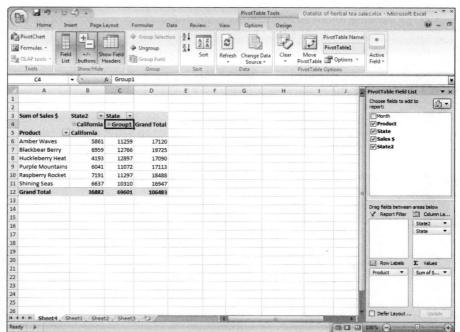

Figure 4-17:
Group data
in a pivot
table.

Selecting this, selecting that

At your disposal is the PivotTable Tools Options tab's Select submenu of commands: Label and Data, Label, Data, Entire Table, and Entire Selection. To display the Select submenu, click the drop-down arrow button to the right of the Options command button. When Excel displays the Options menu, choose the Select command.

Essentially, when you choose one of these submenu commands, Excel selects the referenced item in the table. For example, if you choose Select⇨Label, Excel selects all the labels in the pivot table. Similarly, choose Select⇨Data command, and Excel selects all the data cells in the pivot table.

The only Select menu command that's a little tricky is the Enable Selection command. That command tells Excel to expand your selection to include all the other similar items in the pivot table. For example, suppose that you create a pivot table that shows sales of herbal tea products for California, Oregon, and Washington over the months of the year. If you select the item that shows California sales of Amber Waves and then you choose the Enable Selection command, Excel selects the California sales of all the herbal teas: Amber Waves, Blackbear Berry, Purple Mountains, Shining Seas, and so on.

Where did that cell's number come from?

Here's a neat trick. Right-click a cell and then choose the Show Details command from the shortcuts menu. Excel adds a worksheet to the open workbook and creates an Excel table that summarizes individual records that together explain that cell's value.

For example, I right-click cell C8 in the workbook shown earlier in Figure 4-16 and choose the Show Details command from the shortcut menu. Excel creates a new table, as shown in Figure 4-18. This table shows all the information that gets totaled and then presented in cell C8 in Figure 4-16.

You can also show the detail that explains some value in a pivot table by double-clicking the cell holding the value.

Setting value field settings

The value field settings for a pivot table determine what Excel does with a field when it's cross-tabulated in the pivot table. This process sounds complicated, but this quick example shows you exactly how it works. If you right-click one of the sales revenue amounts shown in the pivot table and choose Value Field Settings from the shortcut menu that appears, Excel displays the Data Field Settings dialog box, as shown in Figure 4-19.

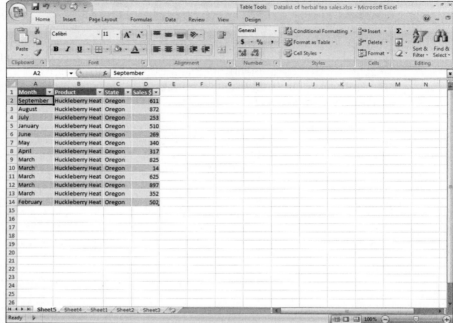

Figure 4-18:
A detail list shows where pivot table cell data comes from.

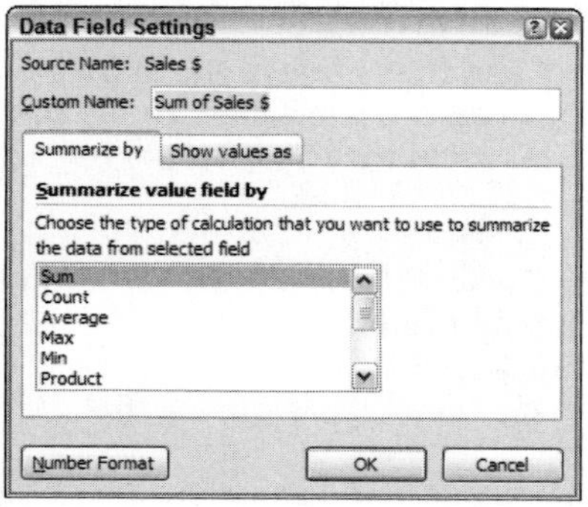

Figure 4-19:
Create field settings here.

Using the Summarize By tab of the Data Field Settings dialog box, you can indicate whether the data item should be summed, counted, averaged, and so on, in the pivot table. By default, data items are summed. But you can also arithmetically manipulate data items in other ways. For example, you can calculate average sales by selecting Average from the list box. You can also find the largest value by using the Max function, the smallest value by using the Min function, the number of sales transactions by using the Count function, and so on. Essentially, what you do with the Data Field Settings dialog box is pick the arithmetic operation that you want Excel to perform on data items stored in the pivot table.

If you click the Number Format button in the Data Field Settings dialog box, Excel displays a scaled-down version of the Format Cells dialog box (see Figure 4-20). From the Format Cells dialog box, you can pick a numeric format for the data item.

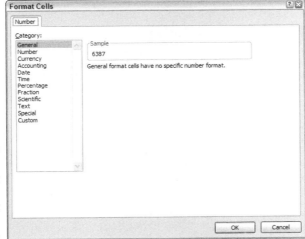

Figure 4-20:
The Format Cells dialog box for pivot tables.

Click the Show Values As tab of the Data Field Settings dialog box, and Excel provides several additional boxes (see Figure 4-21) that enable you to specify how the data item should be manipulated for fancy-schmancy summaries. I postpone a discussion of these calculation options until Chapter 5. There's some background stuff that I should cover before moving on to the subject of custom calculations, which is what these boxes are for.

Figure 4-21:
Make more choices from the expanded PivotTable Field dialog box.

Customizing How Pivot Tables Work and Look

Excel gives you a bit of flexibility over how pivot tables work and how they look. You have options to change their names, formatting, and data manipulation.

Setting pivot table options

Right-click a pivot table and choose the PivotTable Options command from the shortcut menu to display the PivotTable Options dialog box, as shown in Figure 4-22.

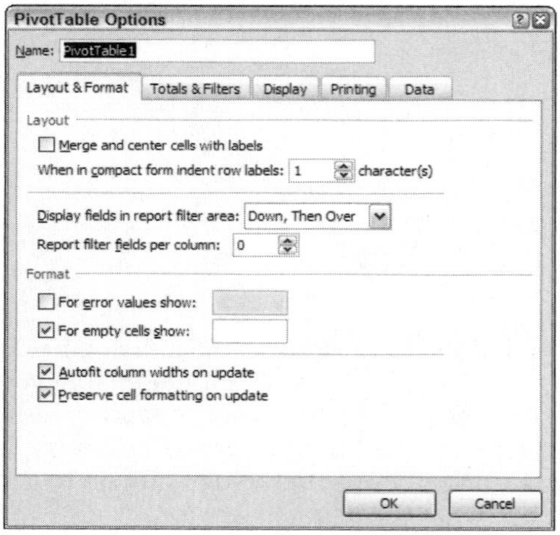

Figure 4-22:
Change a pivot table's look from the PivotTable Options dialog box.

The PivotTable Options dialog box provides several tabs of check and text boxes with which you tell Excel how it should create a pivot table. I do a quick run-through on these tab's options.

Layout & Format tab options

Use the Layout & Format tab's choices (refer to Figure 4-22) to control the appearance of your pivot table. For example, select the Merge And Center Cells with Labels check box to horizontally and vertically center outer row and outer column labels. Use the When in Compact Form Indent Row Labels [X] Character(s) to indent rows with labels when the PivotTable report is displayed using the compact format. Use the Display Fields in Report Filter Area and Report Filter Fields Per Column boxes to specify the ordering of multiple PivotTable filters and the number of filter fields per column.

The Format check boxes appearing on the Layout & Format tab all work pretty much as you would expect. To turn on a particular formatting option — specifying, for example, that Excel should show some specific label or value if the cell formula returns an error or results in an empty cell — select the For Error Values Show or For Empty Cells Show check boxes. To tell Excel to automatically size the column widths, select the Autofit Column Widths on Update check box. To tell Excel to leave the cell-level formatting as is, select the Preserve Cell Formatting On Update check box.

Perhaps the best way to understand what these layout and formatting options do is simply to experiment. Just an idea. . . .

Totals & Filters options

Use the Totals & Filters tab (see Figure 4-23) to specify whether Excel should add grand total rows and columns, whether Excel should let you use more than one filter per field and should subtotal filtered page items, and whether Excel should let you use custom lists when sorting. (Custom sorting lists include the months in a year or the days in the week.)

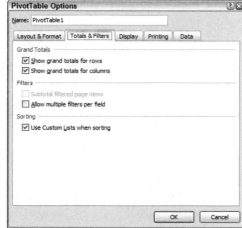

Figure 4-23:
The Totals & Filters tab of the PivotTable Options dialog box.

Display options

Use the Display tab (see Figure 4-24) to specify whether Excel should add expand/collapse buttons, contextual ScreenTips, field captions and filter drop-down list boxes, and similar such PivotTable bits and pieces. The Display tab also lets you return to Excel's old-fashioned (so-called "classic") PivotTable layout, which lets you design your pivot table by dragging fields to an empty PivotTable template in the worksheet.

Figure 4-24:
The Display
tab of the
PivotTable
Options
dialog box.

Again, your best bet with these options is to just experiment. If you're curious about what a check box does, simply mark (select) the check box. You can also click the Help button (the question mark button, top-left corner of the dialog box) and then click the feature that you have a question about.

Printing options

Use the Printing tab (see Figure 4-25) to specify whether Excel should print expand/collapse buttons, whether Excel should repeat row labels on each printed page, and whether Excel should set print titles for printed versions of your PivotTable so that the column and row that label your PivotTable appear on each printed page.

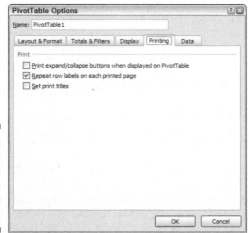

Figure 4-25:
The Printing
tab of the
PivotTable
Options
dialog box.

Data options

The Data tab's check boxes (see Figure 4-26) enable you to specify whether Excel stores data with the pivot table and how easy it is to access the data upon which the pivot table is based. For example, select the Save Source Data with File check box, and the data is saved with the pivot table. Select the Enable Expand to Detail check box, and you can get the detailed information that supports the value in a pivot table cell by right-clicking the cell to display the shortcut menu and then choosing the Show Detail command. Selecting the Refresh Data When Opening the File check box tells Excel to refresh the pivot table's information whenever you open the workbook that holds the pivot table.

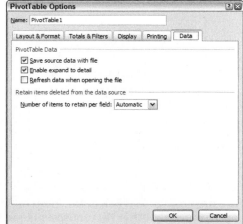

Figure 4-26:
The Data
tab of the
PivotTable
Options
dialog box.

The Number of Items to Retain Per Field box probably isn't something you need to pay attention to. This box lets you set the number of items per field to temporarily save, or cache, with the workbook.

Formatting pivot table information

You can and will want to format the information contained in a pivot table. Essentially, you have two ways of doing this: using standard cell formatting and using an autoformat for the table.

Using standard cell formatting

To format a single cell or a range of cells in your pivot table, select the range, right-click the selection, and then choose Format Cells from the shortcut menu. When Excel displays the Format Cells dialog box, as shown in Figure 4-27, use its tabs to assign formatting to the selected range. For example, if you want to assign numeric formatting, click the Number tab, choose a formatting category, and then provide any other additional formatting specifications appropriate — such as the number of decimal places to be used.

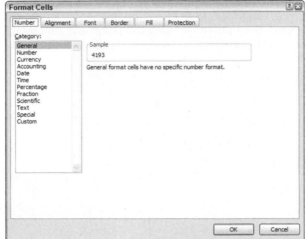

Figure 4-27:
Format one cell or a range of cells here.

Using PivotTable styles for automatic formatting

You can also format an entire pivot table. Just select the PivotTable Tools Design tab and then click the command button that represents the pre-designed PivotTable report format you want. (See Figure 4-28.) Excel uses this format to reformat your pivot table information. Look at Figure 4-29 to see how my running example pivot table of this chapter looks after I apply a PivotTable style.

If you don't look closely at the PivotTable Tools Design tab, you might not see something that's sort of germane to this discussion of formatting PivotTables: Excel provides several rows of PivotTable styles. Do you see the scrollbar along the right edge of this part of the Ribbon? If you scroll down, Excel displays a bunch more rows of predesigned PivotTable report formats — including some report formats that just go ape with color. And if you click the More button below the scroll buttons, the list expands so you can see the Light, Medium, and Dark categories.

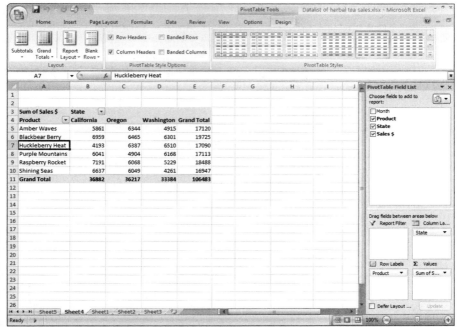

Figure 4-28:
Choose a format for an entire pivot table.

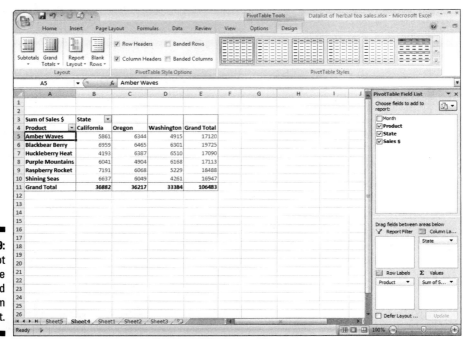

Figure 4-29:
My pivot table formatted from AutoFormat.

Using the lost PivotTable Tools Design tab tools

The PivotTable Tools Design tab supplies Subtotals, Grand Totals, Report Layout, and Blank Rows command buttons. Click one of these buttons and Excel displays a menu of formatting choices related to the command button's name. If you click the Grand Totals button, for example, Excel displays a menu that lets you add and remove grand total rows and columns to the PivotTable.

Finally, just so you don't miss them, notice that the PivotTable Tools Design tab also provides four check boxes — Row Headers, Column Headers, Banded Rows, and Banded Columns — that also let you change the appearance of your PivotTable report. If the check box labels don't tell you what the box does (and the check box labels are pretty self-descriptive), just experiment. You'll easily figure things out, and you can't hurt anything by trying.

Chapter 5

Building PivotTable Formulas

In This Chapter

▶ Adding another standard calculation

▶ Creating custom calculations

▶ Using calculated fields and items

▶ Retrieving data from a pivot table

*M*ost of the techniques that I discuss in this chapter aren't things that you need to do very often. Most frequently, the cross-tabulated data that appears in a pivot table after you run the PivotTable Wizard are almost exactly what you need. And if not, a little bit of fiddling around with the item buttons gets the information into the perfect arrangement for your needs. (For more on the PivotTable Wizard, read through Chapter 4.)

On occasion, however, you'll find that you need to either grab information from a pivot table so that you can use it someplace else or that you need to hard-code calculations and add them to a pivot table. In these special cases, the techniques that I describe in this chapter might save you much wailing and gnashing of teeth.

Adding Another Standard Calculation

Take a look at the pivot table shown in Figure 5-1. This pivot table shows coffee sales by state for an imaginary business that you can pretend that you own and operate. The data item calculated in this pivot table is sales. Sometimes, sales might be the only calculation that you want made. But what if you also want to calculate average sales by product and state in this pivot table?

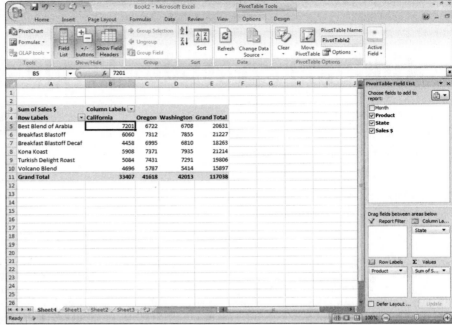

Figure 5-1:
Add
standard
calculations
to basic
pivot tables
for more
complex
data
analysis.

To do this, right-click the pivot table and choose Value Field Settings from the shortcut menu that appears. Then, when Excel displays the Data Field Settings dialog box, as shown in Figure 5-2, select Average from the Summarize Value Field By list box.

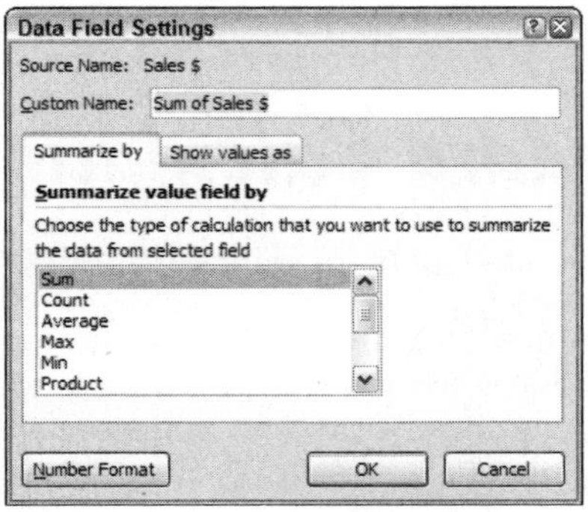

Figure 5-2:
Replace
calculations
here.

Now assume, however, that you don't want to replace the data item that sums sales. Assume instead that you want to add average sales data to the worksheet. In other words, you want your pivot table to show both total sales and average sales.

To add a second summary calculation, or standard calculation, to your pivot table, drag the data item from the PivotTable Field list box to the Σ Values box. Figure 5-3 shows how the roast coffee product sales by state pivot table looks after you drag the sales data item to the pivot table a second time. You may also need to drag the Σ Values entry to the Row Labels box. (See the Row Labels box at the bottom of the PivotTable Field List.)

After you add a second summary calculation — in Figure 5-3, this shows as the Sum of Sales $2 data item — right-click that data item, choose Value Field Settings from the shortcut menu that appears, and use the Data Field Settings dialog box to name the new average calculation and specify that the average calculation should be made. In Figure 5-4, you can see how the Data Field Settings dialog box looks when you make these changes for the pivot table shown in Figure 5-3.

See Figure 5-5 for the new pivot table. This pivot table now shows two calculations: the sum of sales for a coffee product in a particular state and the average sale. For example, in cell B6, you can see that sales for the Best Blend of the Arabia coffee are $7,201 in California. And in cell B7, the pivot table shows that the average sale of the Best Blend of Arabia coffee in California is $554.

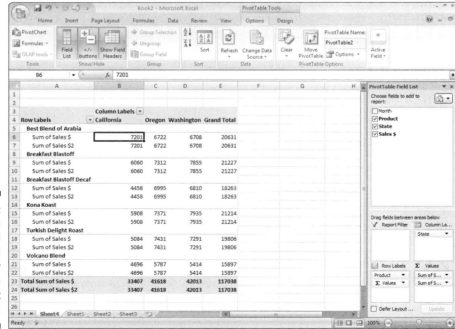

Figure 5-3:
Add a second standard summary calculation to a pivot table.

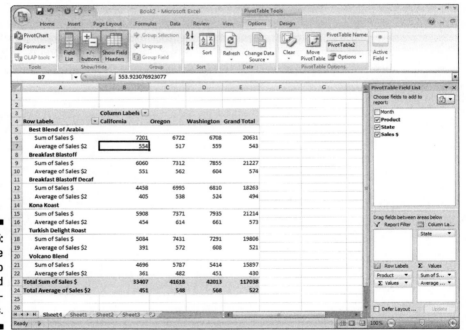

Figure 5-4:
Add a
second
standard
calculation
to a pivot
table.

Figure 5-5:
A pivot table
with two
standard
calcu-
lations.

If you can add information to your pivot table by using a standard calculation, that's the approach you want to take. Using standard calculations is the
easiest way to calculate information, or add formulas, to your pivot tables.

Creating Custom Calculations

Excel pivot tables provide a feature called *Custom Calculations*. Custom Calculations enable you to add many semi-standard calculations to a pivot table. By using Custom Calculations, for example, you can calculate the difference between two pivot table cells, percentages, and percentage differences.

To illustrate how custom calculations work in a pivot table, take a look at Figure 5-6. This pivot table shows coffee product sales by month for the imaginary business that you own and operate. Suppose, however, that you want to add a calculated value to this pivot table that shows the difference between two months' sales. You may do this so that you easily see large changes between two months' sales. Perhaps this data can help you identify new problems or important opportunities.

To add a custom calculation to a pivot table, you need to complete two tasks: You need to add another standard calculation to the pivot table, and you need to then customize that standard calculation to show one of the custom calculations listed in Table 5-1.

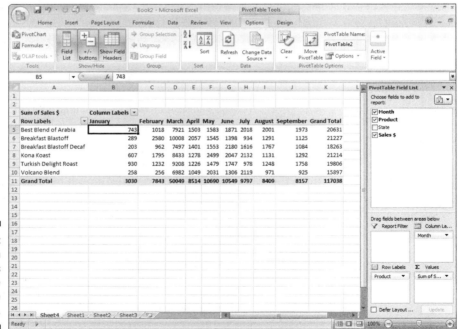

Figure 5-6:
Use custom calculations to compare pivot table data.

Table 5-1	Custom Calculation Options for Pivot Tables
Calculation	*Description*
Normal	You don't want a custom calculation.
Difference From	This is the difference between two pivot table cell values; for example, the difference between this month's and last month's value.
% of	This is the percentage that a pivot table cell value represents compared with a base value.
% Difference From	This is the percentage difference between two pivot table cell values; for example, the percentage difference between this month's and last month's value.
Running Total In	This shows cumulative or running totals of pivot table cell values; for example, cumulative year-to-date sales or expenses.
% of Row	This is the percent that a pivot table cell value represents compared with the total of the row values.
% of Column	This is the percent that a pivot table cell value represents compared with the total of the column values.
% of Total	This is the pivot table cell value as a percent of the grand total value.
Index	Kind of complicated, dude. The index custom calculation uses this formula: ((cell value) x (grand total of grand totals)) / ((grand total row) x (grand total column)).

To add a second standard calculation to the pivot table, add a second data item. For example, in the case of the pivot table shown in Figure 5-6, if you want to calculate the difference in sales from one month to another, you need to drag a second sales data item from the field list to the pivot table. Figure 5-7 shows how your pivot table looks after you make this change.

After you add a second standard calculation to the pivot table, you must customize it by telling Excel that you want to turn the standard calculation into a custom calculation. To do so, follow these steps:

1. **Click the new standard calculation field, right-click, and then choose Value Field Settings from the shortcut menu that appears.**

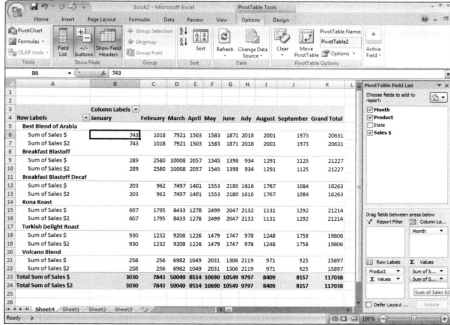

Figure 5-7:
Add a
second
standard
calculation
and then
customize it.

2. **When Excel displays the Data Field Settings dialog box, as shown in Figure 5-8, click the Show Values As tab.**

   The Show Values As tab provides three additional boxes: Show Values As, Base Field, and Base Item.

Click to select a custom calculation.

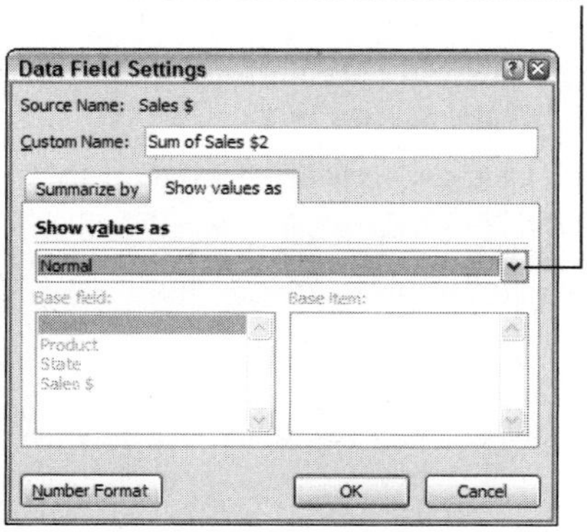

Figure 5-8:
Customize a
standard
calculation
here.

The Base Field and Base Item list box options that Excel offers depend on which type of custom calculation you're making.

3. **Select a custom calculation by clicking the down-arrow at the right side of the Show Values As list box and then selecting one of the custom calculations available in that drop-down list.**

For example, to calculate the difference between two pivot table cells, select the Difference From entry. Refer to Table 5-1 for explanation of the possible choices.

4. **Instruct Excel about how to make the custom calculation.**

After you choose the custom calculation that you want Excel to make in the pivot table, you make choices from the Base Field and Base Item list boxes to specify how Excel should make the calculation. For example, to calculate the difference in sales between the current month and the previous month, select Month from the Base Field list box and Previous from the Base Item list box. Figure 5-9 shows how this custom calculation gets defined.

Figure 5-9:
Define a
custom
calculation
here.

5. **Appropriately name the new custom calculation in the Custom Name text box of the Data Field Settings dialog box.**

For example, to calculate the change between two pivot table cells and the cells supply monthly sales, you may name the custom calculation *Change in Sales from Previous Month.* Or, more likely, you may name the custom calculation *Mthly Change.*

6. **Click OK.**

Excel adds the new custom calculation to your pivot table, as shown in Figure 5-10.

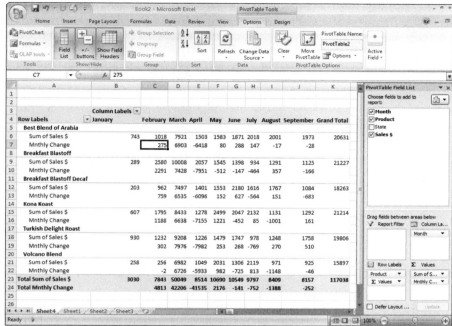

Figure 5-10:
Your pivot table now shows a custom calculation.

Using Calculated Fields and Items

Excel supplies one other opportunity for calculating values inside a pivot table. You can also add calculated fields and items to a table. With these calculated fields and items, you can put just about any type of formula into a pivot table. But, alas, you need to go to slightly more work to create calculated fields and items.

Adding a calculated field

Adding a calculated field enables you to insert a new row or column into a pivot table and then fill the new row or column with a formula. For example, if you refer to the pivot table shown in Figure 5-10, you see that it reports on sales both by product and month. What if you want to add the commissions expense that you incurred on these sales?

Suppose for the sake of illustration that your network of independent sales representatives earns a 25 percent commission on coffee sales. This commission expense doesn't appear in the data list, so you can't retrieve the information from that source. However, because you know how to calculate the commissions expense, you can easily add the commissions expense to the pivot table by using a calculated field.

To add a calculated field to a pivot table, take the following steps:

1. **Identify the pivot table by clicking any cell in that pivot table.**

2. **Tell Excel that you want to add a calculated field.**

   Click the PivotTable Tools Options tab's Formulas command, and then choose Calculated Field from the Formulas menu. Excel displays the Insert Calculated Field dialog box, as shown in Figure 5-11.

Figure 5-11:
Add a
calculated
field here.

3. **In the Name text box, name the new row or column that you want to show the calculated field.**

   For example, if you want to add a row that shows commissions expense, you might name the new field *Commissions*.

4. **Write the formula in the Formula text box.**

   Calculated field formulas work the same way as formulas for regular cells:

   a. Begin the formula by typing the equal (=) sign.

   b. Enter the operator and operands that make up the formula.

      If you want to calculate commissions and commissions equal 25 percent of sales, enter **=.25***.

   c. The Fields box lists all the possible fields that can be included in your formula. To include a choice from the Fields list, click the Sales $ item in the Fields list box and then click the Insert Field button.

See in Figure 5-11 how the Insert Calculated Field dialog box looks after you create a calculated field to show a 25 percent commissions expense.

5. Click OK.

Excel adds the calculated field to your pivot table. Figure 5-12 shows the pivot table with coffee product sales with the Commissions calculated field now appearing.

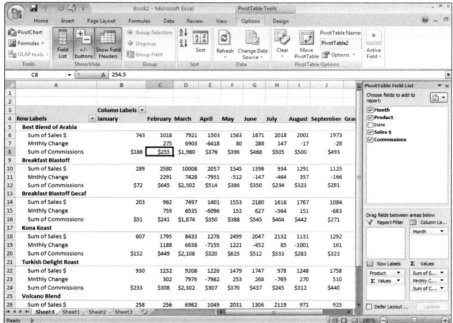

Figure 5-12:
A pivot table with a calculated field.

After you insert a calculated field, Excel adds the calculated field to the PivotTable field list. You can then pretty much work with the calculated item in the same way that you work with traditional items.

Adding a calculated item

You can also add calculated items to a pivot table. Now, frankly, adding a calculated item usually doesn't make any sense. If, for your pivot table, you have retrieved data from a complete, rich Excel list or from some database, creating data by calculating item amounts is more than a little goofy. However, in the spirit of fair play and good fun, here I create a scenario where you might need to do this using the sales of roast coffee products by months.

Assume that your Excel list omits an important product item. Suppose that you have another roast coffee product called *Volcano Blend Decaf.* And even though this product item information doesn't appear in the source Excel list, you can calculate this product item's information by using a simple formula.

Also assume that sales of the Volcano Blend Decaf product equal exactly and always 25 percent of the Volcano Blend product. In other words, even if you don't know or don't have Volcano Blend Decaf product item information available in the underlying Excel data list, it doesn't really matter. If you have information about the Volcano Blend product, you can calculate the Volcano Blend Decaf product item information.

Here are the steps that you take to add a calculated item for Volcano Blend Decaf to the Roast Coffee Products pivot table shown in earlier figures in this chapter:

1. **Select the Product button by simply clicking the Row Labels button in the pivot table.**

2. **Tell Excel that you want to add a calculated item to the pivot table.**

   Click the PivotTable Tools Options tab's Formulas command and then choose Calculated Items from the Formulas submenu that appears. Excel displays the Insert Calculated Item in "Product" dialog box, as shown in Figure 5-13.

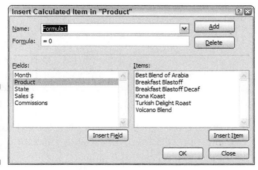

Figure 5-13: Insert a calculated item here.

3. **Name the new calculated item in the Name text box.**

   In the example that I set up here, the new calculated item name is *Volcano Blend Decaf,* so that's what you enter in the Name text box.

4. **Enter the formula for the calculated item in the Formula text box.**

Use the Formula text box to give the formula that calculates the item. In the example here, you can calculate Volcano Blend Decaf sales by multiplying Volcano Blend sales by 25 percent. This formula then is =.25*'Volcano Blend'.

a. To enter this formula into the Formula text box, first type **=.25***.

b. Then select Volcano Blend from the Items list box and click the Insert Item button.

See Figure 5-14 for how the Insert Calculated Item in "Product" dialog box looks after you name and supply the calculated item formula.

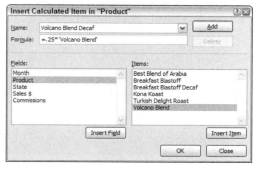

Figure 5-14:
The Insert Calculated Item dialog box after you do your dirty work.

5. **Add the calculated item.**

After you name and supply the formula for the calculated item, click OK. Excel adds the calculated item to the pivot table. Figure 5-15 shows the pivot table of roast coffee product sales by month with the new calculated item, Volcano Blend Decaf. This isn't an item that comes directly from the Excel data list, as you can glean from the preceding discussion. This data item is calculated based on other data items: in this case, based on the Volcano Blend data item.

Removing calculated fields and items

You can easily remove calculated fields and items from the pivot table.

To remove a calculated field, click a cell in the pivot table. Then click the PivotTable Tools Options tab's Formulas command and choose Calculated Field from the Formulas submenu that appears. When Excel displays the Insert Calculated Field dialog box, as shown in Figure 5-16, select the calculated field that you want to remove from the Name list box. Then click the Delete button. Excel removes the calculated field.

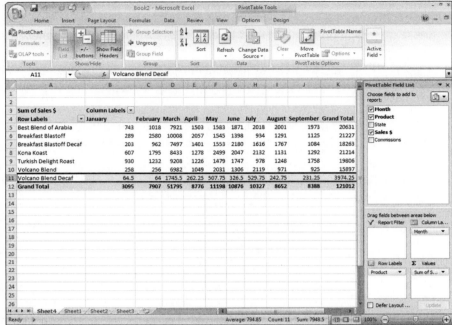

Figure 5-15:
The new pivot table with the inserted calculated item.

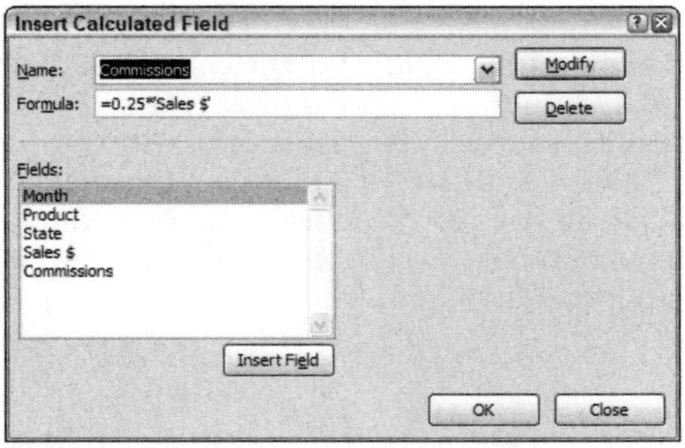

Figure 5-16:
Use the Insert Calculated Field dialog box to remove calculated fields from the pivot table.

To remove a calculated item from a pivot table, perform the following steps:

1. Click the button of the calculated item that you want to remove.

For example, if you want to remove the Volcano Blend Decaf item from the pivot table shown in Figure 5-15, click the Product button.

2. **Click the Options tab's Formulas button and then click Calculated Item from the menu that appears.**

   The Insert Calculated Item dialog box appears.

3. **Select the calculated item from the Name list box that you want to delete.**

4. **Click the Delete button.**

5. **Click OK.**

Figure 5-17 shows the Insert Calculated Item in "Product" dialog box as it looks after you select the Volcano Blend Decaf item to delete it.

Figure 5-17: Delete unwanted items from the Insert Calculated Item dialog box.

Reviewing calculated field and calculated item formulas

If you click the PivotTable Tools Options tab's Formulas command and choose List Formulas from the submenu that appears, Excel adds a new sheet to your workbook. This new sheet, as shown in Figure 5-18, identifies any of the calculated field and calculated item formulas that you add to the pivot table.

For each calculated field or item, Excel reports on the solve order, the field or item name, and the actual formula. If you have only a small number of fields or items, the solve order doesn't really matter. However, if you have many fields and items that need to be computed in a specific order, the Solve Order field becomes relevant. You can pick the order in which fields and items are calculated. The Field and Item columns of the worksheet give a field or item name. The Formula column shows the actual formula.

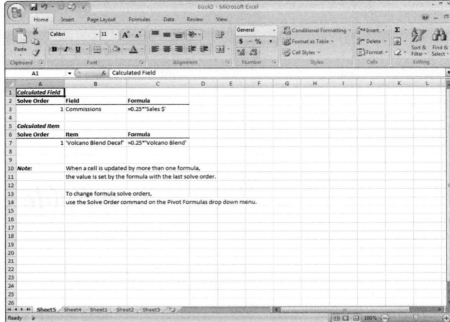

Figure 5-18:
The Calculated Field and Calculated Item list of formulas worksheet.

Reviewing and changing solve order

If you click the PivotTable Tools Options tab's Formulas command and choose Solve Order from the submenu that appears, Excel displays the Calculated Item Solve Order dialog box, as shown in Figure 5-19. In this dialog box, you tell Excel in what order the calculated item formulas should be solved.

In many cases, the solve order doesn't matter. But if, for example, you add calculated items for October, November, and December to the Kona Koast coffee product sales pivot table shown earlier in the chapter (refer to Figure 5-6), the solve order might just matter. For example, if the October calculated item formula depends on the previous three months and the same thing is true for November and December, you need to calculate those item values in chronological order. Use the Calculated Item Solve Order dialog box to do this. To use the dialog box, simply click a formula in the Solve Order list box. Click the Move Up and Move Down buttons to put the formula at the correct place in line.

Retrieving Data from a Pivot Table

You can build formulas that retrieve data from a pivot table. Like, I don't know, say that you want to chart some of the data shown in a pivot table. You can also retrieve an entire pivot table.

Getting all the values in a pivot table

To retrieve all the information in a pivot table, follow these steps:

1. **Select the pivot table by clicking a cell within it.**

2. **Click the PivotTable Tools Options tab's Options command, click Select, and choose Entire Table from the Select submenu that appears.**

   Excel selects the entire pivot table range.

3. **Copy the pivot table.**

   You can copy the pivot table the same way that you would copy any other text in Excel. For example, you can click the Home tab's Copy button or by pressing Ctrl+C. Excel places a copy of your selection onto the Clipboard.

4. **Select a location for the copied data by clicking there.**

5. **Paste the pivot table into the new range.**

   You can paste your pivot table data into the new range in the usual ways: by clicking the Paste button on the Home tab or by pressing Ctrl+V. Note, however, that when you paste a pivot table, you get another pivot table. You don't actually get data from the pivot table.

If you want to get just the data and not the pivot table — in other words, you want a range that includes labels and values, not a pivot table with pivot table buttons — you need to use the Paste Special command. (The Paste Special command is available from the menu that appears when you click the down-arrow button beneath the Paste button.) When you choose the Paste Special command, Excel displays the Paste Special dialog box, as shown in Figure 5-20. In the Paste section of this dialog box, select the Values radio button to indicate that you want to paste just a range of simple labels and values and not a pivot table itself. When you click OK, Excel pastes only the labels and values from the pivot table and not the actual pivot table.

Figure 5-20:
Paste information from a pivot table rather than the entire pivot table.

Getting a value from a pivot table

To get a single value from a paragraph using a formula, create a cell reference. For example, suppose that you want to retrieve the value shown in cell C8 in the worksheet shown in Figure 5-21. Further suppose that you want to place this value into cell C15. To do this, click cell C15, type the = sign, click cell C8, and then press Enter. Figure 5-21 shows how your worksheet looks before you press Enter. The formula shows.

As you can see in Figure 5-21, when you retrieve information from an Excel pivot table, the cell reference isn't a simple cell reference as you might expect. Excel uses a special function to retrieve data from a pivot table because Excel knows that you might change the pivot table. Therefore, upon changing the pivot table, Excel needs more information about the cell value or data value that you want than simply its previous cell address.

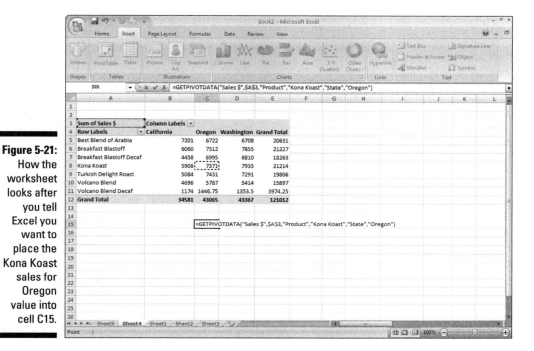

Figure 5-21: How the worksheet looks after you tell Excel you want to place the Kona Koast sales for Oregon value into cell C15.

Look a little more closely at the GET pivot table formula shown in Figure 5-21. The actual formula is

```
=GETPIVOTDATA("Sales$",$A$3,"Product","KonaKoast","State",
"Oregon")
```

The easiest way to understand the GETPIVOTDATA function arguments is by using the Insert Function command. To show you how this works, assume that you enter a GETPIVOTDATA function formula into cell C15. This is the formula that Figure 5-21 shows. If you then click cell C15 and choose the Formulas tab's Function Wizard command, Excel displays the Function Arguments dialog box, as shown in Figure 5-22. The Function Arguments dialog box, as you might already know if you're familiar with Excel functions, enables you to add or change arguments for a function. In essence, the Function Arguments dialog box names and describes each of the arguments used in a function.

Figure 5-22:
The
Function
Arguments
dialog box
for the GET
PIVOTDATA
function.

Arguments of the GETPIVOTDATA function

Here I quickly go through and describe each of the GETPIVOTDATA function arguments. The bulleted list that follows names and describes each argument:

- ✔ data=field: The data_field argument names the data field that you want to grab information from. The data_field name in Figure 5-22 is Sales $. This simply names the item that you drop into the Values area of the pivot table.

- ✔ pivot=table: The pivot=table argument identifies the pivot table. All you need to do here is to provide a cell reference that's part of the pivot table. In the GETPIVOTDATA function that I use in Figure 5-21, for example, the pivot=table argument is $A$3. Because cell A3 is at the top-left corner of the pivot table, this is all the identification that the function needs in order to identify the correct pivot table.

- ✔ field1 and item1: The field1 and item1 arguments work together to identify which product information that you want the GETPIVOTDATA function to retrieve. Cell C8 holds Kona Koast sales information. Therefore, the field1 argument is product, and the item1 argument is Kona Koast. Together, these two arguments tell Excel to retrieve the Kona Koast product sales information from the pivot table.

- ✔ field2 and item2: The field2 and item2 arguments tell Excel to retrieve just Oregon state sales of the Kona Koast product from the pivot table. Field2 shows the argument state. item2, which isn't visible in Figure 5-22, shows as Oregon.

Chapter 6

Working with PivotCharts

In Chapter 4, I discuss how cool it is that Excel easily cross-tabulates data in pivot tables. In this chapter, I cover a closely related topic: how to cross-tabulate data in pivot charts.

You might notice some suspiciously similar material in this chapter compared with Chapter 4. But that's all right. The steps for creating a pivot chart closely resemble those that you take to create a pivot table.

If you've just read the preceding paragraphs and find yourself thinking, "Hmmm. *Cross-tabulate* is a familiar-sounding word, but I can't quite put my finger on what it means," you might want to first peruse Chapter 4. Let me also say that, as is the case when constructing pivot tables, you build pivot charts by using data stored in an Excel table. Therefore, you should also know what Excel tables are and how they work and should look. I discuss this information a little bit in Chapter 4 and a bunch in Chapter 1.

Why Use a PivotChart?

Before I get into the nitty-gritty details of creating a pivot chart, stop and ask a reasonable question: *When would you or should you use a pivot chart?* Well, the correct answer to this question is, "Heck, most of the time you won't use a pivot chart. You'll use a pivot table instead."

Pivot charts, in fact, work only in certain situations: Specifically, pivot charts work when you have only a limited number of rows in your cross-tabulation. Say, less than half a dozen rows. And pivot charts work when it makes sense to show information visually, such as in a bar chart.

These two factors mean that for many cross-tabulations, you won't use pivot charts. In some cases, for example, a pivot chart won't be legible because the underlying cross-tabulation will have too many rows. In other cases, a pivot chart won't make sense because its information doesn't become more understandable when presented visually.

Getting Ready to Pivot

As with a pivot table, in order to create a pivot chart, your first step is to create the Excel table that you want to cross-tabulate. You don't have to put the information into a table, but working with information that's already stored in a table is easiest, so that's the approach that I assume you'll use.

Figure 6-1 shows an example data table — this time, a list of specialty coffee roasts that you can pretend sell to upscale, independent coffeehouses along the West Coast.

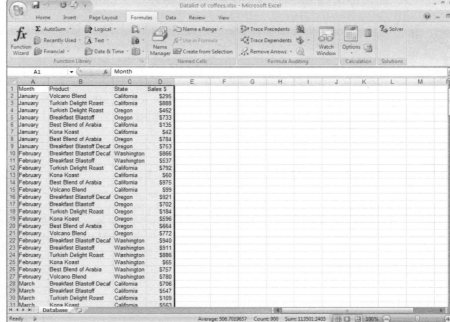

Figure 6-1:
A simple Excel data table that shows sales for your imaginary coffee business.

The roast coffee list workbook is available in the Zip file of example Excel workbooks related to this book and stored at the Dummies Web site. You might want to download this list in order to follow along with the discussion here. The URL is www.dummies.com/go/e2007dafd.

Running the PivotTable Wizard

Because you typically create a pivot chart by starting with the PivotTable Wizard, I describe that approach first. (Actually, the wizard is technically called the PivotTable and PivotChart Wizard, but that gets a little long-winded.) At the very end of the chapter, however, I describe briefly another method for creating a pivot chart: using the Insert Chart command on an existing pivot table.

To run the PivotTable Wizard to create a pivot chart, take the following steps:

1. **Select the Excel table.**

   To do this, just click a cell in the table. After you've done this, Excel assumes you want to work with the entire table.

2. **Tell Excel that you want to create a pivot chart by choosing the Insert tab's PivotChart command.**

   To get to the menu with the PivotChart command, you need to click the down-arrow button that appears beneath the PivotTable button. Excel then displays a menu with two commands: PivotTable and PivotChart. When you choose the PivotChart command, Excel displays the Create PivotTable with PivotChart dialog box, as shown in Figure 6-2.

3. **Answer the question about where the data that you want to analyze is stored.**

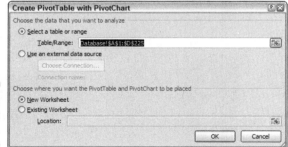

Figure 6-2:
Create pivot tables here.

I recommend you store the to-be-analyzed data in an Excel Table/Range. If you do so, click the Select a Table or Range radio button.

4. **Tell Excel in what worksheet range the to-be-analyzed data is stored.**

If you followed Step 1, Excel should already have filled in the Range text box with the worksheet range that holds the to-be-analyzed data, but you should verify that the worksheet range shown in the Table/Range text box is correct.

If you skipped Step 1, enter the list range into the Table/Range text box. You can do so in two ways. You can type the range coordinates. For example, if the range is cell A1 to cell D225, you can type **$A$1:$D$225**. Alternatively, you can click the button at the right end of the Range text box. Excel collapses the Create PivotTable with PivotChart dialog box, as shown in Figure 6-3. Now use the mouse or the navigation keys to select the worksheet range that holds the list you want to pivot.

After you select the worksheet range, click the range button again. Excel redisplays the Create PivotTable with PivotChart dialog box. (Refer to Figure 6-2.)

5. **Tell Excel where to place the new pivot table report that goes along with your pivot chart.**

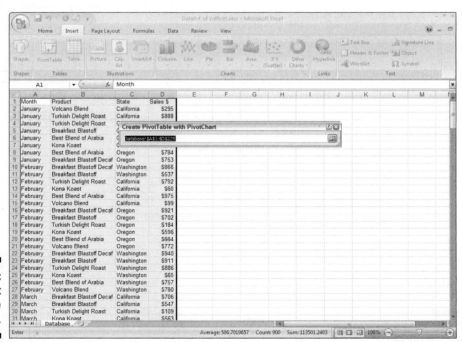

Figure 6-3:
Enter a pivot table range here.

Select either the New Worksheet or Existing Worksheet radio button to select a location for the new pivot table that supplies the data to your pivot chart. Most often, you want to place the new pivot table onto a new worksheet in the existing workbook — the workbook that holds the Excel table that you're analyzing with a pivot chart. However, if you want, you can place the new pivot table into an existing worksheet. If you do this, you need to select the Existing Worksheet radio button and also make an entry in the Existing Worksheet text box to identify the worksheet range. To identify the worksheet range here, enter the cell name in the top-left corner of the worksheet range.

You don't tell Excel where to place the new pivot chart, by the way. Excel inserts a new chart sheet in the workbook that you use for the pivot table and uses that new chart sheet for the pivot table.

6. **When you finish with the Create PivotTable with PivotChart dialog box, click OK.**

   Excel displays the new worksheet with the partially constructed pivot chart in it, as shown in Figure 6-4.

7. **Select the data series.**

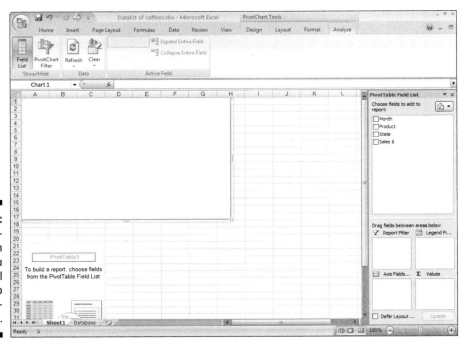

Figure 6-4: A cross-tabulation before you tell Excel what to cross-tabulate.

You need to decide first what you want to plot in the chart — or what data series should show in a chart.

If you haven't worked with Excel charting tools before, determining what the right data series are seems confusing at first. But this is another one of those situations where somebody's taken a ten-cent idea and labeled it with a five-dollar word. *Charts* show data series. And a *chart legend* names the *data series* that a chart shows. For example, if you want to plot sales of coffee products, those coffee products are your data series.

After you identify your data series — suppose that you decide to plot coffee products — you drag the field from the PivotTable Field List box to the Legend Field (Series) box. To use coffee products as your data series, for example, drag the Product field to the Legend Field (Series) box. Using the example data from Figure 6-1, after you do this, the partially constructed Excel pivot chart looks like the one shown in Figure 6-5.

8. **Select the data category.**

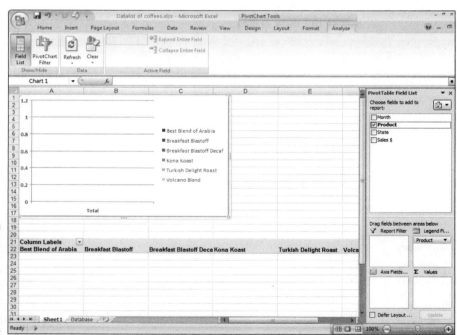

Figure 6-5:
The cross-tabulation after you select a data series.

Your second step in creating a pivot chart is to select the data category. The data category organizes the values in a data series. That sounds complicated, but in many charts, identifying the data category is easy. In any chart (including a pivot chart) that shows how some value changes over time, the data category is *time*. In the case of this example pivot chart, to show how coffee product sales change over time, the data category is *time*. Or, more precisely, the data category uses the Month field.

After you make this choice, you drag the data category field item from the PivotTable Field list to the box marked Axis Fields. Figure 6-6 shows the way that the partially constructed pivot chart looks after you specify the data category as Months.

9. **Select the data item that you want to chart.**

After you choose the data series and data category for your pivot chart, you indicate what piece of data that you want plotted in your pivot chart. For example, to plot sales revenue, drag the Sales $ item from the PivotTable Field List to the box labeled Σ Values.

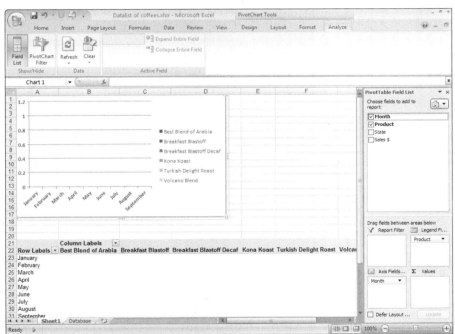

Figure 6-6: And it just gets better.

Figure 6-7 shows the pivot table after the Data Series (Step 7), Data Category (Step 8), and Data (Step 9) items have been selected. This is a completed pivot chart. Note that it cross-tabulates information from the Excel list shown in Figure 6-1. Each bar in the pivot chart shows sales for a month. Each bar is made up of colored segments that represent the sales contribution made by each coffee product. Obviously, you can't see the colors in a black-and-white image like the one shown in Figure 6-7. But on your computer monitor, you can see the colored segments and the bars that they make.

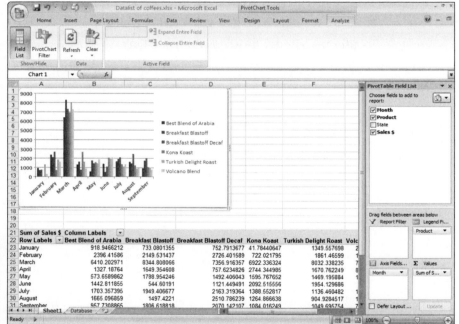

Figure 6-7: The completed pivot chart.

Fooling Around with Your Pivot Chart

After you construct your pivot chart, you can further analyze your data. Here I briefly describe some of the cool tools that Excel provides for manipulating information in a pivot chart.

Pivoting and re-pivoting

The thing that gives the pivot tables and pivot charts their names is that you can continue cross-tabulating, or pivoting, the data. For example, you could take the data shown in Figure 6-7 and by swapping the data series and data categories — you do this merely by dragging the State and Product buttons — you can flip-flop the organization of the pivot chart.

One might also choose to pivot new data. For example, the chart in Figure 6-8 shows the same information as Figure 6-7. The difference is that the new pivot chart uses the State field rather than the Month field as the data category. The new pivot chart continues to use the Product field as the data series.

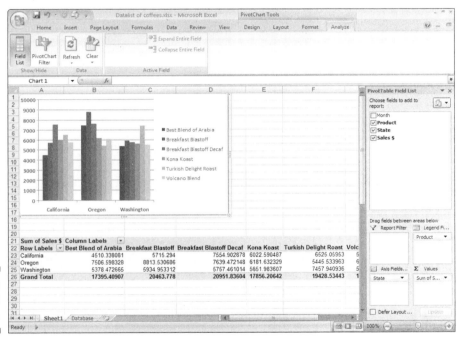

Figure 6-8:
A re-pivoted
pivot chart.

Filtering pivot chart data

You can also segregate data by putting information on different charts. For example, if you drag the Month data item to the Report Filter box (in the bottom half of the PivotTable Field List), Excel creates the pivot table shown in Figure 6-9. This pivot table lets you view sales information for all the months, as shown in Figure 6-9, or just one of the months. In Figure 6-9, note the Month drop-down box in the upper-left corner of the pivot table. This box is by default set to display all the months (All), so the chart in Figure 6-9 looks just like Figure 6-8. Things really start to happen, however, when you want to look at just one month's data.

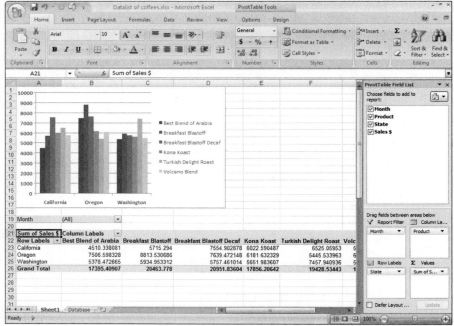

Figure 6-9:
Whoa. Now
I use
months to
cross-
tabulate.

To show sales for only a single month, click the down-arrow button to the right of the Month drop-down list. When Excel displays the drop-down list, select the month that you want to see sales for and then click OK. Figure 6-10 shows sales for just the month of January.

To remove an item from the pivot chart, simply drag the item's button back to the PivotTable Field list.

You can also filter data based on the data series or the data category. In the case of the pivot chart shown in Figure 6-10, you can indicate that you want to see only a particular data series information by clicking the arrow button to the right of the Column Labels drop-down list. When Excel displays the drop-down list of coffee products, select the coffee that you want to see sales for. You can use the Row Labels drop-down list in a similar fashion to see sales for only a particular state.

Let me mention one other tidbit about pivoting and re-pivoting. If you've worked with pivot tables, you might remember that you can cross-tabulate by more than one row or column items. You can do something very similar with pivot charts. You can become more detailed in your data series or data categories by dragging another field item to the Legend Fields or Axis Fields box.

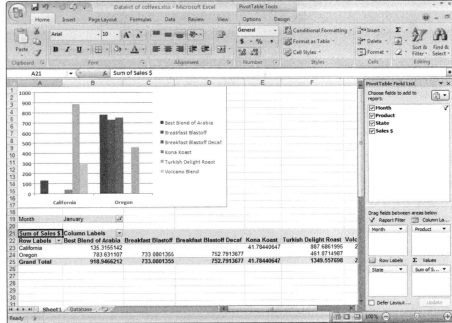

Figure 6-10:
You can
filter pivot
chart
information,
too.

Figure 6-11 shows how the pivot table looks if you use State to add granularity to the Product data series.

Sometimes lots of granularity in a cross-tabulation makes sense. But having multiple row items and multiple column items in a pivot table makes more sense than adding lots of granularity to pivot charts by creating superfine data series or data categories. Too much granularity in a pivot chart turns your chart into an impossible-to-understand visual mess, a bit like the disaster that I show in Figure 6-11.

Refreshing pivot chart data

As the data in an Excel table changes, you need to update the pivot chart. You have two methods for telling Excel to refresh your chart:

- ✔ **You can click the Refresh command** on the PivotTable Tools Options tab. (See Figure 6-12.)

- ✔ **You can choose the Refresh Data command** from the shortcut menu that Excel displays when you right-click a pivot chart.

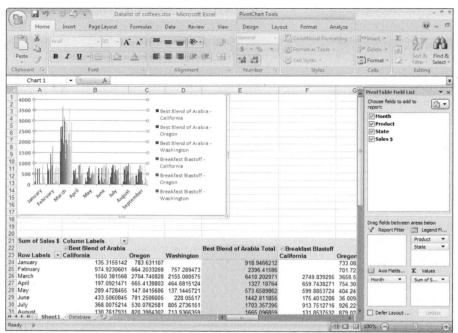

Figure 6-11: Yet another cross-tabulation of the data.

 Point to an Excel ribbon button, and Excel displays pop-up ScreenTips that give the command button name.

Grouping and ungrouping data items

You can group together and ungroup values plotted in a pivot chart. For example, suppose that you want to take the pivot chart shown in Figure 6-13 — which is very granular — and hide some of the detail. You might want to combine the detailed information shown for Breakfast Blend and Breakfast Blend Decaf and show just the total sales for these two related products. To do this, select a Row Labels cell or the Column Labels cell that you want to group, right-click your selection, and choose Group from the shortcut menu. Next, right-click the new group and choose Collapse from the shortcut menu.

After you group and collapse, Excel shows just the group totals in the PivotTable and PivotChart. As shown in Figure 6-14, the combined Breakfast Blast sales are labeled as Group1.

Click to refresh your chart.

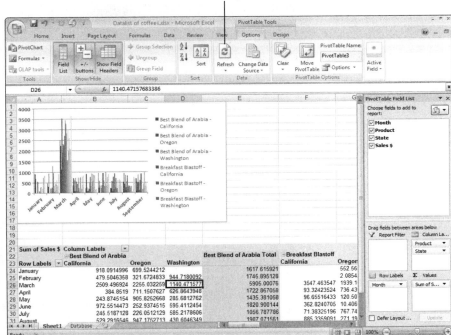

Figure 6-12:
The
PivotTable
Tools Option
tab provides
a Refresh
command.

To show previously collapsed detail, right-click the Row Labels or Column Labels cell that shows the collapsed grouping. Then choose Expand/Collapse⊏ Expand from the menu that appears.

To show previously grouped detail, right-click the Row Labels or Column Labels cell that shows the grouping. Then choose Ungroup from the menu that appears.

Using Chart Commands to Create Pivot Charts

You can also use Excel's standard charting commands to create charts of pivot table data. You might choose to use the Charts toolbar on the Insert tab when you've already created a pivot table and now want to use that data in a chart.

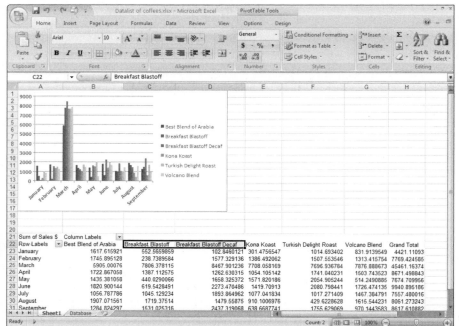

Figure 6-13:
A pivot chart with too much detail.

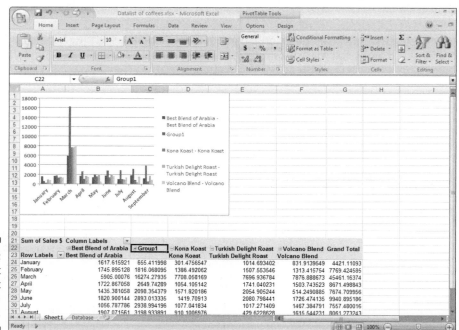

Figure 6-14:
A pivot chart that looks a little bit better.

How about just charting pivot table data?

You can chart a pivot table, too. I mean, if you just want to use pivot table data in a regular old chart, you can do so. Here's how. First, copy the pivot table data to a separate range, using the Paste Special command to just grab values. Then chart the data by clicking the Insert tab's charting commands.

To create a regular old chart using PivotTable data, follow these steps:

1. **Create a pivot table.**

   For help on how to do this, refer to Chapter 4 for the blow-by-blow account.

2. **Select the worksheet range in the pivot table that you want to chart.**

3. **Tell Excel to create a pivot chart by choosing the appropriate charting command from the Insert tab.**

   The Chart Wizard creates a pivot chart that matches your pivot table.

For normal charting, by the way, you set up a worksheet with the data that you want to plot in a chart. Then you select the data and tell Excel to plot the data in a chart by choosing one of the Insert tab's chart commands.

By the way, in this chapter, I don't describe how to customize the actual pivot chart . . . but I didn't forget that topic. Pivot chart customization as a subject is so big that it gets its own chapter: Chapter 7.

Chapter 7

Customizing PivotCharts

Although you usually get pretty good-looking pivot charts by using the wizard, you'll sometimes want to customize the charts that Excel creates. Sometimes you'll decide that you want a different type of chart . . . perhaps to better communicate the chart's message. And sometimes you want to change the colors so that they match the personality of the presentation or the presenter. In this chapter, I describe how to make these and other changes to your pivot charts.

Selecting a Chart Type

The first step in customizing a pivot chart is to choose the chart type that you want. When the active sheet in an Excel workbook shows a chart or when a chart object in the active sheet is selected, Excel adds the Design and Layout tabs to the Ribbon to allow you to customize the chart. The leftmost command on the Design tab is Change Chart Type. If you click the Change Chart Type command button, Excel displays the Change Chart Type dialog box, as shown in Figure 7-1.

The Change Chart Type dialog box has two lists from which you pick the type of chart that you want. The left chart type list identifies each of the 11 chart types that Excel plots. You can choose chart types such as Column, Line, Pie, Bar, and so on. For each chart type, Excel also displays several subtypes; pictographs of these subtypes display on the right side of the Change Chart Type dialog box. You can think of a chart subtype as a flavor or model or mutation. You choose a chart type and chart subtype by selecting a chart from the chart type list and then clicking one of the chart subtype buttons.

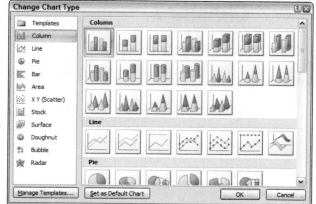

Figure 7-1:
Select your
chart type
here.

Working with Chart Layouts

Excel provides several chart layouts, which are also available on the Design tab of the Ribbon. You choose a chart layout by clicking its button. Do note that although the Design tab provides space for only three chart layout buttons to be displayed at a time, you can scroll down and see other chart layout options, too.

Working with Chart Styles

Excel also provides several dozen chart styles on the Design tab. As with chart layouts, you select a chart style by clicking its button. Also as with chart styles, the Design tab provides space for only a subset of the available chart style buttons to be displayed at a time. You need to scroll down to see the other chart style options.

Setting Chart Options

Choosing the Layout tab displays the command you can use to customize just about any element of your pivot chart, including titles, legends, data labels, data tables, axes, and gridlines.

Chart titles

The Chart Title and Axis Titles commands on the Layout tab open menus of commands that you can use to provide your chart with a title and to add titles to the vertical, horizontal, and depth axes of your chart.

After you choose a command, Excel adds a placeholder box to the chart. Figure 7-2, for example, shows the placeholder added for a chart title. To replace the placeholder title text, click the placeholder and type the title you want.

The last command on the Chart menu, More Title Options, and the last command on the Axis Titles submenus, More Primary [X] Axis Title Options, display simple-to-understand dialog boxes you can use to control the appearance of the box that the chart or axis title sits in.

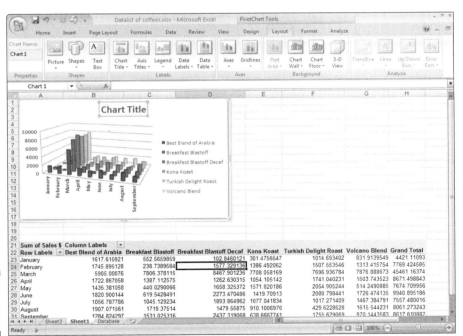

Figure 7-2:
A chart title placeholder.

Figure 7-3, for example, shows the Format Chart Title dialog box, which is the dialog box that appears when you choose the More Title Options command from the Chart Title menu. The Format Chart Title dialog box, for example, provides a set of Fill options that let you fill in the chart title box with color or a pattern. (If you do select a fill color or pattern, Excel adds buttons and boxes to the set of Fill options so you can specify what the color or pattern should be.)

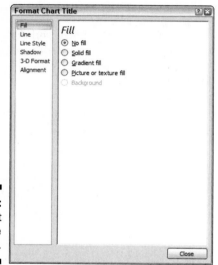

Figure 7-3:
The Format
Chart Title
dialog box.

The Format Chart Title dialog box and the equivalent Format Axis Title boxes also provide buttons and boxes for you to specify how you want any lines drawn for the chart title box or axis title to look in terms of thickness, color, and style.

Chart legend

Use the Legend command on the Layout tab to add or remove a legend to a pivot chart. When you click this command button, Excel displays a menu of commands with each command corresponding to a location in which the chart legend can be placed. A *chart legend* simply identifies the data series plotted in your chart.

You can also choose the More Legend Options command, which is the last command on the Legend menu, to display the Format Legend dialog box. (See Figure 7-4.) The Format Legend dialog box allows you to select a location for the legend and also to specify how Excel should draw the legend.

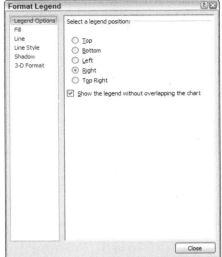

Chart data labels

The Data Labels command on the Layout tab allows you to label data markers with pivot table information or table information. When you click the command button, Excel displays a menu with commands corresponding to locations for the data labels: None, Center, Left, Right, Above, and Below. None signifies that no data labels should be added to the chart and Show signifies heck yes, add data labels. The menu also displays a More Data Label Options command. To add data labels, just select the command that corresponds to the location you want. To remove the labels, select the None command. Figure 7-5 shows a chart with data labels.

If you want to specify what Excel should use for the data label, choose the More Data Labels Options command from the Data Labels menu. Excel displays the Format Data Labels dialog box (see Figure 7-6). Check the box that corresponds to the bit of pivot table or Excel table information that you want to use as the label. For example, if you want to label data markers with a pivot table chart using data series names, select the Series Name check box. If you want to label data markers with a category name, select the Category Name check box. To label the data markers with the underlying value, select the Value check box.

Different chart types supply different data label options. Your best bet, therefore, is to experiment with data labels by selecting and deselecting the check boxes in the Label Contains area of the Data Labels tab.

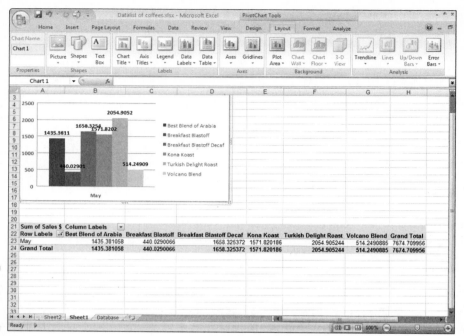

Figure 7-5:
A chart with
data labels.

Figure 7-6:
Set data
labels here.

Note: The Label Options tab also provides a Separator drop-down list box, from which you can select the character or symbol (a space, comma, colon, and so on) that you want Excel to use to separate data labeling information.

Selecting the Include Legend Key In Label check box tells Excel to display a small legend key next to data markers to visually connect the data marker to the legend. This sounds complicated, but it's not. Just select the check box to see what it does. (You have to select one of the Label Contains check boxes before this check box is active.)

Chart data tables

A *data table* just shows the plotted values in a table and adds the table to the chart. A data label might make sense for non-pivot charts, but not for pivot charts. (A data table duplicates the pivot table data that Excel creates as an intermediate step in creating the pivot chart.) Nevertheless, just because I have an obsessive-compulsive personality, I'll explain what the Data Table tab does.

When you choose the Data Table command from the Layout menu, Excel displays a menu of commands: None, Show Data Table, Show Data Table With Legend Keys, and More Data Table Options. To add a data table to your chart, select the Show Data Table or the Show Data Table with Legend Keys command. Figure 7-7 shows you what a data table looks like.

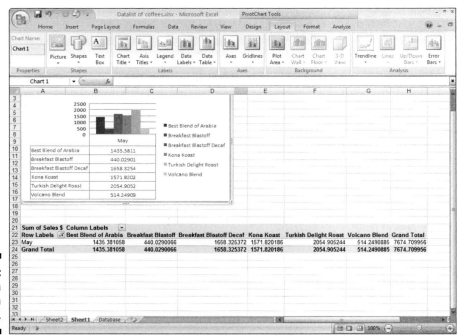

Figure 7-7:
Add a data
table to a
chart here.

To customize the appearance of your data table, choose the Data Table menu's last command, More Data Table Options. Excel displays the Format Data Table dialog box (see Figure 7-8). You can use its boxes and buttons to change the appearance of the data table.

Figure 7-8:
Add a data
table to a
pivot chart.

Chart axes

The Axes command on the Layout tab provides access to menu commands (actually submenu commands) that let you control the placement and scaling of the horizontal and vertical axes for your chart simply by choosing the command that corresponds to the axis placement and scaling you want.

You can also choose either the More Primary Horizontal Axis Options command or the More Primary Vertical Axis Options command to display a Format Axis dialog box (see Figure 7-9).

The best way to find out what these radio buttons do is to just experiment with them. In some cases, selecting the different axis radio button has no effect. For example, you can't select the Date Axis option under Axes Type unless your chart shows time series data — and Excel realizes it.

Tips for scaling a pivot chart's axes

A couple of options on the Format Axis dialog box are worth discussing in a bit more detail. First, the Display Units drop-down list enables you to choose a display scaling unit for the chart, such as Hundreds, Thousands, Millions, and so on. If you don't want to use some display scaling unit, select None from the Display Units drop-down list.

Second, don't ignore the Values in Reverse Order or the Logarithmic Scale boxes. They can be pretty darn useful at times:

✔ **Values in Reverse Order:** Select the Values in Reverse Order check box to tell Excel to flip the chart upside down and plot the minimum value at the top of the scale and the maximum value at the bottom of the scale. If this description sounds confusing — and I guess it is — just try this reverse order business with a real chart. You'll instantly see what I mean.

✔ **Logarithmic Scale:** Select the Logarithmic Scale check box to tell Excel to logarithmically scale a chart's gridlines. A *logarithmic scale*, by the way, lets you view rates of change in your plotted data rather than absolute changes.

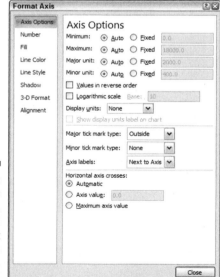

Figure 7-9: Control axis appearance, scaling, and placement with this dialog box.

Note: When you format an axis, you tell Excel how to scale a chart's axes and, as a result, where to draw gridlines. If you select the Auto check boxes, for example, you tell Excel to automatically scale the gridline minimum, maximum, major unit, minor unit, and for 3-D charts, the floor. To manually control scaling, select the Fixed check box and then enter a value into its corresponding text box. To manually set the minimum, for example, select the Minimum Fixed check box and then enter the minimum value that you want into the Minimum text box.

Chart gridlines

The Gridlines command on the Layout tab displays a menu of commands that enables you to add and remove horizontal and vertical gridlines to your chart. To add or remove gridlines to either axis, simply select the appropriate command from the Primary Horizontal Gridlines or Primary Vertical Gridlines menu. Note, too, that the More Gridlines Options command, the last one listed on the Gridlines menu, displays the Format Gridlines dialog box (see Figure 7-10). Use this dialog box's boxes and buttons to customize the appearance of the gridlines.

Figure 7-10:
The Format
Gridlines
dialog box.

Changing a Chart's Location

When you choose the Design tab's Move Chart Location command, Excel displays the Move Chart dialog box, as shown in Figure 7-11. From here, you tell Excel where it should move a chart. In the case of a pivot chart, this means that you're telling Excel to move the pivot chart to some new chart sheet or to a worksheet. When you move a pivot chart to a worksheet, the pivot chart becomes a chart object in the worksheet.

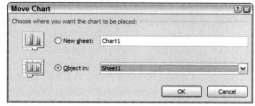

Figure 7-11:
Move a
pivot chart
from here.

To tell Excel to place the pivot table on to a new sheet, select the New Sheet radio button. Then name the new sheet that Excel should create by entering some clever sheet name in the New Sheet text box.

To tell Excel to add the pivot chart to some existing chart sheet or worksheet as an object, select the Object In radio button. Then select the name of the chart sheet or worksheet from the Object In drop-down list box.

Check out Figure 7-12 to see how a pivot chart looks when it appears on its own sheet.

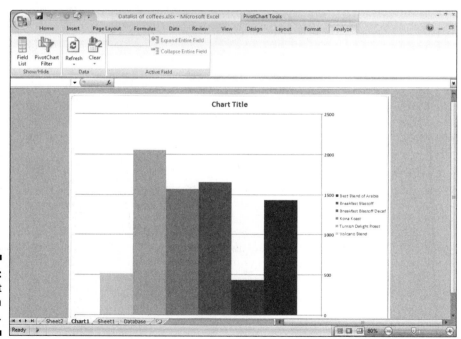

Figure 7-12:
Give a chart
its own
sheet.

Formatting the Plot Area

If you right-click a pivot chart's plot area — the area that shows the plotted data — Excel displays a shortcut menu. Choose the last command on this menu, Format Plot Area, and Excel displays the Format Plot Area dialog box, as shown in Figure 7-13. This dialog box provides several collections of buttons and boxes you can use to specify the line background fill color and pattern, the line and line style, any shadowing, and any third-dimension visual effect for the chart.

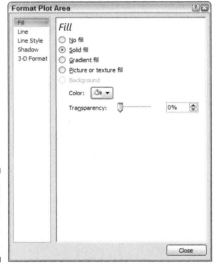

Figure 7-13:
Add fill
colors for a
plot area
here.

For example, to add a background fill to the plot area, select Fill from the list box on the left side of the Format Plot Area dialog box. Then make your choices from the radio buttons, drop-down list, and slider buttons available.

I could spend pages describing in painful and tedious detail the buttons and boxes that these formatting choices provide, but I have a better idea. If you're really interested in fiddling with the pivot chart plot area fill effects, just noodle around. You'll easily be able to see what effect your changes and customizations have.

Formatting the Chart Area

If you right-click a chart sheet or object outside of the plot area and then choose the Format Chart Area command from the shortcuts menu, Excel displays the Format Chart Area dialog box. From here you can set chart area fill patterns, line specifications (see Figure 7-14), line styles, shadowing effects, and 3-D effects for your charts.

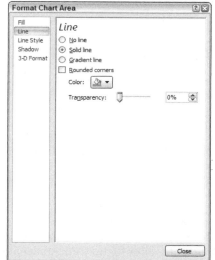

Figure 7-14:
The Format
Chart Area
dialog box.

Chart fill patterns

The Fill options of the Format Chart Area dialog box look and work like the Fill options of the Format Plot area dialog box. (Refer to Figure 7-13.) To choose a fill pattern, select the Solid Fill, Gradient Fill, or Picture or Texture Fill options. Use the Color drop-down list to select the fill color and the Transparency slider button or spin box to select the color transparency.

Note: Different fill pattern options have different buttons and boxes.

Chart area fonts

To format chart text, right-click the text. When you do, Excel displays the formatting menu — which means you have access to its buttons and boxes for changing the font, adding boldfacing and italics, resizing the font, coloring the font, and so forth.

If you have questions about which formatting buttons and boxes do what, don't worry. As you make your changes, Excel updates the chart text.

Formatting 3-D Charts

If you choose to create a three-dimensional (3-D) pivot chart, you should know about a couple of commands that apply specifically to this case: the Format Walls command and the 3-D View command.

Formatting the walls of a 3-D chart

After you create a 3-D pivot chart, you can format its walls if you want. Just right-click the wall of the chart and choose the Format Walls command from the shortcut menu that appears. Excel then displays the Format Walls dialog box. The Format Walls dialog box provides the expected fill, line, line style, and shadow formatting options as well as a couple of formatting options related to the third dimension of the chart: 3-D Format and 3-D Rotation.

The walls of the 3-D chart are its sides and backs — the sides of the 3-D cube, in other words.

Use the 3-D Format options to specify the beveling, illusion of depth, contouring, and surface of the 3-D chart. Use the 3-D Rotation options to specify how you want to rotate, or turn, the chart to show off its three-dimensionality to maximum effect. Note that the 3-D Rotation options also include buttons you can click to incrementally rotate the chart.

Using the 3-D View command

After you create a 3-D pivot chart, you can also change the appearance of its 3-D view. Just right-click the chart and choose the 3-D View command from the shortcut menu that appears. Excel then displays the Format Chart Area dialog box (as shown earlier in Figure 7-14 and which I sort of discussed earlier).

Part III
Advanced Tools

The 5th Wave   By Rich Tennant

"Our customer survey indicates 30% of our customers think our service is inconsistent, 40% would like a change in procedures, and 50% think it would be real cute if we all wore matching colored vests."

In this part . . .

Read here to find out about some mighty useful whistles and bells available to advanced Excel users. It'd be a shame if you didn't at least know what they are and the basic steps that you need to use them. In Part III, I cover using database and statistical functions, descriptive and inferential statistics, and how to use the Excel Solver.

Chapter 8

Using the Database Functions

*E*xcel provides a special set of functions, called *database functions,* especially for simple statistical analysis of information that you store in Excel tables. In this chapter, I describe and illustrate these functions.

Are you interested in statistical analysis of information that's *not* stored in an Excel table? Then you can use this chapter as a resource for descriptions of functions that you use for analysis when your information isn't in an Excel table.

Note: Excel also provides a rich set of statistical functions, which are also wonderful tools for analyzing information in an Excel table. Skip to Chapter 9 for details on these statistical functions.

Quickly Reviewing Functions

The Excel database functions work like other Excel functions. In a nutshell, when you want to use a function, you create a formula that includes the function. Because I don't discuss functions in detail anywhere else in this book — and because you need to be relatively proficient with the basics of using functions in order to employ them in any data analysis — I review some basics here, including function syntax and entering functions.

Understanding function syntax rules

Most functions need arguments, or *inputs*. In particular, all database functions need arguments. You include these arguments inside parentheses. If a function needs more than one argument, you can separate arguments by using commas.

For illustration purposes, here are a couple of example formulas that use simple functions. These aren't database functions, by the way. I get to those in later sections of this chapter. Read through these examples to become proficient with the everyday functions. (Or just breeze through these as a refresher.)

You use the SUM function to sum, or add up, the values that you include as the function arguments. In the following example, these arguments are 2, 2, the value in cell A1, and the values stored in the worksheet range B3:G5.

```
=SUM(2,2,A1,B3:G5)
```

Here's another example. The following AVERAGE function calculates the average, or arithmetic mean, of the values stored in the worksheet range B2:B100.

```
=AVERAGE(B2:B100)
```

Simply, that's what functions do. They take your inputs and perform some calculation, such as a simple sum or a slightly more complicated average.

Entering a function manually

How you enter a function-based formula into a cell depends on whether you're familiar with how the function works — at least roughly.

If you're familiar with how a function works — or at the very least, you know its name — you can simply type the function name into the cell. SUM and AVERAGE are good examples of easy-to-remember function names. When you type that first parenthesis [(] after entering the full function name, Excel displays a pop-up ScreenTip that names the function arguments and shows their correct order. (Refer to the previous section, "Understanding function syntax rules," if you need to brush up on some mechanics.) In Figure 8-1, for example, you can see how this looks in the case of the loan payment function, which is named PMT.

If you point to the function name in the ScreenTip, Excel turns the function name into a hyperlink. Click the hyperlink to open the Excel Help file and see its description and discussion of the function.

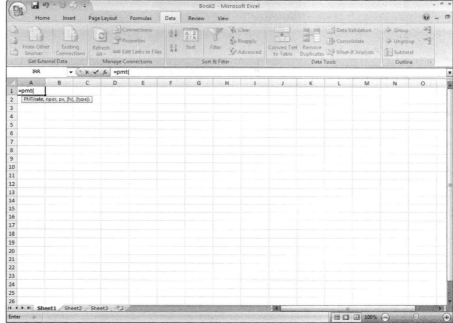

Figure 8-1:
The
ScreenTip
for the PMT
function
identifies
function
arguments
and shows
their correct
order.

Entering a function with the Function command

If you're not familiar with how a function works — maybe you're not even sure what function that you want to use — you need to use the Formulas tab's Insert Function command to find the function and then correctly identify the arguments.

To use the Function Wizard command in this manner, follow these steps:

1. **Position the cell selector at the cell into which you want to place the function formula.**

   You do this in the usual way. For example, you can click the cell. Or you can use the navigation keys, such as the arrow keys, to move the cell selector to the cell.

2. **Choose the Formulas tab's Function Wizard command.**

   Excel displays the Insert Function dialog box, as shown in Figure 8-2.

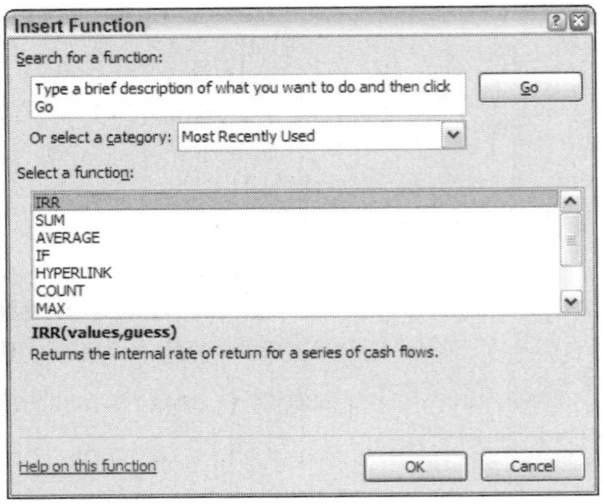

Figure 8-2:
Select a
function
here.

3. **In the Search for a Function text box, type a brief description of what you want to calculate by using a function.**

   For example, if you want to calculate a standard deviation for a sample, type something like **standard deviation**.

4. **Click the Go button.**

   In the Select a Function list box, Excel displays a list of the functions that might just work for you, as shown in Figure 8-3.

   Note: The STDEVPA function in Figure 8-3 isn't a database function, so I don't describe it in this chapter. Read through Chapter 9 for more on this function.

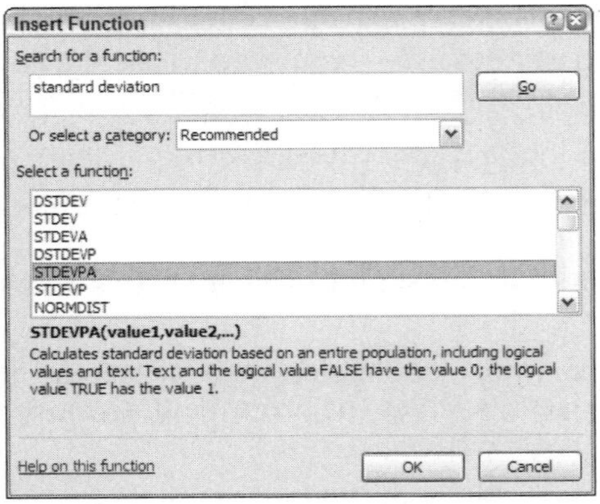

Figure 8-3:
Let Excel
help you
narrow
down the
function
choices.

5. Find the right function.

To find the right function for your purposes, first select a function in the Select a Function list. Then read the full description of the function, which appears beneath the function list. If the function you select isn't the one you want, select another function and read its description. Repeat this process until you find the right function.

If you get to the end of the list of functions and still haven't found what you want, consider repeating Step 3, but this time use a different (and hopefully better) description of the calculation you want to make.

6. After you find the function you want, select it and then click OK.

Excel displays the Function Arguments dialog box, as shown in Figure 8-4.

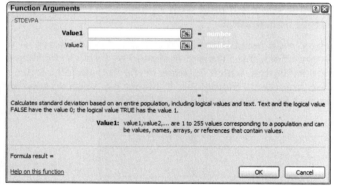

Figure 8-4:
Supply
function
arguments
here.

7. Supply the arguments.

To supply the arguments that a function needs, click an argument text box (Value1 and Value2 in Figure 8-4). Next, read the argument description, which appears at the bottom of the dialog box. Then supply the argument by entering a value, formula, or cell or range reference into the argument text box.

If a function needs more than one argument, repeat this step for each argument.

Excel calculates the function result based on the arguments that you enter and displays this value at the bottom of the dialog box next to Formula Result =, as shown in Figure 8-5.

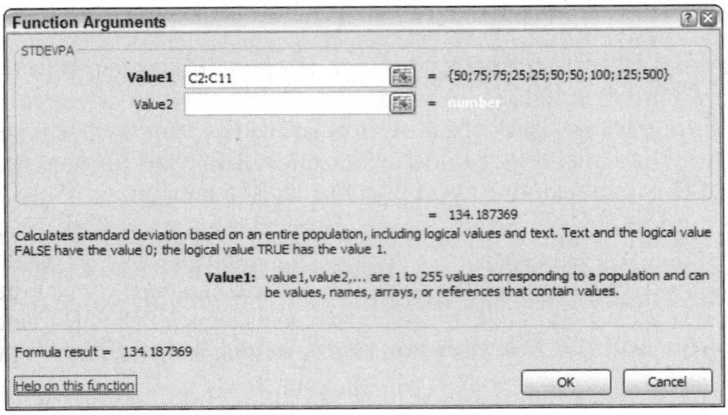

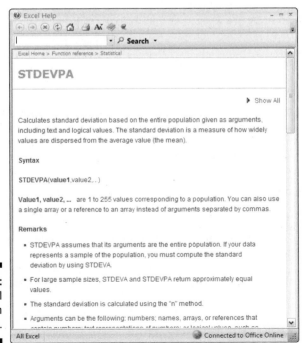

Figure 8-5:
Enter
arguments,
and Excel
calculates
them for
you.

8. **(Optional) If you need help with a particular function, browse the Excel Help information.**

If you need help using some function, your first resource — yes, even before you check this chapter — should be to click the Help on This Function hyperlink, which appears in the bottom-left corner of the Function Arguments dialog box. In Figure 8-6, you can see the help information that Excel displays for the STDEVPA function.

Figure 8-6:
Ask Excel
for function
help.

The Or Select a Category drop-down list

After you learn your way around Excel and develop some familiarity with its functions, you can also narrow down the list of functions by selecting a function category from the Or Select a Category drop-down list in the Insert Function dialog box. For example, if you select Database from this drop-down list, Excel displays a list of its database functions. In some cases, this category-based approach works pretty darn well. It all depends, really, on how many functions Excel puts into a category. Excel provides 12 database functions, so that's a pretty small set. Other sets, however, are much larger. For example, Excel supplies more than 70 statistical functions. For large categories, such as the statistical functions category, the approach that I suggest in the section "Entering a function with the Function command" (see Step 3 there) usually works best.

9. **When you're satisfied with the arguments that you enter in the Function Arguments dialog box, click OK.**

And now it's party time. In the next section, I describe each of the database statistical functions that Excel provides.

Using the DAVERAGE Function

The DAVERAGE function calculates an average for values in an Excel list. The unique and truly useful feature of DAVERAGE is that you can specify that you want only list records that meet specified criteria included in your average.

If you want to calculate a simple average, use the AVERAGE function. In Chapter 9, I describe and illustrate the AVERAGE function.

The DAVERAGE function uses the following syntax:

```
=DAVERAGE(database,field,criteria)
```

where *database* is a range reference to the Excel table that holds the value you want to average, *field* tells Excel which column in the database to average, and *criteria* is a range reference that identifies the fields and values used to define your selection. The *field* argument can be a cell reference holding the field name, the field name enclosed in quotation marks, or a number that identifies the column (1 for the first column, 2 for the second column, and so on).

As an example of how the DAVERAGE function works, suppose that you've constructed the worksheet shown in Figure 8-7. Notice that the worksheet range holds a small table. Row 1 predictably stores field names: Name, State, and Donation. Rows 2–11 store individual records.

If you're a little vague on what an Excel table (or list) is, you should take a peek at Chapter 1. Excel database functions analyze information from Excel tables, so you need to know how tables work in order to easily use database functions.

Rows 14 and 15 store the criteria range. The *criteria range* typically duplicates the row of field names. The criteria range also includes at least one other row of labels or values or Boolean logic expressions that the DAVERAGE function uses to select records from the list. In Figure 8-7, for example, note the Boolean expression in cell C15, <500, which tells the function to include only records where the Donation field shows a value less than 500.

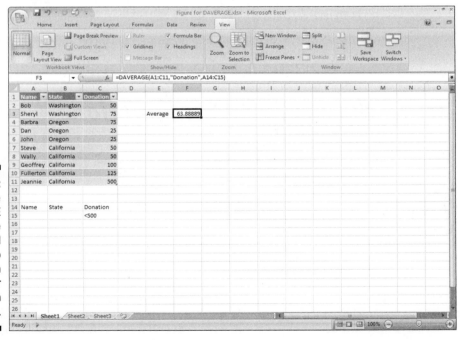

Figure 8-7:
Use the DAVERAGE database statistical functions to calculate an average for values in an Excel table.

The DAVERAGE function, which appears in cell F3, is

```
=DAVERAGE(A1:C11,"Donation",A14:C15)
```

and it returns the average donation amount shown in the database list excluding the donation from Jeannie in California because that amount isn't less than 500. The actual function result is 63.88889.

Although I mention this in a couple of other places in this book, I want to be a little redundant about something important: Each row in your criteria range is used to select records for the function. For example, if you use the criteria range shown in Figure 8-8, you select records using two criteria. The criterion in row 15 tells the DAVERAGE function to select records where the donation is less than 500. The criterion in row 16 tells the DAVERAGE function to select records where the state is California. The DAVERAGE function, then, uses every record in the list because every record meets at least one of the criteria. The records in the list don't have to meet both criteria; just one of them.

To combine criteria — suppose that you want to calculate the DAVERAGE for donations from California that are less than 500 — you put both the criteria into the same row, as shown in row 15 of Figure 8-9.

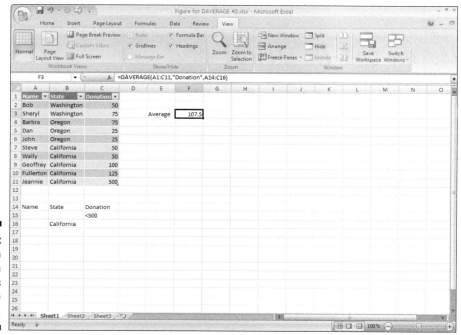

Figure 8-8:
Using a criteria range that's a little more complicated.

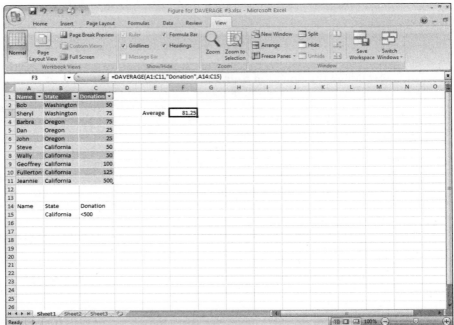

Figure 8-9:
You can
combine the
criteria in a
range.

Using the DCOUNT and DCOUNTA Functions

The DCOUNT and DCOUNTA functions count records in a database table that match criteria that you specify. Both functions use the same syntax, as shown here:

```
=DCOUNT(database,field,criteria)
=DCOUNTA(database,field,criteria)
```

where *database* is a range reference to the Excel table that holds the value that you want to count, *field* tells Excel which column in the database to count, and *criteria* is a range reference that identifies the fields and values used to define your selection criteria. The *field* argument can be a cell reference holding the field name, the field name enclosed in quotation marks, or a number that identifies the column (1 for the first column, 2 for the second column, and so on).

TIP

Excel provides several other functions for counting cells with values or labels: COUNT, COUNTA, COUNTIF, and COUNTBLANK. Refer to Chapter 9 or the Excel online help for more information about these tools.

The functions differ subtly, however. DCOUNT counts fields with values; DCOUNTA counts fields that aren't empty.

As an example of how the DCOUNT and DCOUNTA functions work, suppose that you've constructed the worksheet shown in Figure 8-10, which contains a list of players on a softball team. Row 1 stores field names: Player, Age, and Batting Average. Rows 2–11 store individual records.

Rows 14 and 15 store the criteria range. Field names go into the first row. Subsequent rows provide labels or values or Boolean logic expressions that the DCOUNT and DCOUNTA functions use to select records from the list for counting. In Figure 8-10, for example, there's a Boolean expression in cell B15, >8, which tells the function to include only records where the Age shows a value greater than eight. In this case, then, the functions count players on the team who are older than 8.

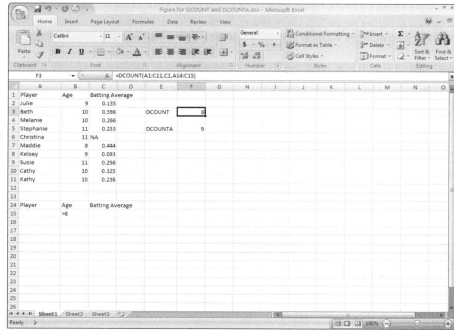

Figure 8-10: Use the DCOUNT and DCOUNTA database statistical functions to count records in a database list.

The DCOUNT function, which appears in cell F3, is

```
=DCOUNT(A1:C11,C1,A14:C15)
```

The function counts the players on the team who are older than 8. But because the DCOUNT function looks only at players with a batting average in the Batting Average field, it returns 8. Another way to say this same thing is that in this example, DCOUNT counts the number of players on the team who are older than 8 and have a batting average.

If you want to get fancy about using Boolean expression to create your selection criteria, take a peek at the earlier discussion of the DAVERAGE function. In that section, "Using the DAVERAGE Function," I describe how to create compound selection criteria.

The DCOUNTA function, which appears in cell F5, is

```
=DCOUNTA(A1:C11,3,A14:C15)
```

The function counts the players on the team who are older than 8 and have some piece of information entered into the Batting Average field. The function returns the value 9 because each of the players older than 8 have something stored in the Batting Average field. Eight of them, in fact, have batting average values. The fifth player (Christina) has the text label NA.

If you just want to count records in a list, you can omit the field argument from the DCOUNT and DCOUNTA functions. When you do this, the function just counts the records in the list that match your criteria without regard to whether some field stores a value or is nonblank. For example, both of the following functions return the value 9:

```
=DCOUNT(A1:C11,,A14:C15)
=DCOUNTA(A1:C11,,A14:C15)
```

Note: To omit an argument, you just leave the space between the two commas empty.

Using the DGET Function

The DGET function retrieves a value from a database list according to selection criteria. The function uses the following syntax:

```
=DGET(database,field,criteria)
```

where *database* is a range reference to the Excel table that holds the value you want to extract, *field* tells Excel which column in the database to extract, and *criteria* is a range reference that identifies the fields and values used to define your selection criteria. The *field* argument can be a cell reference holding the field name, the field name enclosed in quotation marks, or a number that identifies the column (1 for the first column, 2 for the second column, and so on).

Go back to the softball players list example in the preceding section. Suppose that you want to find the batting average of the single eight-year-old player. To retrieve this information from the list shown in Figure 8-11, enter the following formula into cell F3:

```
=DGET(A1:C11,3,A14:C15)
```

This function returns the value 0.444 because that's the eight-year-old's batting average.

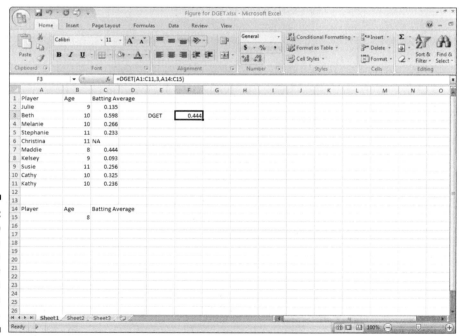

Figure 8-11:
Use DGET to retrieve a value from a database list based on selection criteria.

By the way, if no record in your list matches your selection criteria, DGET returns the #VALUE error message. For example, if you construct selection criteria that look for a twelve-year-old on the team, DGET returns #VALUE because there aren't any twelve-year-old players. Also, if multiple records in your list match your selection criteria, DGET returns the #NUM error message. For example, if you construct selection criteria that look for a ten-year-old, DGET returns the #NUM error message because four ten-year-olds are on the team.

Using the DMAX and DMAX Functions

The DMAX and DMIN functions find the largest and smallest values, respectively, in a database list field that match the criteria that you specify. Both functions use the same syntax, as shown here:

```
=DMAX(database,field,criteria)
=DMIN(database,field,criteria)
```

where *database* is a range reference to the Excel table, *field* tells Excel which column in the database to look in for the largest or smallest value, and *criteria* is a range reference that identifies the fields and values used to define your selection criteria. The *field* argument can be a cell reference holding the field name, the field name enclosed in quotation marks, or a number that identifies the column (1 for the first column, 2 for the second column, and so on).

Excel provides several other functions for finding the minimum or maximum value, including MAX, MAXA, MIN, and MINA. Turn to Chapter 9 for more information about using these related functions.

As an example of how the DMAX and DMIN functions work, suppose you construct a list of your friends and some important statistical information, including their typical golf scores and their favorite local courses, as shown in Figure 8-12. Row 1 stores field names: Friend, Golf Score, and Course. Rows 2–11 store individual records.

Rows 14 and 15 store the criteria range. Field names go into the first row. Subsequent rows provide labels or values or Boolean logic expressions that the DMAX and DMIN functions use to select records from the list for counting. In Figure 8-12, for example, note the text label in cell C15, Snohomish, which tells the function to include only records where the Course field shows the label Snohomish.

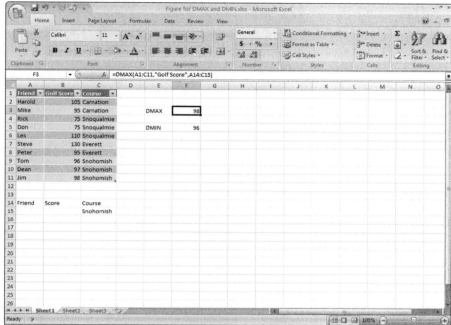

Figure 8-12:
Use the
DMAX and
DMIN
database
statistical
functions to
find the
largest and
smallest
values.

The DMAX function, which appears in cell F3, is

```
=DMAX(A1:C11,"Golf Score",A14:C15)
```

The function finds the highest golf score of the friends who favor the Snohomish course, which happens to be 98.

If you want to get fancy about using Boolean expression to create your selection criteria, take a peek at the earlier discussion of the DAVERAGE function. In that section, "Using the DAVERAGE Function," I describe how to create compound selection criteria.

The DMIN function, which appears in cell F5, is

```
=DMIN(A1:C11,"Golf Score",A14:C15)
```

The function counts the lowest score of the friends who favor the Snohomish course, which happens to be 96.

Using the DPRODUCT Function

The DPRODUCT function is weird. And I'm not sure why you would ever use it. Oh sure, I understand what it does. The DPRODUCT function multiplies the values in fields from a database list based on selection criteria. I just can't think of a general example about why you would want to do this.

The function uses the syntax

```
=DPRODUCT(database,field,criteria)
```

where *database* is a range reference to the Excel table that holds the value you want to multiply, *field* tells Excel which column in the database to extract, and *criteria* is a range reference that identifies the fields and values used to define your selection criteria. If you're been reading this chapter from the very start, join the sing-along: The *field* argument can be a cell reference holding the field name, the field name enclosed in quotation marks, or a number that identifies the column (1 for the first column, 2 for the second column, and so on).

I can't construct a meaningful example of why you would use this function, so no worksheet example this time. Sorry.

Note: Just so you don't waste time looking, the Excel Help file doesn't provide a good example of the DPRODUCT function either.

Using the DSTDEV and DSTDEVP Functions

The DSTDEV and DSTDEVP functions calculate a standard deviation. DSTDEV calculates the standard deviation for a sample. DSTDEVP calculates the standard deviation for a population. As with other database statistical functions, the unique and truly useful feature of DSTDEV and DSTDEVP is that you can specify that you want only list records that meet the specified criteria you include in your calculations.

If you want to calculate standard deviations without first applying selection criteria, use one of the Excel non-database statistical functions such as STDEV, STDEVA, STDEVP, or STDEVPA. In Chapter 9, I describe and illustrate these other standard deviation functions.

The DSTDEV and DSTDEVP functions use the same syntax:

```
=DSTDEV(database,field,criteria)
=DSTDEVP(database,field,criteria)
```

where *database* is a range reference to the Excel table that holds the values for which you want to calculate a standard deviation, *field* tells Excel which column in the database to use in the calculations, and *criteria* is a range reference that identifies the fields and values used to define your selection criteria. The *field* argument can be a cell reference holding the field name, the field name enclosed in quotation marks, or a number that identifies the column (1 for the first column, 2 for the second column, and so on).

As an example of how the DSTDEV function works, suppose you construct the worksheet shown in Figure 8-13. (This is the same basic worksheet as shown in Figure 8-7, in case you're wondering.)

The worksheet range holds a small list with row 1 storing field names (Name, State, and Donation) and rows 2 through 11 storing individual records.

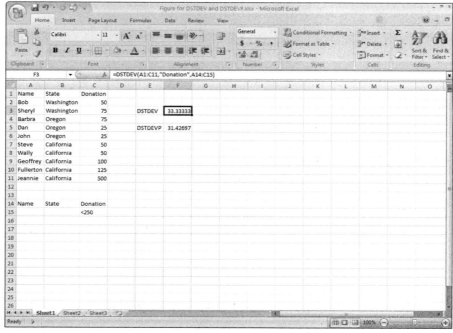

Figure 8-13: Calculate a standard deviation with the DSTDEV and DSTDEVP functions.

Rows 14 and 15 store the criteria range. The criteria range typically duplicates the row of field names. The criteria range also includes at least one other row of labels or values or Boolean logic expressions that the DSTDEV and DSTDEVP functions use to select records from the list. In Figure 8-13, for example, note the Boolean expression in cell C15, <250, which tells the function to include only records where the Donation field shows a value less than 250.

The DSTDEV function, which appears in cell F3, is

```
=DSTDEV(A1:C11,"Donation",A14:C15)
```

and it returns the sample standard deviation of the donation amounts shown in the database list excluding the donation from Jeannie in California because that amount is not less than 250. The actual function result is 33.33333.

The DSTDEVP function, which appears in cell F5, is

```
=DSTDEVP(A1:C11,"Donation",A14:C15)
```

and returns the population standard deviation of the donation amounts shown in the database list excluding the donation from Jeannie in California because that amount isn't less than 250. The actual function result is 31.42697.

You wouldn't, by the way, simply pick one of the two database standard deviation functions willy-nilly. If you're calculating a standard deviation using a sample, or subset of items, from the entire data set, or population, you use the DSTDEV function. If you're calculating a standard deviation using all the items in the population, use the DSTDEVP function.

Using the DSUM Function

The DSUM function adds values from a database list based on selection criteria. The function uses the syntax:

```
=DSUM(database,field,criteria)
```

where *database* is a range reference to the Excel table, *field* tells Excel which column in the database to sum, and *criteria* is a range reference that identifies the fields and values used to define your selection criteria. The *field* argument can be a cell reference holding the field name, the field name enclosed in quotation marks, or a number that identifies the column (1 for the first column, 2 for the second column, and so on).

Figure 8-14 shows a simple bank account balances worksheet that illustrates how the DSUM function works. Suppose that you want to find the total of the balances that you have in open accounts paying more than 0.02, or 2 percent, interest. The criteria range in A14:D15 provides this information to the function. Note that both criteria appear in the same row. This means that a bank account must meet both criteria in order for its balance to be included in the DSUM calculation.

The DSUM formula appears in cell F3, as shown here:

```
=DSUM(A1:C11,3,A14:D15)
```

This function returns the value 39000 because that's the sum of the balances in open accounts that pay more than 2 percent interest.

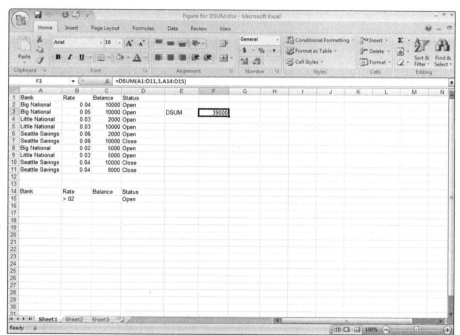

Figure 8-14:
Add values
from a
database
list with
DSUM.

Using the DVAR and DVARP Functions

The DVAR and DVARP functions calculate a variance, which is another measure of dispersion — and actually, the square of the standard deviation. DVAR calculates the variance for a sample. DVARP calculates the variance for a population. As with other database statistical functions, using DVAR and DVARP enable you to specify that you want only those list records that meet selection criteria included in your calculations.

If you want to calculate variances without first applying selection criteria, use one of the Excel non-database statistical functions such as VAR, VARA, VARP, or VARPA. In Chapter 9, I describe and illustrate these other variance functions.

The DVAR and DVARP functions use the same syntax:

```
=DVAR(database,field,criteria)
=DVARP(database,field,criteria)
```

where *database* is a range reference to the Excel table that holds the values for which you want to calculate a variance, *field* tells Excel which column in the database to use in the calculations, and *criteria* is a range reference that identifies the fields and values used to define your selection criteria. The *field* argument can be a cell reference holding the field name, the field name enclosed in quotation marks, or a number that identifies the column (1 for the first column, 2 for the second column, and so on).

As an example of how the DVAR function works, suppose you've constructed the worksheet shown in Figure 8-15. (Yup, this is the same worksheet as shown in Figure 8-12.)

The worksheet range holds a small list with row 1 storing field names and rows 2–11 storing individual records.

Rows 14–17 store the criteria, which stipulate that you want to include golfing buddies in the variance calculation if their favorite courses are Snohomish, Snoqualmie, or Carnation. The first row, row 14, duplicates the row of field names. The other rows provide the labels or values or Boolean logic expressions — in this case, just labels — that the DVAR and DVARP functions use to select records from the list.

The DVAR function, which appears in cell F3, is

```
=DVAR(A1:C11,"Golf Score",A14:C17)
```

and it returns the sample variance of the golf scores shown in the database list for golfers who golf at Snohomish, Snoqualmie, or Carnation. The actual function result is 161.26786.

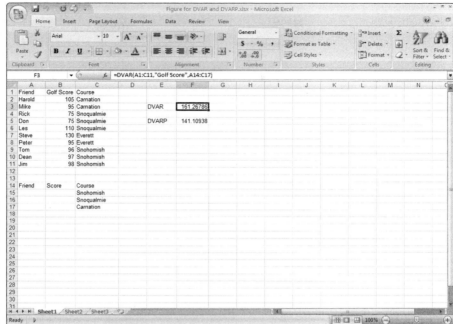

Figure 8-15:
Calculate a
variance
with the
DVAR and
DVARP
functions.

The DVARP function, which appears in cell F5, is

```
=DVARP(A1:C11,"Golf Score",A14:C17)
```

and it returns the population variance of the golf scores shown in the database list for golfers who golf at Snohomish, Snoqualmie, and Carnation. The actual function result is 141.10938.

As when making standard deviation calculations, you don't simply pick one of the two database variances based on a whim, the weather outside, or how you're feeling. If you're calculating a variance using a sample, or subset of items, from the entire data set, or population, you use the DVAR function. To calculate a variance using all the items in the population, you use the DVARP function.

Chapter 9

Using the Statistics Functions

*E*xcel supplies a bunch of statistical functions . . . more than 70, in fact. These functions help you dig more deeply into the characteristics of data that you've stored in an Excel worksheet, list, or pivot table. In this chapter, I discuss and illustrate each of the statistical functions that you're likely to use. I also briefly describe some of the very esoteric statistical functions.

Counting Items in a Data Set

Excel provides four useful statistical functions for counting cells within a worksheet or list: COUNT, COUNTA, COUNTBLANK, and COUNTIF. Excel also provides two useful functions for counting permutations and combinations: PERMUT and COMBIN.

COUNT: Counting cells with values

The COUNT function counts the number of cells within a specified range that hold values. The function, however, doesn't count cells containing the logical values TRUE or FALSE or cells that are empty. The function uses the syntax

```
=COUNT(value1,[value2])
```

If you want to use the COUNT function to count the number of values in the range B1:B10 in the worksheet shown in Figure 9-1, you might enter the formula

```
=COUNT(B1:B10)
```

into cell G2, as shown in the figure. The function returns the value 9.

Note: You can include several arguments as part of the range argument in the COUNT function. For example, in Figure 9-1, you might also use the syntax =COUNT(B1,B2:B5,B6:B7,B8,B9), which would return the same result as the formula shown in the figure.

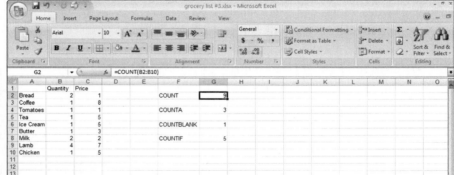

Figure 9-1: A worksheet fragment for illustrating the counting functions.

COUNTA: Alternative counting cells with values

The COUNTA function counts the number of cells within a specified range that aren't empty. The function uses the syntax

```
=COUNTA(value1,[value2])
```

If you want to use the COUNTA function to count the number of non-empty cells in the range A1:B2 in the worksheet shown in Figure 9-1, for example, enter the formula

```
=COUNTA(A1:B2)
```

into cell G4. The function returns the value 3.

COUNTBLANK: Counting empty cells

The COUNTBLANK function counts the number of cells within a specified range that are empty. The function uses the syntax

```
=COUNTBLANK(value1,[value2])
```

To use the COUNTBLANK function to count the number of empty cells in the range A1:B2 in the worksheet shown in Figure 9-1, for example, you could enter the formula

```
=COUNTBLANK(A1:B2)
```

into cell G6. The function returns the value 1.

COUNTIF: Counting cells that match criteria

The COUNTIF function counts the number of cells within a specified range that match criteria that you specify. The function uses the syntax

```
=COUNTIF(range,criteria)
```

where *range* is the worksheet range in which you count cells and *criteria* is a Boolean expression, enclosed in quotation marks, that describes your criteria.

As an example of how this works, suppose you want to use the COUNTIF function to count the number of cells within the worksheet range C1:C10 that hold values greater than 4. To make this count, you use the following formula:

```
=COUNTIF(C1:C10,">4")
```

This formula appears in cell G8 of the worksheet shown in Figure 9-1.

 You can use other Boolean operators to construct other match criteria: Use the < operator for a less-than comparison, the <= operator for a less-than-or-equal-to comparison, the >= operator for a greater-than-or-equal-to comparison, the = operator for the equal-to comparison, and the <> operator for a not-equal-to comparison.

PERMUT: Counting permutations

The PERMUT function counts the number of permutations possible when selecting a sample from a population. Note that for a permutation, the order does matter in which items are selected. The function uses the syntax

```
=PERMUT(number,number_chosen)
```

where *number* is the number of items in the population and *number_chosen* is the number of items selected. Given a population of six items and three selections, for example, you calculate the number of permutations by using the formula

```
=PERMUT(6,3)
```

The function returns the value 120, indicating that 120 different ways exist in which three items can be selected from a set of six.

COMBIN: Counting combinations

If the order in which items are selected doesn't matter, you use the combination function, COMBIN, which uses the syntax

```
=COMBIN(number,number_chosen)
```

The number of combinations possible when three items are selected from a set of six can be calculated using the formula

```
=COMBIN(6,3)
```

This function returns the value 20. The COMBIN function isn't technically an Excel statistical function, by the way. But it seems so closely related to the PERMUT function that I include a description here.

Means, Modes, and Medians

Excel provides a handful of functions for calculating means, modes, and medians.

AVEDEV: An average absolute deviation

The AVEDEV function provides a measure of dispersion for a set of values. To do this, the function looks at a set of values and calculates the average absolute deviation from the mean of the values. The function uses the syntax

```
=AVEDEV(number1,[number2])
```

where `number1,[number2]` is a worksheet reference to the range that stores the values.

Note: As is the case with many other simple statistical functions, you can include several arguments as part of the range argument in the AVEDEV function. For example, the formulas =AVEDEV(B1,B2:B5,B6:B7,B8,B9) and =AVEDEV(B1:B9) are equivalent.

Suppose you have three values — 100, 200, and 300 — in the worksheet range that you supply to the AVEDEV function. The average of these three values is 200, calculated as (100+200+300)/3. The average of the deviations from the mean is 66.6667, calculated as:

```
(|100-200|+|200-200|+|300-200|)/3
```

Note: The AVEDEV function calculates the average of the absolute value of the deviation. For this reason, the function calculates absolute differences, or deviations, from the mean.

The AVEDEV function isn't used in practice. Mostly a teaching tool, educators and trainers sometimes use the average deviation measure of dispersion to introduce the more useful but also more complicated measures of dispersion: the standard deviation and variance.

AVERAGE: Average

The AVERAGE function calculates the arithmetic mean for a set of values. The function uses the syntax

```
=AVERAGE(number1,[number2])
```

where `number1,[number2]` is a worksheet reference to the range that stores the values.

If your argument includes the three values — 100, 200, and 300 — the function returns the value 200 because (100+200+300)/3 equals 200.

AVERAGEA: An alternate average

The AVERAGEA function, like the AVERAGE function, calculates the arithmetic mean for a set of values. The difference with the AVERAGEA function, however, is that AVERAGEA includes cells with text and the logical value for FALSE in its calculations as 0. The AVERAGEA function includes the logical value for TRUE in its calculations as 1. The function uses the syntax

```
=AVERAGEA(number1,[number2])
```

where *number1*, [*number2*] is a worksheet reference to the range that stores the values — and possibly text as well as logical values.

If your argument includes three values — 100, 200, and 300 — and three text labels in the worksheet range that you supply to the AVERAGEA function, the function returns the value 100 because (100+200+300+0+0+0)/6 equals 100.

Note: As is the case with the AVERAGE function, you can supply up to 255 arguments to the AVERAGEA function.

TRIMMEAN: Trimming to a mean

The TRIMMEAN function calculates the arithmetic average of a set of values but only after discarding a specified percentage of the lowest and highest values from the set. The function uses the syntax

```
=TRIMMEAN(array,percent)
```

where *array* is the range holding the values and *percent* is the decimal value that gives the percentage of values that you want to discard. For example, to calculate the arithmetic mean of the values stored in the worksheet range C2:C10 in Figure 9-2 only after discarding 10 percent of the data — the top 5 percent and the bottom 5 percent — you use the following formula:

```
=TRIMMEAN(C2:C10,0.1)
```

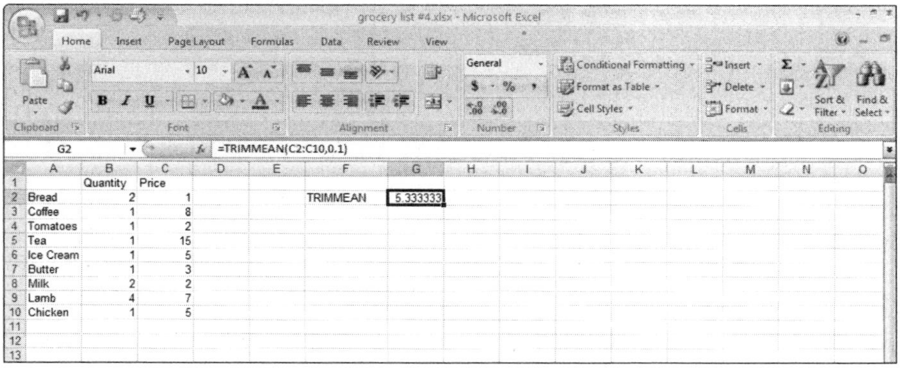

Figure 9-2:
A worksheet
fragment
that shows
how
TRIMMEAN
works.

MEDIAN: Median value

The MEDIAN function finds the middle value in a set of values: Half the values fall below and half the values fall above the median. The function uses the syntax

```
=MEDIAN(number1,[number2])
```

If you use the MEDIAN function to find the median of a range holding the values 1, 2, 3, 4, and 5, for example, the function returns the value 3.

Note: You can supply up to 255 arguments to the MEDIAN function.

If you use the MEDIAN function to find the median of a range holding the values 1, 2, 3, and 4, the function returns the value 2.5. Why? Because if you have an even number of data entries, Excel calculates a median by averaging the two middle values.

MODE: Mode value

The MODE function finds the most common value in your data set, but the function ignores empty cells and cells that store text or return logical values. The function uses the syntax

```
=MODE(number1,[number2])
```

If you use the MODE function to find the most common value in a range holding the values 1, 2, 3, 4, 4, and 4, the function returns the value 4.

Note: You can supply up to 255 arguments to the MODE function.

GEOMEAN: Geometric mean

The GEOMEAN function calculates the geometric mean of a set of values. The *geometric mean* equals the *n*th root of the product of the numbers. The function uses the syntax

```
=GEOMEAN(number1,[number2]...)
```

where *number1* and, optionally, other similar arguments supply the values that you want to geometrically average.

HARMEAN: Harmonic mean

The HARMEAN function calculates the reciprocal of the arithmetic mean of the reciprocals of a data set. The function uses the syntax

```
=HARMEAN(number1,[number2]...)
```

where *number1* and, optionally, other similar arguments supply the values that you want to harmonically average.

Finding Values, Ranks, and Percentiles

Excel provides functions for finding the largest or smallest values in a data set and also for finding values with a particular rank and for ranking values within the data set. Excel also provides a couple of tangentially related functions for calculating frequency distributions and simple probabilities for data sets. I describe all these function tools in the next sections.

MAX: Maximum value

The MAX function finds the largest value in your data. The function ignores blank cells and cells containing text or logical values such as TRUE and FALSE and uses the syntax

```
=MAX(number1,[number2])
```

If the largest value in the range A1:G500 is 50, the function =MAX(A1:G500) returns the value 50.

Note: You can supply up to 255 arguments to the MAX function.

MAXA: Alternate maximum value

In a fashion similar to the MAX function, the MAXA function also finds the largest value in your data. However, unlike the MAX function, the MAXA function includes logical values and text. The logical value TRUE equals 1, the logical value FALSE equals 0, and text also equals 0. The MAXA function uses the syntax

```
=MAXA(number1,[number2])
```

MIN: Minimum value

The MIN function finds the smallest value in your data. The function ignores blank cells and cells containing text or logical values such as TRUE and FALSE and uses the syntax

```
=MIN(number1,[number2])
```

If the smallest value in the range A1:G500 is 1, the function =MIN(A1:G500) returns the value 1.

MINA: Alternate minimum value

The MINA function also finds the smallest value in your data, but the MINA function includes logical values and text. The logical value TRUE equals 1, the logical value FALSE equals 0, and text also equals 0. The MINA function uses the syntax

```
=MINA(number1,[number2])
```

If the smallest value in the range A1:G500 is 1 but this range also includes text values, the function =MINA(A1:G500) returns the value 0.

LARGE: Finding the kth largest value

You can use the LARGE function to find the kth largest value in an array. The function uses the syntax

```
=LARGE(array,k)
```

where *array* is the array of values and k identifies which value you want the function to return. For example, if you store the values 1, 3, 5, 8, and 9 in the worksheet range A1:A5 and you want the function to return the second largest value, use the following formula:

```
=LARGE(A1:A5,2)
```

The function returns the value 8 because that's the second largest value in the array.

SMALL: Finding the kth smallest value

The SMALL function finds the *k*th smallest value in an array. The function uses the syntax

```
=SMALL(array,k)
```

where *array* is the array of values and *k* identifies which value you want to find and have the function return. For example, if you store the values 1, 3, 5, 8, and 9 in the worksheet range A1:A5 and you want the function to return the second smallest value, use the following formula:

```
=SMALL(A1:A5,2)
```

The function returns the value 3 because that's the second smallest value in the array.

RANK: Ranking an array value

The RANK function determines the rank, or position, of a value in an array. The formula uses the syntax

```
=RANK(number,ref,[order])
```

where *number* is the value you want to rank, *ref* is the array of values, and optionally *order* indicates whether array values should be arranged in descending order (indicated with a 0 or logical FALSE value) or in ascending order (indicated with a 1 or logical TRUE value). By the way, Excel ranks duplicate values the same, but these duplicates do affect the rank of subsequent numbers. If you leave out the *order* argument, Excel ranks values in descending order.

To demonstrate how the RANK function works, suppose you want to rank the values shown in the worksheet range A1:A9 in Figure 9-3.

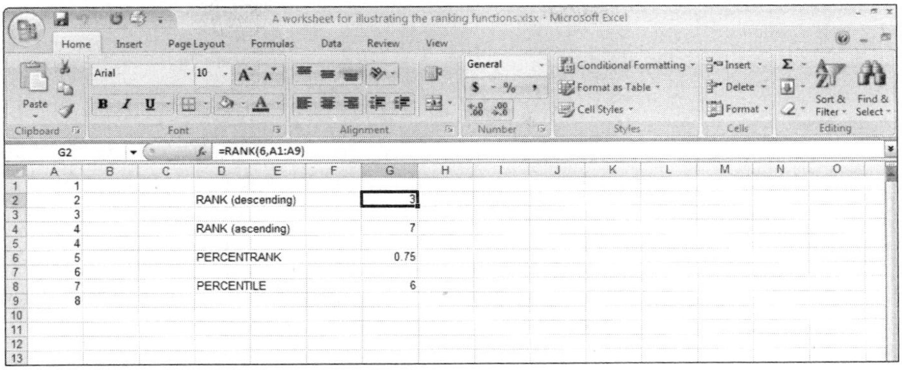

Figure 9-3:
A worksheet
fragment
with the
array 1, 2, 3,
4, 4, 5, 6, 7, 8.

The formula in cell G2

```
=RANK(6,A1:A9)
```

returns the value 3, indicating that when a descending order is used, the value 6 is the third value in the array.

The formula in cell G4

```
=RANK(6,A1:A9,1)
```

returns the value 7, indicating that when an ascending order is used, the value 6 is the seventh value in the array.

PERCENTRANK: Finding a percentile ranking

The PERCENTRANK function determines the percentage rank, or percentile, of a value in an array. The formula uses the syntax

```
=PERCENTRANK(array,x,[significance])
```

where *array* gives the array of values, *x* identifies the value you want to rank, and *significance* identifies the number of decimal places that you want in the percentage. The *significance* argument is optional. If you omit the argument, Excel assumes that you want three significant digits.

To demonstrate how the PERCENTRANK function works, again suppose you want to rank the values shown in the worksheet range A1:A9 in Figure 9-3 — only this time, you rank the values using percentages.

The formula in cell G6

```
=PERCENTRANK(A1:A9,6,2)
```

returns the value 0.75, which is the same thing as 75 percent.

Excel calculates the percentage rank by looking at the number of array values greater than the x value and the number of array values smaller than the x value. The array shown earlier in Figure 9-3 includes the values 1, 2, 3, 4, 4, 5, 6, 7, 8. The percent rank of 6 in the array equals 0.75 because six array values are smaller than 6 and two array values are larger than 6. The actual formula that the function calculates is 6/(2+6), which equals 0.75.

PERCENTILE: Finding a percentile ranking

The PERCENTILE function determines the array value at a specified percentile in an array. The formula uses the syntax

```
=PERCENTILE(array,k)
```

where *array* gives the array of values and k gives the percentile of the value that you want to find.

To find the value at the 75-percent percentile in the array of values shown in the worksheet range A1:A9 in Figure 9-3, use the formula

```
=PERCENTILE(A1:A9,.75)
```

The function returns the value 6 because the value 6 is at the 75th percentile in this array. This formula appears in cell G8 in the worksheet shown in Figure 9-3.

To repeat something in the earlier discussion of the PERCENTRANK function, note that Excel calculates the percentage rank by looking at the number of array values greater than the x value and the number of array values smaller than the x value. For the array shown in Figure 9-3, the array includes the values 1, 2, 3, 4, 4, 5, 6, 7, 8. The percent rank of 6 in the array equals 0.75 because six array values are smaller than 6 and two array values are larger than 6.

FREQUENCY: Frequency of values in a range

The FREQUENCY function counts the values in an array that fall within a range, or bin. The function uses the syntax

    =FREQUENCY(data_array,bins_array)

where *data_array* is the worksheet range that holds the values that you want to count and *bins_array* is a worksheet range that identifies the ranges of values, or bins, that you want to use to create a frequency distribution. Take a look at Figure 9-4, for example.

To categorize the values in the worksheet range A2:A20 using the bins shown in B2:B6, select the worksheet range C2:C6 and enter the formula

    =FREQUENCY(A2:A20,B2:B6)

Then press Ctrl+Shift+Enter to tell Excel that the function formula should be entered as an array. Excel enters your formula into each of the cells in the worksheet range C2:C6, with the result shown in Figure 9-4.

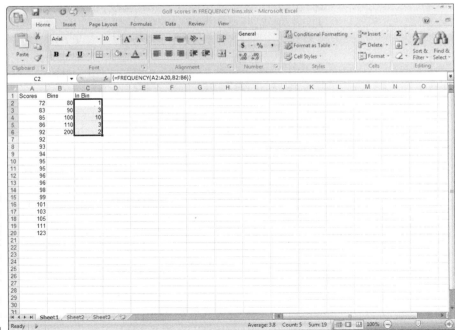

Figure 9-4:
A worksheet that illustrates how the FREQUENCY function works.

Working with array formulas

You can use array formulas to return arrays. For example, you can create an array formula that adds the array 1, 2, 3 to the array 4, 5, 6. This formula produces an array result: 5, 7, 9. The worksheet fragment below shows this. The array in range A1:C1 is added to the array in range A2:C2, and the resulting array is placed into the range A3:C3.

If you want to try entering this formula yourself, create a worksheet that holds the values shown in A1:C2. Then, select the range A3:C3, type the formula **=A1:C1+A2:C2**, and press Ctrl+Shift+Enter. Excel enters the same formula, {=A1:C1+A2:C2}, into each of the cells in the worksheet range

A3:C3. You don't enter the braces, by the way. Excel enters those for you when you press Ctrl+Shift+Enter. The array formula tells Excel to calculate different values for different cells. Excel calculates the value for cell A3 by adding the values in A1 and A2. Excel calculates the value in cell B3 by adding the values in B1 and B2, and so on.

A3			f_x	{=A1:C1+A2:C2}	
	A	B	C	D	E
1	1	2	3		
2	4	5	6		
3	5	7	9		
4					

In cell C2, the function uses the bin value in cell B2 to count up all the data values greater than 0 and less than or equal to 80. In cell C3, the function counts up all the data values greater than 80 but less than 90, and so on. Note that you need to arrange your bin range values in ascending order.

PROB: Probability of values

The PROB function uses a set of values and associated probabilities to calculate the probability that a variable equals some specified value or that a variable falls with a range of specified values. The function uses the syntax

```
=PROB(x_range,prob_range,lower_limit,[upper_limit])
```

where *x_range* equals the worksheet range that holds your values and *prob_range* holds the worksheet range that specifies the probabilities for the values from *x_range*. To calculate the probability that a variable equals a specified value, enter that value using the *lower_limit* argument. To calculate the probability that a variable falls within a range, enter the bounds of that range using the *lower_limit* and *upper_limit* arguments.

Although the PROB function seems complicated at first blush, take a peek at the worksheet shown in Figure 9-5. The worksheet range A1:A10 holds the values, and the worksheet range B1:B10 holds the probability of those values.

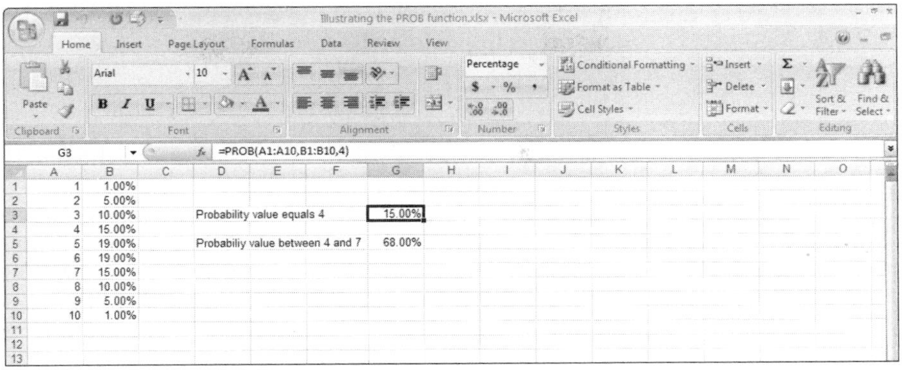

Figure 9-5:
A worksheet fragment for demonstrating the PROB function.

To calculate the probability that a value equals 4, use the formula

```
=PROB(A1:A10,B1:B10,4)
```

In what shouldn't be a surprise to you, given the value shown in cell B4, this function returns the value 15.00%, as shown in cell G3 in Figure 9-5. To calculate the probability that a value falls from 4 to 7, use the formula

```
=PROB(A1:A10,B1:B10,4,7)
```

The function returns the value 68.00%, which is the sum of the values in the range B4:B7. Figure 9-5 also shows this formula result in cell G5.

Standard Deviations and Variances

I'm sure that this will be a big surprise to you. Excel provides almost a dozen functions for calculating standard deviations and variances. A *standard deviation,* by the way, describes dispersion (spread of data) about (around) the data set's mean. You can kind of think of a standard deviation as an *average* deviation from the mean. A *variance* is just the squared standard deviation. You often use variances and standard deviations in other statistical calculations and as arguments to other statistical functions.

STDEV: Standard deviation of a sample

The STDEV function calculates the standard deviation of a sample, a measure of how widely values in a data set vary around the mean — and a common input to other statistical calculations. The function uses the syntax

```
=STDEV(number1,[number2])
```

To calculate the standard deviation of the worksheet range A1:A5 using the STDEV function, for example, use the formula

```
=STDEV(A1:A5)
```

If the worksheet range holds the values 1, 4, 8, 9, and 11, the function returns the standard deviation value 4.037326.

The STDEV function lets you include up to 255 arguments as inputs; those arguments can be values, cell references, formulas, and range references. The STDEV function ignores logical values, text, and empty cells.

STDEVA: Alternate standard deviation of a sample

The STDEVA function calculates the standard deviation of a sample, but unlike the STDEV function, STDEVA doesn't ignore the logical values TRUE (which is 1) and FALSE (which is 0). The function uses the syntax

```
=STDEVA(number1,[number2])
```

STDEVA arguments, which can number up to 255, can be values, cell references, formulas, and range references.

STDEVP: Standard deviation of a population

The STDEVP function calculates the standard deviation of a population to measure how widely values vary around the mean. The function uses the syntax

```
=STDEVP(number1,[number2])
```

To calculate the standard deviation of the worksheet range A1:A5 using the STDEVP function, for example, use the formula

```
=STDEVP(A1:A5)
```

If the worksheet range holds the values 1, 4, 8, 9, and 11, the function returns the standard deviation value 3.611094.

The STDEVP function lets you include up to 255 arguments as inputs; the arguments can be values, cell references, formulas, and range references. The STDEV function ignores logical values, text, and empty cells.

STDEVPA: Alternate standard deviation of a population

The STDEVPA function calculates the standard deviation of a population, but unlike the STDEVP function, STDEVPA doesn't ignore the logical values TRUE (which is 1) and FALSE (which is 0). The function uses the syntax

```
=STDEVPA(number1,[number2])
```

STDEVPA arguments, which can number up to 255, can be values, cell references, formulas, and range references.

VAR: Variance of a sample

The VAR function calculates the variance of a sample, another measure of how widely values in a data set vary around the mean. The VAR function uses the syntax

```
=VAR(number1,[number2])
```

A standard deviation is calculated by finding the square root of the variance.

To calculate the variance of the worksheet range A1:A5 using the VAR function, for example, use the formula

```
=VAR(A1:A5)
```

If the worksheet range holds the values 1, 4, 8, 9, and 11, the function returns the standard deviation value 16.3.

The VAR function lets you include up to 255 arguments as inputs; the arguments can be values, cell references, formulas, and range references. The VAR function ignores logical values, text, and empty cells.

VARA: Alternate variance of a sample

The VARA function calculates the variance of a sample, but unlike the VAR function, VARA doesn't ignore the logical values TRUE (which is 1) and FALSE (which is 0). The function uses the syntax

```
=VARA(number1,[number2])
```

VARA arguments, which can number up to 255, can be values, cell references, formulas, and range references.

VARP: Variance of a population

The VARP function calculates the variance of a population. The function uses the syntax

```
=VARP(number1,[number2])
```

To calculate the variance of the worksheet range A1:A5 using the VARP function, for example, use the formula

```
=VARP(A1:A5)
```

If the worksheet range holds the values 1, 4, 8, 9, and 11, the function returns the standard deviation value 13.04.

The VARP function lets you include up to 255 arguments as inputs; the arguments can be values, cell references, formulas, and range references. The VARP function ignores logical values, text, and empty cells.

VARPA: Alternate variance of a population

The VARPA function calculates the variance of a population, but unlike the VARP function, VARPA doesn't ignore the logical values TRUE (which is 1) and FALSE (which is 0). The function uses the syntax

```
=VARPA(number1,[number2])
```

VARPA arguments, which can number up to 255, can be values, cell references, formulas, and range references.

COVAR: Covariance

The COVAR function calculates a covariance, which is the average of the products of the deviations between pairs of values. The function uses the syntax

```
=COVAR(array1,array2)
```

where *array1* is the worksheet range holding the first values in the pair and *array2* is the worksheet range holding the second values in the pair.

DEVSQ: Sum of the squared deviations

The DEVSQ function calculates the deviations of values from a mean, squares those deviations, and then adds them up. The function uses the syntax

```
=DEVSQ(number1,[number2]...)
```

where *number1* and, optionally, *number2* are worksheet ranges or arrays that hold your values.

Normal Distributions

Excel provides five useful functions for working with normal distributions. Normal distributions are also known as *bell curves* or *Gaussian distributions*.

Pssst. Hey buddy, wanna to see how a normal distribution changes when you noodle with its mean and standard deviation? Visit the Stanford University Web page at

```
http://www-stat.stanford.edu/~naras/jsm/NormalDensity/
        NormalDensity.html
```

NORMDIST: Probability X falls at or below a given value

The NORMDIST function calculates the probability that variable X falls below or at a specified value. The NORMDIST function uses the syntax

```
=NORMDIST(x,mean,standard_dev,cumulative)
```

where x is the variable that you want to compare, *mean* is the population mean, *standard_dev* is the population standard deviation, and *cumulative* is a logical value that tells Excel whether you want a cumulative probability or a discrete probability.

Here's an example of how you might use the NORMDIST function: Suppose you want to calculate the probability that some goofball with whom you work actually does have an IQ above 135 like he's always bragging. Further suppose that the population mean IQ equals 100 and that the population standard deviation for IQs is 15. (I don't know whether these numbers are true. I do vaguely remember reading something about this in *Zen and the Art of Motorcycle Maintenance* when I was in high school.)

In this case, you use the following formula:

```
=NORMDIST(135,100,15,1)
```

The function returns the value .990185, indicating that if the inputs are correct, roughly 99 percent of the population has an IQ at or below 135. Or, slightly restated, this means the chance that your co-worker has an IQ above 135 is less than 1 percent.

If you want to calculate the probability that your co-worker has an IQ equal to exactly 135, use the following formula:

```
=NORMDIST(135,100,15,0)
```

This function returns the value .001748 indicating that .1748 percent, or roughly one-sixth of a percent, of the population has an IQ equal to 135.

To be very picky, statisticians might very well tell you that you can't actually calculate the probability of a single value, such as the probability that somebody's IQ equals 135. When you set the cumulative argument to 0, therefore, what actually happens is that Excel roughly estimates the probability by using a small range about the single value.

NORMINV: X that gives specified probability

The NORMINV function makes the inverse calculation of the NORMDIST function. NORMINV calculates the variable X that gives a specified probability. The NORMINV function uses the syntax

```
=NORMINV(probability,mean,standard_dev)
```

where *probability* is the percentage that you want the variable X value to fall at or below, *mean* is the population mean, and *standard_dev* is the population standard deviation.

Okay, here's something that I do remember from *Zen and the Art of Motorcycle Maintenance*. In that book, the protagonist says that he has an IQ that occurs only once in every 50,000 people. You can turn this into a percentile using the formula 1–1/50000, which returns the value .99998.

To calculate the IQ level (which is the variable X) that occurs only every 50,000 people and again assuming that the IQ mean is 100 and that the standard deviation is 15 IQ points, you use the following formula:

```
=NORMINV(.99998,100,15)
```

The formula returns the value 162, when rounded to the nearest whole number.

NORMSDIST: Probability variable within z-standard deviations

For normal distributions, the NORMSDIST function calculates the probability that a random variable is within z-standard deviations of the mean. The function uses the syntax

```
=NORMSDIST(z)
```

To find the probability that a randomly selected variable from a data set is within 2 standard deviations from the mean, use the following formula:

```
=NORMSDIST(2)
```

which returns the value 0.97725, indicating that there is a 97.725-percent chance that the variable falls within 2 standard deviations of the mean.

NORMSINV: z-value equivalent to a probability

The NORMSINV function is the inverse of the NORMSDIST function. If you know the probability that a randomly selected variable is within a certain distance of the mean, you can calculate the z-value by using the NORMSINV function to describe the distance in standard deviations. The function uses the syntax

```
=NORMSINV(probability)
```

where *probability* is a decimal value between 0 and 1. To find the z-value for 99 percent, for example, you use the following formula:

```
=NORMSINV(0.99)
```

The function returns the z-value 2.326348, indicating that there is a 99-percent chance that a randomly selected variable is within 2.326348 standard deviations of the mean.

STANDARDIZE: z-value for a specified value

The STANDARDIZE function returns the z-value for a specified variable. The z-value describes the distance between a value and the mean in terms of standard deviations. The function uses the syntax

```
=STANDARDIZE(x, mean, standard_dev)
```

where *x* is the variable for which you want to calculate a z-value, *mean* is the arithmetic mean, and *standard_dev* is the standard deviation.

For example, to calculate the z-value for the variable 6600 given a mean equal to 6000 and a standard deviation equal to 800, you use the following formula:

```
=STANDARDIZE(6600,6000,800)
```

The function returns the z-value 0.75.

With a z-value, you can use the NORMSDIST function to calculate the probability that a randomly selected variable falls within the area calculated as the mean plus or minus the z-value. The probability that a randomly selected variable falls within the area that equals the mean plus or minus the z-value 0.75 is calculated using the formula =NORMSDIST(0.75). This function returns the probability value 0.773373, indicating that there's a 77.3373 chance that a variable will fall within 0.75 standard deviations of the mean.

CONFIDENCE: Confidence interval for a population mean

The CONFIDENCE function calculates a value that you can use to create a confidence interval for the population mean based on the sample mean. This definition amounts to a mouthful, but in practice what the CONFIDENCE function does is straightforward.

Suppose that, based on a sample, you calculate that the mean salary for a chief financial officer for a particular industry equals $100,000. You might wonder how close this sample mean is to the actual population mean. Specifically, you might want to know what range of salaries, working at a 95-percent confidence level, includes the population mean.

The CONFIDENCE function calculates the number that you use to create this interval using the syntax

```
=CONFIDENCE(alpha,standard_dev,size)
```

where *alpha* equals 1 minus the confidence level, *standard_dev* equals the standard deviation of the population, and *size* equals the number of values in your sample.

If the standard deviation for the population equals $20,000 and the sample size equals 100, use the formula

```
=CONFIDENCE(1-.95,20000,100)
```

The function returns the value $3920 (rounded to the nearest dollar). This interval suggests that if the average chief financial officer's salary in your sample equals $100,000, there's a 95-percent chance that the population mean of the chief financial officers' salaries falls within the range $96,080 to $103,920.

KURT: Kurtosis

The KURT function measures the tails in a distribution. The function uses the syntax

```
=KURT(number1,[number2]...)
```

where *number1* is a value, cell reference, or range reference. Optionally, you can include additional arguments that provide values, cell references, and ranges.

The kurtosis of a normal distribution equals 0. A kurtosis greater than 0 means the distribution's tails are larger than for a normal distribution. A kurtosis less than 0 means the distribution's tails are smaller than for a normal distribution.

SKEW: Skewness of a distribution

The SKEW function measures the symmetry of a distribution of values. The function uses the syntax

```
=SKEW(number1,[number2])
```

The skewness of a symmetrical distribution, such as a normal distribution, equals 0. For example, the formula

```
=SKEW(1,2,3,4,5,6,7,8)
```

returns the value 0.

If a distribution's values *tail* (that is, stretch out) to the right, it means the distribution includes greater numbers of large values (or larger values) than a symmetrical distribution would. Thus the skewness is positive. For example, the formula

```
=SKEW(1,2,3,4,5,6,8,8)
```

returns the value 0.09884.

If the distribution's values tail (stretch out) to the left, meaning that the distribution includes greater numbers of small values or smaller values than a symmetrical observation would, the skewness is negative. For example, the formula

```
=SKEW(1,1,3,4,5,6,7,8)
```

returns the value -0.09884.

t-distributions

When you're working with small samples — less than 30 or 40 items — you can use what's called a *student t-value* to calculate probabilities rather than the usual z-value, which is what you work with in the case of normal distributions. Excel provides three t-distribution functions, which I discuss in the following paragraphs.

TDIST: Probability of given t-value

The TDIST function returns the probability of a given t-value. The function uses the syntax

```
=TDIST(x,deg_freedom,tails)
```

where *x* equals the t-value, `deg_freedom` equals the degrees of freedom, and `tails` indicates whether you want to calculate the probability assuming one tail or two tails: This value can be either 1 or 2. For example, to calculate the two-tailed probability of the t-value 2.093025 given 19 degrees of freedom, you use the following formula:

```
=TDIST(2.093025,19,2)
```

which returns the value 0.05, including that there's a 5-percent chance that a value will fall within the range calculated as the mean plus or minus 2.093025 t-values.

Student t-distribution measures let you estimate probabilities for normally distributed data when the sample size is small (say, 30 items or fewer). You can calculate the degrees of freedom argument by subtracting 1 from the sample size. For example, if the sample size is 20, the degrees of freedom equal 19.

TINV: t-value of a given probability

The TINV function calculates the t-value for a given probability. The function uses the syntax

```
=TINV(probability,deg_freedom)
```

where `probability` is the probability percentage and `deg_freedom` equals the degrees of freedom. To calculate the t-value given a 5-percent probability and 19 degrees of freedom, for example, use the following formula:

```
=TINV(0.05,19)
```

which returns the t-value 2.093025.

TTEST: Probability two samples from same population

The TTEST function returns the probability that two samples come from the same populations with the same mean. The function uses the syntax

```
=TTEST(array1,array2,tails,type)
```

where *array1* is a range reference holding the first sample, *array2* is a range reference holding the second sample, *tails* is either the value 1 (representing a one-tailed probability) or 2 (representing a two-tailed probability), and *type* tells Excel which type of t-test calculation to make. You set *type* to 1 to perform a paired t-test, to 2 to perform a *homoscedastic* test (a test with two samples with equal variance), or to 3 to perform a *heteroscedastic* test (a test with two samples with unequal variance).

f-distributions

f-distributions are probability distributions that compare the ratio in variances of samples drawn from different populations. That comparison produces a conclusion regarding whether the variances in the underlying populations resemble each other.

FDIST: f-distribution probability

The FDIST function returns the probability of observing a ratio of two samples' variances as large as a specified f-value. The function uses the syntax

```
=FDIST(x,deg_freedom1,deg_freedom2)
```

where *x* is specified f-value that you want to test; *deg_freedom1* is the degrees of freedom in the first, or numerator, sample; and *deg_freedom2* is the degrees of freedom in the second, or denominator, sample.

As an example of how the FDIST function works, suppose you compare two sample's variances, one equal to 2 and one equal to 4. This means the f-value equals 0.5. Further assume that both samples number 10 items, which means both samples have degrees of freedom equal to 9. The formula

```
=FDIST(2/4,9,9)
```

returns the value 0.841761297, suggesting that there's roughly an 84-percent probability that you might observe an f-value as large as 0.5 if the samples' variances were equivalent.

FINV: f-value given f-distribution probability

The FINV function returns the f-value equivalent to a given f-distribution probability. The function uses the syntax

```
=FINV(probability,deg_freedom1,deg_freedom2)
```

where `probability` is probability of the f value that you want to find; `deg_freedom1` is the degrees of freedom in the first, or numerator, sample; and `deg_freedom2` is the degrees of freedom in the second, or denominator, sample.

FTEST: Probability data set variances not different

The FTEST function compares the variances of two samples and returns the probability that variances aren't significantly different. The function uses the syntax

```
=FTEST(array1,array2)
```

where `array1` is a worksheet range holding the first sample and `array2` is a worksheet range holding the second sample.

Binomial Distributions

Binomial distributions let you calculate probabilities in two situations:

- When you have a limited number of independent trials, or tests, which can either succeed or fail
- When success or failure of any one trial is independent of other trials

I also discuss Excel's sole hypergeometric distribution function here with the binomial functions because, as you'll see if you slog through this discussion, hypergeometric distributions are related to binomial distributions.

BINOMDIST: Binomial probability distribution

The BINOMDIST function finds the binomial distribution probability. The function uses the syntax

```
=BINOMDIST(number_s,trials,probability_s,cumulative)
```

where *number_s* is the specified number of successes that you want, *trials* equals the number of trials you'll look at, *probability_s* equals the probability of success in a trial, and *cumulative* is a switch that's set to either the logical value TRUE (if you want to calculate the cumulative probability) or the logical value FALSE (if you want to calculate the exact probability).

For example, if a publisher wants to know the probability of publishing three best-selling books out of a set of ten books when the probability of publishing a best-selling book is ten percent, the formula is:

```
=BINOMDIST(3,10,.1,FALSE)
```

which returns the value 0.0574. This indicates that there's roughly a 6-percent chance that in a set of ten books, a publisher will publish exactly three best-selling books.

To calculate the probability that a publisher will publish either one, two, or three bestsellers in a set of ten books, the formula is

```
=BINOMDIST(3,10,.1,TRUE)
```

which returns the value 0.9872, which indicates that there is roughly a 99-percent chance that a publisher will publish between one and three best-sellers in a set of ten books.

NEGBINOMDIST: Negative binominal distribution

The NEGBINOMDIST function finds the probability that a specified number of failures will occur before a specified number of successes based on a probability-of-success constant. The function uses the syntax

```
=NEGBINOMDIST(number_f,number_s,probability_s)
```

where *number_f* is the specified number of failures, *number_s* is the specified number of successes, and *probability_s* is the probability of success.

For example, suppose you're a wildcat oil operator and you want to know the chance of failing to find oil in exactly ten wells before you find oil in exactly 1 well. If the chance for success is 5 percent, you can find the chance that you'll fail ten times before drilling and finding oil by using the formula

```
=NEGBINOMDIST(10,2,.05)
```

which returns the value 0.016465266, indicating that there's less than a 2-percent chance that you'll fail ten times before hitting a gusher.

CRITBINOM: Cumulative binomial distribution

The CRITBINOM function finds the smallest value for which the cumulative binomial distribution equals or exceeds a criterion value. The function uses the syntax

```
=CRITBINOM(trials,probability_s,alpha)
```

where *trials* is the number of Bernoulli trials, *probability_s* is the probability of success for each trial, and *alpha* equals your criterion value. Both the *probability_s* and *alpha* arguments must fall between 0 and 1.

HYPGEOMDIST: Hypergeometric distribution

The HYPERGEOMETRIC function returns the probability of a specified number of sample successes. A hypergeometric distribution resembles a binomial distribution except with a subtle difference. In a hypergeometric distribution, the success in one trial affects the success in another trial. Typically, you use a the HYPGEOMDIST function when you take samples from a finite population and don't replace the samples for subsequent trials. The function uses the syntax

```
=HYPGEOMDIST(sample_s,number_sample,population_s,number_
         pop)
```

where *sample_s* equals the specified number of sample successes, *number_sample* gives the size of the sample, *population_s* gives the number of successes in the population, and *number_pop* gives the size of the population.

As an example of a hypergeometric distribution, suppose you want to calculate the probability that in a sample of 30 items, 5 will be successful. Further suppose you know that within a 4,000-item population, 1,000 are successful. You use the following formula to make this calculation:

```
=HYPGEOMDIST(5,30,1000,4000)
```

which returns the value 0.01046, indicating that the chances that exactly 5 items will be successful in a set of 30 items given the characteristics of the population equals roughly 10 percent.

Chi-Square Distributions

I get very confused, personally, when I start working with statistical measures that are more complicated than those simple calculations that you learn in junior high. Yet the chi-square functions, which I discuss next, really are practical. I take this one slow and use an easy-to-understand example.

Even if you're going to use only one of the chi-square functions, read through all three function descriptions. Viewed as a set of statistical tools, the functions make quite a bit more sense.

CHIDIST: Chi-square distribution

The CHIDIST function calculates a level of significance using the chi-square value and the degrees of freedom. The chi-square value equals the sum of the squared standardized scores. The function uses the syntax

```
=CHIDIST(x,deg_freedom)
```

where x equals the chi-square value and $deg\_freedom$ equals the degrees of freedom.

As an example of how all this works, suppose you're more than a little suspicious of some slot machine that shows one of six pictures: diamonds, stars, cowboy boots, cherries, oranges, or pots of gold. With six possibilities, you might expect that in a large sample, each of the six possibilities would appear roughly one-sixth of the time. Say the sample size is 180, for example. In this case, you might expect that each slot machine possibility appears 30 times because 180/6 equals 30. If you built worksheet fragment like the one shown in Figure 9-6, you could analyze the one-armed bandit.

To calculate the level of significance using the data shown in Figure 9-6 and the chi-square distribution function, you could enter the following formula into D10:

```
=CHIDIST(D8,5)
```

The function returns the value 0.010362338, which is the level of significance that a chi-square value of 15 is due to sampling error.

Cell D8 holds the chi-square value, which is simply the sum of the squared differences between the observed and expected values. For example, the value in cell D2 is calculated using the formula =+(B2–C2)^2/C2 to return the value 3.333333333. Predictably, similar formulas in the range D3:D7 calculate the squared differences for the other slot machine symbols. And, oh, by the way, the formula in cell D8 is =SUM(D2:D7).

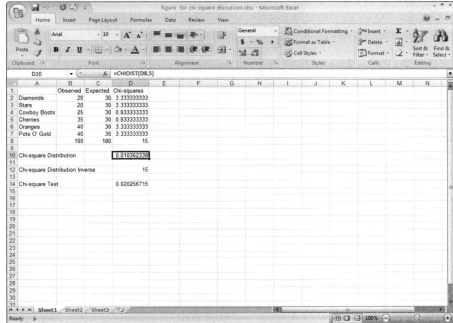

Figure 9-6:
A worksheet fragment we'll use to look at chi-square measures.

The bottom line: It doesn't look good, does it? I mean, that there's only a 1-percent chance that the slot machine that you're worried about could actually produce the observed values due to chance. Very suspicious. . . .

CHIINV: Chi-square value for a given level of significance

The CHIINV function returns the chi-square value equivalent to a specified level of confidence. The function uses the syntax

```
=CHIINV(probability,deg_freedom)
```

where *probability* equals the level of significance and *deg_freedom* equals the degrees of freedom.

To show you an example of the CHIINV function, refer to the worksheet fragment shown in Figure 9-6. With six possible outcomes on the slot machine, you have five degrees of freedom. Therefore, if you want to calculate the chi-square that's equivalent to a 0.010362338 level of significance, you could enter the following formula into cell D12:

```
=CHIINV(D10,5)
```

This function returns the value 14.99996888, which is pretty darn close to 15 . . . so I call it 15. Note that I use D10 as the first probability argument because that cell holds the level of significance calculated by the CHIDIST function.

CHITEST: Chi-square test

The chi-square test function lets you assess whether differences between the observed and expected values represent chance, or *sampling error*. The function uses the syntax

```
=CHITEST(actual_range,expected_range)
```

Again referring to the example of the suspicious slot machine shown in Figure 9-6, you could perform a chi-square test by entering the following formula into cell D14 and then comparing what you observe with what you expect:

```
=CHITEST(B2:B7,C2:C7)
```

The function returns the p-value, or probability, shown in Figure 9-6 in cell D14, indicating that only a 2.0256715-percent chance exists that the differences between the observed and expected outcomes stem from sampling error.

A common feature of a chi-square test is comparison of the p-value — again the value that the CHITEST function returns — to a level of significance. For example, in the case of the suspicious slot machine, you might say, "Because it's not possible to be 100-percent sure, we'll say that we want a 95-percent probability, which corresponds to a 5-percent level of significance." If the p-value is less than the level of significance, you assume that something is fishy. Statisticians, not wanting to sound so earthy, have another phrase for this something-is-fishy conclusion: *rejecting the null hypothesis.*

Regression Analysis

Excel's regression functions let you perform regression analysis. In a nutshell, *regression analysis* involves plotting pairs of independent and dependent variables in an XY chart and then finding a linear or exponential equation that describes the plotted data.

FORECAST: Forecast dependent variables using a best-fit line

The FORECAST function finds the y-value of a point on a best-fit line produced by a set of x- and y-values given the x-value. The function uses the syntax

```
=FORECAST(x,known_y's,known_x's)
```

where *x* is the independent variable value, *known_y's* is the worksheet range holding the dependent variables, and *known_x's* is the worksheet range holding the independent variables.

The FORECAST function uses the *known_y's* and *known_x's* values that you supply as arguments to calculate the y=mx+b equation that describes the best-fit straight line for the data. The function then solves that equation using the x argument that you supply to the function.

To use the linear regression functions such as the FORECAST function, remember the equation for a line is *y=mx+b*. *y* is the dependent variable, *b* is the y-intercept or constant, *m* is the slope, and *x* gives the value of the independent variable.

INTERCEPT: y-axis intercept of a line

The INTERCEPT function finds the point where the best-fit line produced by a set of x- and y-values intersects the y-axis. The function uses the syntax

```
=INTERCEPT(known_y's,known_x's)
```

where *known_y's* is the worksheet range holding the dependent variables and *known_x's* is the worksheet range holding the independent variables.

If you've ever plotted pairs of data points on an XY graph, the way the INTERCEPT function works is pretty familiar. The INTERCEPT function uses the *known_y's* and *known_x's* values that you supply as arguments to calculate the best-fit straight line for the data — essentially figuring out the *y=mx+b* equation for the line. The function then returns the *b* value because that's the value of the equation when the independent, or *x*, variable equals zero.

LINEST

The LINEST function finds the *m* and *b* values for a line based on sets of known_ys and known_xs variables. The function uses the syntax

```
=LINEST(known_y's,[known_x's],[const],[stats])
```

where *known_y's* equals the array of y-values that you already know, *known_x's* supplies the array of x-values that you may already know, *const* is a switch set to either TRUE (which means the constant *b* equals 0) or to TRUE (which means the constant *b* is calculated), and *stats* is another switch set to either TRUE (which means the function returns a bunch of other regression statistics) or FALSE (which means *enough already*).

SLOPE: Slope of a regression line

The SLOPE function calculates the slope of a regression line using the x- and y-values. The functions uses the syntax

```
=SLOPE(known_y's,known_x's)
```

An upward slope indicates that the independent, or *x*, variable positively affects the dependent, or *y*, variable. In other words, an increase in *x* produces an increase in *y*. A downward slope indicates that the independent, or *x*, variable negatively affects the dependent, or *y*, variable. The steeper the slope, the greater the effect of the independent variable on the dependent variable.

STEYX: Standard error

The STEYX function finds the standard error of the predicted y-value of each of the x-values in a regression. The function uses the syntax

```
=STEYX(known_y's,known_x's)
```

TREND

The TREND function finds values along a trend line, which the function constructs using the method of least squares. The syntax looks like this:

```
=TREND(known_y's,[known_x's],[new_x's],[const])
```

LOGEST: Exponential regression

The LOGEST function returns an array that describes an exponential curve that best fits your data. The function uses the syntax

```
=LOGEST(known_y's,[known_x's],[const],[stats])
```

where *known_y's* is the set of y-values, *known_x's* is the set of x-values, *const* is a switch set to either TRUE (which means that *b* is calculated normally) or FALSE (which means that *b* is forced to equal 1), and *stats* is a switch that's set to either TRUE (in which case, the LOGEST function returns a bunch of additional regression statistics) or FALSE (which tells the function to skip returning all the extra information).

In an exponential regression, Excel returns an equation that takes the form $y=ab^x$ that best fits your data set.

GROWTH: Exponential growth

The GROWTH function calculates exponential growth for a series of new x-values based on existing x-values and y-values. The function uses the syntax

```
=GROWTH(known_y's,[known_x's],[new_x's],[const])
```

where *known_y's* is the set of y-values, *known_x's* is the set of x-values, *new_x's* is the set of x-values for which you want to calculate new y-values, and *const* is a switch set to either TRUE (which means that *b* is calculated normally) or FALSE (which means that *b* is forced to equal 1).

Correlation

Excel's correlation functions let you quantitatively explore the relationships between variables.

CORREL: Correlation coefficient

The CORREL function calculates a correlation coefficient for two data sets. The function uses the syntax

```
=CORREL(array1,array2)
```

where *array1* is a worksheet range that holds the first data set and *array2* is a worksheet range that holds the second data set. The function returns a value between -1 (which would indicate a perfect, negative linear relationship) and +1 (which would indicate a perfect, positive linear relationship).

PEARSON: Pearson correlation coefficient

The PEARSON calculates a correlation coefficient for two data sets by using a different formula than the CORREL function does but one that should return the same result. The function uses the syntax

```
=PEARSON(array1,array2)
```

where *array1* is a worksheet range that holds the first data set and *array2* is a worksheet range that holds the second data set. The function returns a value between -1 (which would indicate a perfect, negative linear relationship) and +1 (which would indicate a perfect, positive linear relationship).

RSQ: r-squared value for a Pearson correlation coefficient

The RSQ function calculates the r-squared square of the Pearson correlation coefficient. The function uses the syntax

```
=RSQ(known_y's,known_x's)
```

where *known_y's* is an array or worksheet range holding the first data set and *known_x's* is an array or worksheet range holding the second data set. The r-squared value describes the proportion of the variance in *y* stemming from the variance in *x*.

FISHER

The FISHER function converts Pearson's r-squared value to the normally distributed variable *z* so you can calculate a confidence interval. The function uses the syntax

```
=FISHER(r)
```

FISHERINV

The FISHERINV function, the inverse of the FISHER function, converts *z* to Pearson's r-squared value. The function uses the syntax

```
=FISHERINV(y)
```

Some Really Esoteric Probability Distributions

Excel supplies several other statistical functions for working with probability distributions. It's very unlikely, it seems to me, that you'll ever work with any of these functions except in an upper-level college statistics course. Thus I go over these tools quickly here. A couple of them, though — the ZTEST and the POISSON functions, in particular — are actually pretty useful.

BETADIST: Cumulative beta probability density

The BETADIST function finds the cumulative beta probability density — something that you might do to look at variation in the percentage of some value in your sample data. The Excel online Help file, for example, talks about using the function to look at the fraction of the day that people spend watching television. And I recently read a fisheries management study that uses beta probability distributions to report on the effects of setting aside a percentage of marine habitat for reserves. The function uses the syntax

```
=BETADIST(x,alpha,beta,[A],[B])
```

where *x* is a value between the optional bounds *A* and *B*, and `alpha` and `beta` are the two positive parameters. If *x* equals .5, `alpha` equals 75, `beta` equals 85, *A* equals 0, and *B* equals 1, use following formula:

```
=BETADIST(.5,75,85,0,1)
```

This function returns the value 0.786080098.

If you leave out the optional bounds arguments, Excel assumes that A equals 0 and that B equals 1. The function =BETADIST(.5,75,85), for example, is equivalent to =BETADIST(.5,75,85,0,1).

BETAINV: Inverse cumulative beta probability density

The BETAINV function returns the inverse of the cumulative beta probability density function. That is, you use the BETADIST function if you know *x* and want to find the probability; and you use the BETAINV function if you know the probability and want to find *x*. The BETAINV function uses the syntax

```
=BETAINV(probability,alpha,beta,[A],[B])
```

EXPONDIST: Exponential probability distribution

The EXPONDIST function calculates an exponential distribution, which can be used to describe the probability that an event takes a specified amount of time. The function uses the syntax

```
=EXPONDIST(x,lambda,cumulative)
```

where *x* is the value you want to evaluate, *lambda* is the inverse of the mean, and *cumulative* is a switch set to either TRUE (if you want the function to return the probability up to and including the *x* value) or FALSE (if you want the function to return the exact probability of the *x* value).

For example, suppose that at a certain poorly run restaurant, you usually have to wait 10 minutes for your waitperson to bring a glass of water. That's the *average wait time,* in other words. To determine the probability that you'll get your water in 5 minutes or less, use the formula

```
=EXPONDIST(5,1/10,TRUE)
```

which returns the value 0.393469, indicating you have (roughly) a 39-percent chance of getting something to drink in 5 minutes or less.

To determine the probability that you'll get your water in exactly 5 minutes, you use the formula

```
=EXPONDIST(5,1/10,FALSE)
```

which returns the value 0.060653, indicating there's roughly a 6-percent chance that you'll get something to drink in exactly 5 minutes.

GAMMADIST: Gamma distribution probability

The GAMMADIST function finds the gamma distribution probability of the random variable *x*. The function uses the syntax

```
=GAMMADIST(x,alpha,beta,cumulative)
```

where *x* equals the random variable, *alpha* and *beta* describe the constant rate, and *cumulative* is a switch set to TRUE if you want a cumulative probability and FALSE if you want an exact probability.

If *x* equals 20, *alpha* equals 5, *beta* equals 2, and *cumulative* is set to TRUE, you use the formula

```
=GAMMADIST(20,5,2,TRUE)
```

which returns the value 0.97075, indicating the probability equals roughly 97 percent.

If *x* equals 20, *alpha* equals 5, *beta* equals 2, and *cumulative* is set to FALSE, you use the formula

```
=GAMMADIST(20,5,2,FALSE)
```

which returns the value 0.00946, indicating the probability is less than 1 percent.

GAMMAINV: X for a given gamma distribution probability

The GAMMAINV function finds the *x* value associated with a given gamma distribution probability. The function uses the syntax

```
=GAMMAINV(probability,alpha,beta)
```

where *probability* equals the probability for the *x* value you want to find and *alpha* and *beta* are the parameters to the distribution.

GAMMALN: Natural logarithm of a gamma distribution

The GAMMALN function finds the natural logarithm of the gamma function. The GAMMALN function uses the syntax

```
=GAMMALN(x)
```

LOGNORMDIST: Probability of lognormal distribution

The LOGNORMDIST function calculates the probability associated with a lognormal distribution. The function uses the syntax

```
=LOGNORMDIST(x,mean,standard_dev)
```

where x is the value for which you want to find the probability, $mean$ is the arithmetic mean, and $standard\_dev$, of course, equals the standard deviation.

LOGINV: Value associated with lognormal distribution probability

The LOGINV function calculates the value associated with a lognormal distribution probability. The function uses the syntax

```
=LOGINV(probability,mean,standard_dev)
```

where $probability$ is the probability of a lognormal distribution, $mean$ is the arithmetic mean, and $standard\_dev$ is the standard deviation.

POISSON: Poisson distribution probabilities

The POISSON function calculates probabilities for Poisson distributions. The function uses the syntax

```
=POISSON(x,mean,cumulative)
```

where x is the number of events, $mean$ is the arithmetic mean, and $cumulative$ is a switch. If set to TRUE, this switch tells Excel to calculate the Poisson probability of a variable being less than or equal to x; if set to FALSE, it tells Excel to calculate the Poisson probability of a variable being exactly equal to x.

To illustrate how the Poisson function works, suppose you want to look at some probabilities associated with cars arriving as a drive-through car wash. (This type of analysis of events occurring over a specified time interval is a common application of Poisson distributions.) If on average, 20 cars drive up an hour, you can calculate the probability that exactly 15 cars will drive up using the formula

```
=POISSON(15,20,FALSE)
```

This function returns the value 0.051648854, indicating that there's roughly a 5-percent chance that exactly 15 cars will drive up in an hour.

To calculate the probability that 15 cars or fewer will drive up in an hour, use the following formula:

```
=POISSON(15,20,TRUE)
```

This function returns the value 0.156513135, indicating that there's roughly a 16-percent chance that 15 or fewer cars will drive up in an hour.

WEIBULL: Weibull distribution

The WEIBULL function returns either the cumulative distribution or the probability mass for a Weibull distribution. The function uses the syntax

```
=WEIBULL(x,alpha,beta,cumulative)
```

where *x* is the value for which you want to calculate the distribution; *alpha* and *beta* are, respectively, the alpha and beta parameters to the Weibull equation, and *cumulative* is a switch. That switch, if set to TRUE, tells the function to return the cumulative distribution function; if set to FALSE, it tells the function to return the probability mass function.

Visit the Web page

```
http://www.windpower.dk/tour/wres/weibull/index.htm
```

to see Weibull distributions for wind speed information.

ZTEST: Probability of a z-test

The ZTEST function calculates the probability that a value comes from the same population as a sample. The function uses the syntax

```
=ZTEST(array,x,[sigma])
```

where *array* is the worksheet range holding your sample, *x* is the value you want to test, and (optionally) *sigma* is the standard deviation of the population. If you omit *sigma*, Excel uses the sample standard deviation.

For example, to find the probability that the value 75 comes from the population as the sample stored in the worksheet range A1:A10, use the following formula:

```
=ZTEST(A1:A10,75)
```

Chapter 10

Descriptive Statistics

· ·

· ·

*I*n this chapter, I describe and discuss the simple descriptive statistical data analysis tools that Excel supplies through the Data Analysis add-in. I also describe some of the really simple-to-use and easy-to-understand inferential statistical tools provided by the Data Analysis add-in — including the tools for calculating moving and exponential averages as well as the tools for generating random numbers and sampling.

Descriptive statistics simply summarize large (sometimes overwhelming) data sets with a few, key calculated values. For example, when you say something like, "Well, the biggest value in that data set is 345," that's a descriptive statistic.

The simple-yet-powerful Data Analysis tools can save you a lot of time. With a single command, for example, you can often produce a bunch of descriptive statistical measures such as mean, mode, standard deviation, and so on. What's more, the other cool tools that you can use for preparing histograms, percentile rankings, and moving average schedules can really come in handy.

Perhaps the best thing about these tools, however, is that even if you've had only a little exposure to basic statistics, none of them are particularly difficult to use. All the hard work and all the dirty work gets done by Excel. All you have to do is describe where the input data is.

Note: You must usually install the Data Analysis tools before you can use them. To install them, choose Office➪Excel Options. When Excel displays the Excel Options dialog box, select the Add-Ins item from the left box that appears along the left edge of the dialog box. Excel next displays a list of the possible add-ins — including the Analysis ToolPak add-in. (The Analysis ToolPak is what the Data Analysis tools are called.) Select the Analysis ToolPak item and click Go. Excel displays the Add-Ins dialog box. Select Analysis ToolPak from this dialog box and click OK. Excel installs the Analysis ToolPak add-in.

Using the Descriptive Statistics Tool

Perhaps the most common Data Analysis tool that you'll use is the one for calculating descriptive statistics. To see how this works, take a look at the worksheet shown in Figure 10-1. It summarizes sales data for a book publisher. In column A, the worksheet shows the suggested retail price (SRP). In column B, the worksheet shows the units sold of each book through one popular bookselling outlet. You might choose to use the Descriptive Statistics tool to summarize this data set.

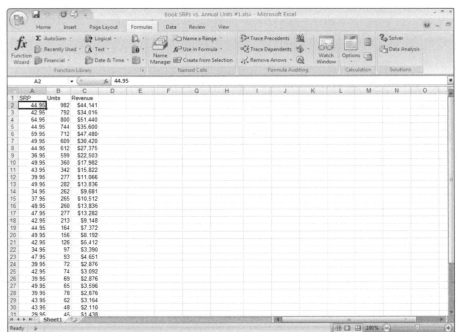

Figure 10-1:
A sample
data set.

To calculate descriptive statistics for the data set shown in Figure 10-1, follow these steps:

1. Click the Data tab's Data Analysis command button to tell Excel that you want to calculate descriptive statistics.

Excel displays the Data Analysis dialog box, as shown in Figure 10-2.

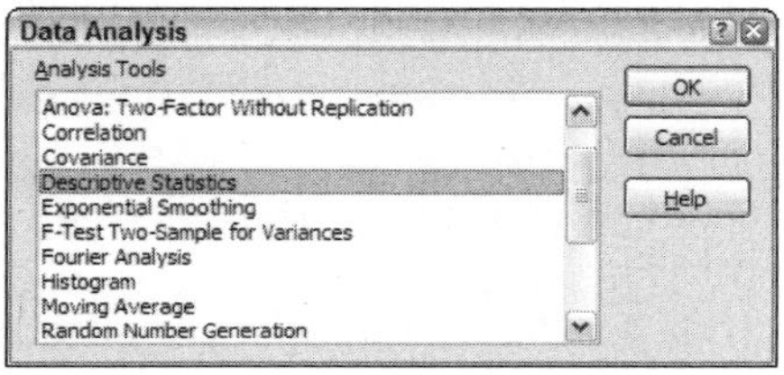

Figure 10-2:
The Data
Analysis
dialog box.

2. In Data Analysis dialog box, highlight the Descriptive Statistics entry in the Analysis Tools list and then click OK.

Excel displays the Descriptive Statistics dialog box, as shown in Figure 10-3.

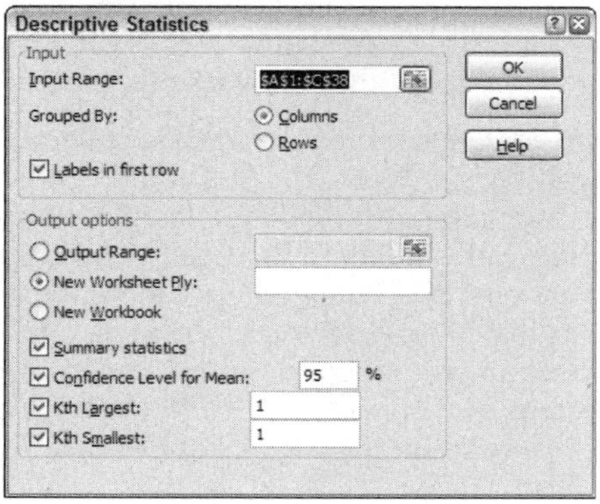

Figure 10-3:
The
Descriptive
Statistics
dialog box.

3. In the Input section of the Descriptive Statistics dialog box, identify the data that you want to describe.

- *To identify the data that you want to describe statistically:* Click the Input Range text box and then enter the worksheet range reference for the data. In the case of the worksheet shown earlier in Figure 10-1, the input range is $A$1:$C$38. Note that Excel wants the range address to use absolute references — hence, the dollar signs.

To make it easier to see or select the worksheet range, click the worksheet button at the right end of the Input Range text box. When Excel hides the Descriptive Statistics dialog box, select the range that you want by dragging the mouse. Then click the worksheet button again to redisplay the Descriptive Statistics dialog box.

- *To identify whether the data is arranged in columns or rows:* Select either the Columns or the Rows radio button.

- *To indicate whether the first row holds labels that describe the data:* Select the Labels in First Row check box. In the case of the worksheet shown in Figure 10-1, the data is arranged in columns, and the first row does hold labels, so you select the Columns radio button *and* the Labels in First Row check box.

4. **In the Output Options area of the Descriptive Statistics dialog box, describe where and how Excel should produce the statistics.**

- *To indicate where the descriptive statistics that Excel calculates should be placed:* Choose from the three radio buttons here — Output Range, New Worksheet Ply, and New Workbook. Typically, you place the statistics onto a new worksheet in the existing workbook. To do this, simply select the New Worksheet Ply radio button.

- *To identify what statistical measures you want calculated:* Use the Output Options check boxes. Select the Summary Statistics check box to tell Excel to calculate statistical measures such as mean, mode, and standard deviation. Select the Confidence Level for Mean check box to specify that you want a confidence level calculated for the sample mean. (*Note:* If you calculate a confidence level for the sample mean, you need to enter the confidence level percentage into the text box provided.) Use the Kth Largest and Kth Smallest check boxes to indicate you want to find the largest or smallest value in the data set.

After you describe where the data is and how the statistics should be calculated, click OK. Figure 10-4 shows a new worksheet with the descriptive statistics calculated, added into a new sheet, Sheet 2. Table 10-1 describes the statistics that Excel calculates.

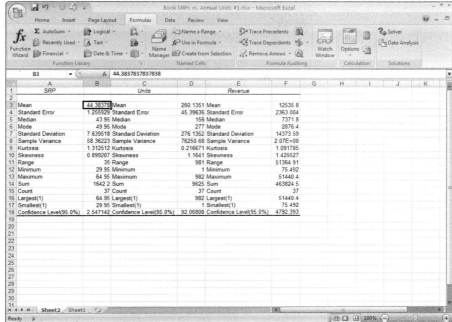

Figure 10-4:
A new
worksheet
with the
descriptive
statistics
calculated.

Table 10-1	The Measures That the Descriptive Statistics Tool Calculates
Statistic	*Description*
Mean	Shows the arithmetic mean of the sample data.
Standard Error	Shows the standard error of the data set (a measure of the difference between the predicted value and the actual value).
Median	Shows the middle value in the data set (the value that separates the largest half of the values from the smallest half of the values).
Mode	Shows the most common value in the data set.
Standard Deviation	Shows the sample standard deviation measure for the data set.
Sample Variance	Shows the sample variance for the data set (the squared standard deviation).

(continued)

Table 10-1 *(continued)*

Statistic	Description
Kurtosis	Shows the kurtosis of the distribution.
Skewness	Shows the skewness of the data set's distribution.
Range	Shows the difference between the largest and smallest values in the data set.
Minimum	Shows the smallest value in the data set.
Maximum	Shows the largest value in the data set.
Sum	Adds all the values in the data set together to calculate the sum.
Count	Counts the number of values in a data set.
Largest(X)	Shows the largest X value in the data set.
Smallest(X)	Shows the smallest X value in the data set.
Confidence Level(X) Percentage	Shows the confidence level at a given percentage for the data set values.

Creating a Histogram

Use the Histogram Data Analysis tool to create a frequency distribution and, optionally, a histogram chart. A frequency distribution shows just how values in a data set are distributed across categories. A histogram shows the same information in a cute little column chart. Here's an example of how all this works — everything will become clearer if you're currently confused.

To use the Histogram tool, you first need to identify the bins (categories) that you want to use to create a frequency distribution. The histogram plots out how many times your data falls into each of these categories. Figure 10-5 shows the same worksheet as Figure 10-2, only this time with bins information in the worksheet range E1:E12. The bins information shows Excel exactly what bins (categories) you want to use to categorize the unit sales data. The bins information shown in the worksheet range E1:E12, for example, create hundred-unit bins: 0-100, 101-200, 201-300, and so on.

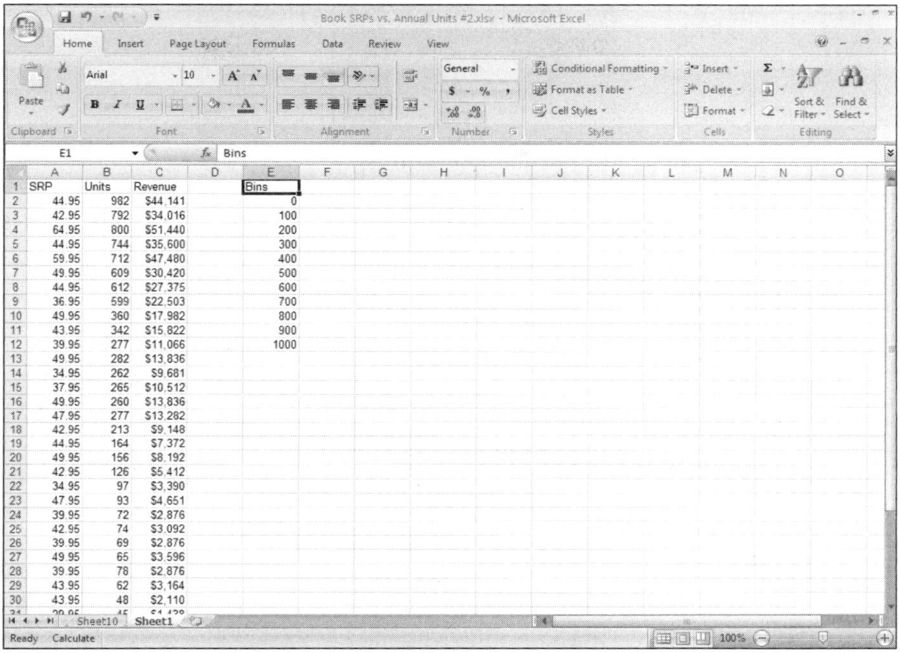

	SRP	Units	Revenue		Bins
2	44.95	982	$44,141		0
3	42.95	792	$34,016		100
4	64.95	800	$51,440		200
5	44.95	744	$35,600		300
6	59.95	712	$47,480		400
7	49.95	609	$30,420		500
8	44.95	612	$27,375		600
9	36.95	599	$22,503		700
10	49.95	360	$17,982		800
11	43.95	342	$15,822		900
12	39.95	277	$11,066		1000
13	49.95	282	$13,836		
14	34.95	262	$9,681		
15	37.95	265	$10,512		
16	49.95	260	$13,836		
17	47.95	277	$13,282		
18	42.95	213	$9,148		
19	44.95	164	$7,372		
20	49.95	156	$8,192		
21	42.95	126	$5,412		
22	34.95	97	$3,390		
23	47.95	93	$4,651		
24	39.95	72	$2,876		
25	42.95	74	$3,092		
26	39.95	69	$2,876		
27	49.95	65	$3,596		
28	39.95	78	$2,876		
29	43.95	62	$3,164		
30	43.95	48	$2,110		

Figure 10-5: Another version of the book sales information worksheet.

To create a frequency distribution and a histogram using the data shown in Figure 10-5, follow these steps:

1. **Click the Data tab's Data Analysis command button to tell Excel that you want to create a frequency distribution and a histogram.**
2. **When Excel displays the Data Analysis dialog box (refer to Figure 10-2), select Histogram from the Analysis Tools list and click OK.**
3. **In the Histogram dialog box that appears, as shown in Figure 10-6, identify the data that you want to analyze.**

   Use the Input Range text box to identify the data that you want to use to create a frequency distribution and histogram. If you want to create a frequency distribution and histogram of unit sales data, for example, enter the worksheet range **$B$1:$B$38** into the Input Range text box.

   To identify the bins that you use for the frequency distribution and histogram, enter the worksheet range that holds the bins into the Bin Range text box. In the case of the example worksheet shown in Figure 10-5, the bin range is $E$1:$E$12.

   If your data ranges include labels (as they do in Figure 10-5), select the Labels check box.

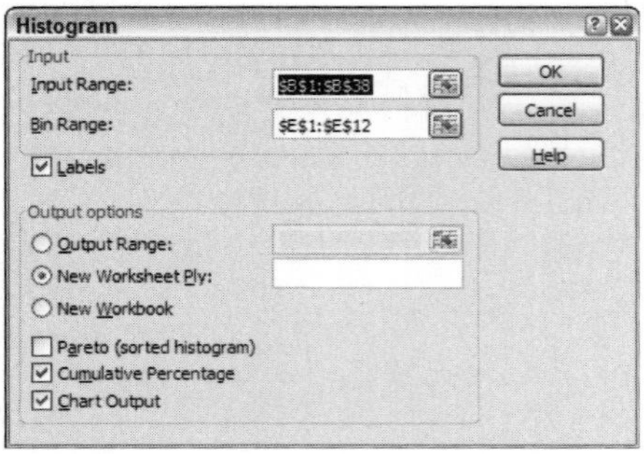

Figure 10-6:
Create a
histogram
here.

4. **Tell Excel where to place the frequency distribution and histogram.**

   Use the Output Options buttons to tell Excel where it should place the frequency distribution and histogram. To place the histogram in the current worksheet, for example, select the Output Range radio button and then enter the range address into its corresponding Output Range text box.

   To place the frequency distribution and histogram in a new worksheet, select the New Worksheet Ply radio button. Then, optionally, enter a name for the worksheet into the New Worksheet Ply text box. To place the frequency distribution and histogram information in a new workbook, select the New Workbook radio button.

5. **(Optional) Customize the histogram.**

   Make choices from the Output Options check boxes to control what sort of histogram Excel creates. For example, select the Pareto (Sorted Histogram) check box, and Excel sorts bins in descending order. Conversely, if you don't want bins sorted in descending order, leave the Pareto (Sorted Histogram) check box clear.

   Selecting the Cumulative Percentage check box tells Excel to plot a line showing cumulative percentages in your histogram.

   Optionally, select the Chart Output check box to have Excel include a histogram chart with the frequency distribution. If you don't select this check box, you don't get the histogram — only the frequency distribution.

6. **Click OK.**

   Excel creates the frequency distribution and, optionally, the histogram. Figure 10-7 shows the frequency distribution for the workbook data shown in Figure 10-5.

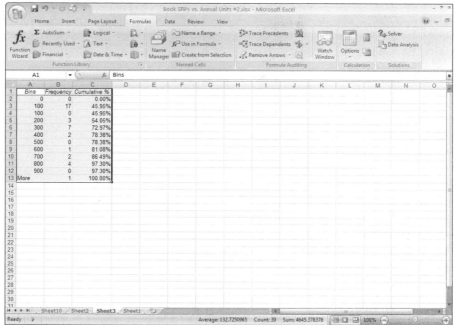

Figure 10-7:
Create a
frequency
distribution
to show
how values
in your
data set
spread out.

Note: Excel also provides a Frequency function with which you use can use arrays to create a frequency distribution. For more information about how the Frequency function works, see Chapter 9.

Ranking by Percentile

The Data Analysis collection of tools includes an option for calculating rank and percentile information for values in your data set. Suppose, for example, that you want to rank the sales revenue information shown in Figure 10-8. To calculate rank and percentile statistics for your data set, take the following steps.

1. **Begin to calculate ranks and percentiles by clicking the Data tab's Data Analysis command button.**

2. **When Excel displays the Data Analysis dialog box, select Rank and Percentile from the list and click OK.**

   Excel displays the Rank and Percentile dialog box, as shown in Figure 10-9.

	A	B	C
1	SRP	Units	Revenue
2	44.95	982	$44,141
3	42.95	792	$34,016
4	64.95	800	$51,440
5	44.95	744	$35,600
6	59.95	712	$47,480
7	49.95	609	$30,420
8	44.95	612	$27,375
9	36.95	599	$22,503
10	49.95	360	$17,982
11	43.95	342	$15,822
12	39.95	277	$11,066
13	49.95	282	$13,836
14	34.95	262	$9,681
15	37.95	265	$10,512
16	49.95	260	$13,836
17	47.95	277	$13,282
18	42.95	213	$9,148
19	44.95	164	$7,372
20	49.95	156	$8,192
21	42.95	126	$5,412
22	34.95	97	$3,390
23	47.95	93	$4,651
24	39.95	72	$2,876
25	42.95	74	$3,092
26	39.95	69	$2,876
27	49.95	65	$3,596
28	39.95	78	$2,876
29	43.95	62	$3,164
30	43.95	48	$2,110
31	29.95	45	$1,438

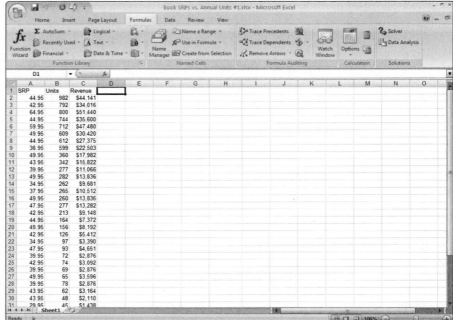

Figure 10-8: The book sales information (yes, again).

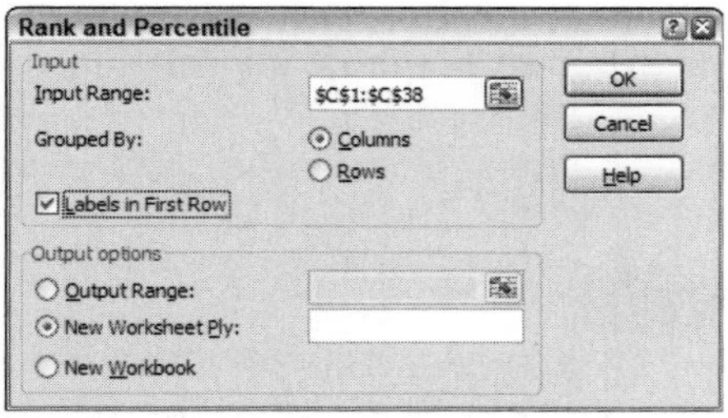

Figure 10-9: Calculate ranks and percentiles here.

3. **Identify the data set.**

   Enter the worksheet range that holds the data into the Input Range text box of the Ranks and Percentiles dialog box.

   To indicate how you have arranged data, select one of the two Grouped By radio buttons: Columns or Rows. To indicate whether the first cell in the input range is a label, select or deselect the Labels In First Row check box.

4. **Describe how Excel should output the data.**

Select one of the three Output Options radio buttons to specify where Excel should place the rank and percentile information.

5. **After you select an output option, click OK.**

Excel creates a ranking like the one shown in Figure 10-10.

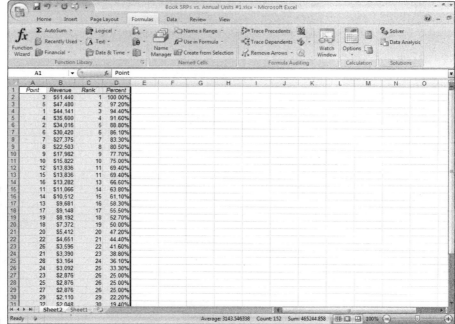

Figure 10-10: A rank and percentile worksheet based on the data from Figure 10-8.

Calculating Moving Averages

The Data Analysis command also provides a tool for calculating moving and exponentially smoothed averages. Suppose, for sake of illustration, that you've collected daily temperature information like that shown in Figure 10-11. You want to calculate the three-day moving average — the average of the last three days — as part of some simple weather forecasting. To calculate moving averages for this data set, take the following steps.

1. **To calculate a moving average, first click the Data tab's Data Analysis command button.**

2. **When Excel displays the Data Analysis dialog box, select the Moving Average item from the list and then click OK.**

Excel displays the Moving Average dialog box, as shown in Figure 10-12.

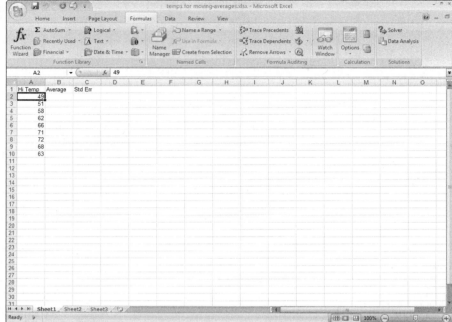

Figure 10-11:
A worksheet for calculating a moving average of temperatures.

Figure 10-12:
Calculate moving averages here.

3. **Identify the data that you want to use to calculate the moving average.**

   Click in the Input Range text box of the Moving Average dialog box. Then identify the input range, either by typing a worksheet range address or by using the mouse to select the worksheet range.

   Your range reference should use absolute cell addresses. An *absolute cell address* precedes the column letter and row number with $ signs, as in $A$1:$A$10.

   If the first cell in your input range includes a text label to identify or describe your data, select the Labels in First Row check box.

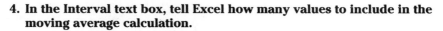

4. **In the Interval text box, tell Excel how many values to include in the moving average calculation.**

You can calculate a moving average using any number of values. By default, Excel uses the most recent three values to calculate the moving average. To specify that some other number of values be used to calculate the moving average, enter that value into the Interval text box.

5. **Tell Excel where to place the moving average data.**

Use the Output Range text box to identify the worksheet range into which you want to place the moving average data. In the worksheet example shown in Figure 10-11, for example, I place the moving average data into the worksheet range B2:B10. (See Figure 10-12.)

6. **(Optional) Specify whether you want a chart.**

If you want a chart that plots the moving average information, select the Chart Output check box.

7. **(Optional) Indicate whether you want standard error information calculated.**

If you want to calculate standard errors for the data, select the Standard Errors check box. Excel places standard error values next to the moving average values. (In Figure 10-11, the standard error information goes into C2:C10.)

8. **After you finish specifying what moving average information you want calculated and where you want it placed, click OK.**

Excel calculates moving average information, as shown in Figure 10-13.

Note: If Excel doesn't have enough information to calculate a moving average for a standard error, it places the error message #N/A into the cell. In Figure 10-13, you can see several cells that show this error message as a value.

Exponential Smoothing

The Exponential Smoothing tool also calculates the moving average. However, exponential smoothing weights the values included in the moving average calculations so that more recent values have a bigger effect on the average calculation and old values have a lesser effect. This weighting is accomplished through a smoothing constant.

To illustrate how the Exponential Smoothing tool works, suppose that you're again looking at the average daily temperature information. (I repeat this worksheet in Figure 10-14.)

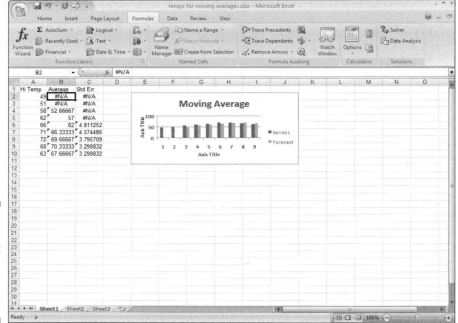

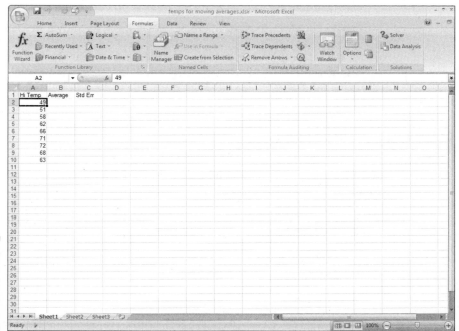

To calculate weighted moving averages using exponential smoothing, take the following steps:

1. **To calculate an exponentially smoothed moving average, first click the Data tab's Data Analysis command button.**

2. **When Excel displays the Data Analysis dialog box, select the Exponential Smoothing item from the list and then click OK.**

   Excel displays the Exponential Smoothing dialog box, as shown in Figure 10-15.

3. **Identify the data.**

   To identify the data for which you want to calculate an exponentially smoothed moving average, click in the Input Range text box. Then identify the input range, either by typing a worksheet range address or by selecting the worksheet range. If your input range includes a text label to identify or describe your data, select the Labels check box.

4. **Provide the smoothing constant.**

   Enter the smoothing constant value in the Damping Factor text box. The Excel Help file suggests that you use a smoothing constant of between 0.2 and 0.3. Presumably, however, if you're using this tool, you have your own ideas about what the correct smoothing constant is. (If you're clueless about the smoothing constant, perhaps you shouldn't be using this tool.)

5. **Tell Excel where to place the exponentially smoothed moving average data.**

   Use the Output Range text box to identify the worksheet range into which you want to place the moving average data. In the worksheet example shown in Figure 10-14, for example, you place the moving average data into the worksheet range B2:B10.

6. **(Optional) Chart the exponentially smoothed data.**

To chart the exponentially smoothed data, select the Chart Output check box.

7. (Optional) Indicate that you want standard error information calculated.

To calculate standard errors, select the Standard Errors check box. Excel places standard error values next to the exponentially smoothed moving average values.

8. After you finish specifying what moving average information you want calculated and where you want it placed, click OK.

Excel calculates moving average information, as shown in Figure 10-16.

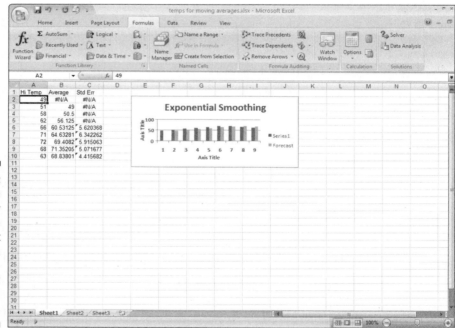

Figure 10-16: The average daily temperature worksheet with exponentially smoothed values.

Generating Random Numbers

The Data Analysis command also includes a Random Number Generation tool. The Random Number Generation tool is considerably more flexible than the =Rand() function, which is the other tool that you have available within Excel to produce random numbers. The Random Number Generation tool isn't really a tool for descriptive statistics. You would probably typically use the tool to help you randomly sample values from a population, but I describe it here in this chapter, anyway, because it works like the other descriptive statistics tools.

To produce random numbers, take the following steps:

1. **To generate random numbers, first click the Data tab's Data Analysis command button.**

   Excel displays the Data Analysis dialog box.

2. **In the Data Analysis dialog box, select the Random Number Generation entry from the list and then click OK.**

   Excel displays the Random Number Generation dialog box, as shown in Figure 10-17.

Figure 10-17: Generate random numbers here.

3. **Describe how many columns and rows of values that you want.**

   Use the Number of Variables text box to specify how many columns of values you want in your output range. Similarly, use the Number of Random Numbers text box to specify how many rows of values you want in the output range.

   You don't absolutely need to enter values into these two text boxes, by the way. You can also leave them blank. In this case, Excel fills all the columns and all the rows in the output range.

4. **Select the distribution method.**

   Select one of the distribution methods from the Distribution drop-down list. The Distribution drop-down list provides several distribution methods: Uniform, Normal, Bernoulli, Binomial, Poisson, Patterned, and Discrete. Typically, if you want a pattern of distribution other than

Uniform, you'll know which one of these distribution methods is appropriate. For example, if you want to pull random numbers from a data set that's normally distributed, you might select the Normal distribution method.

5. **(Optional) Provide any parameters needed for the distribution method.**

   If you select a distribution method that requires parameters, or input values, use the Parameters text box (Value and Probability Input Range) to identify the worksheet range that holds the parameters needed for the distribution method.

6. **(Optional) Select a starting point for the random number generation.**

   You have the option of entering a value that Excel will use to start its generation of random numbers. The benefit of using a Random Seed value, as Excel calls it, is that you can later produce the same set of random numbers by planting the same "seed."

7. **Identify the output range.**

   Use the Output Options radio buttons to select the location that you want for random numbers.

8. **After you describe how you want Excel to generate random numbers and where those numbers should be placed, click OK.**

   Excel generates the random numbers.

Sampling Data

One other data analysis tool — the Sampling tool — deserves to be discussed someplace. I describe it here, even if it doesn't fit perfectly.

Truth be told, both the Random Number Generation tool (see the preceding section) and the Sampling tool are probably what you would use while preparing to perform inferential statistical analysis of the sort that I describe in Chapter 11. But because these tools work like (and look like) the other descriptive statistics tools, I describe them here.

With the Sampling tool that's part of the Data Analysis command, you can randomly select items from a data set or select every nth item from a data set. For example, suppose that as part of an internal audit, you want to randomly select five titles from a list of books. To do so, you could use the Sampling tool. For purposes of this discussion, pretend that you're going to use the list of books and book information shown in Figure 10-18.

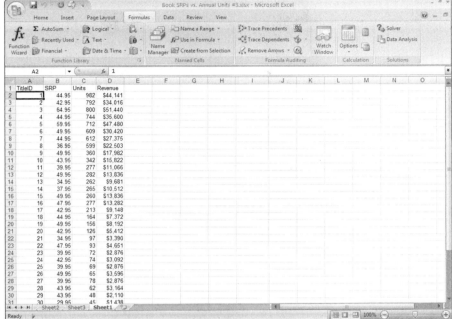

To sample items from a worksheet like the ones shown in Figure 10-18, take the following steps:

1. **To tell Excel that you want to sample data from a data set, first click the Data tab's Data Analysis command button.**

2. **When Excel displays the Data Analysis dialog box, select Sampling from the list and then click OK.**

   Excel displays the Sampling dialog box, as shown in Figure 10-19.

3. **Identify the input range.**

   Use the Input Range text box to describe the worksheet range that contains enough data to identify the values in the data set. For example, in the case of the data set like the one shown in Figure 10-18, the information in column A — `TitleID` — uniquely identifies items in the data set. Therefore, you can identify (or uniquely locate) items using the input range A1:A38. You can enter this range into the Input Range text box either by directly typing it or by clicking in the text box and then dragging the cursor from cell A1 to cell A38.

   If the first cell in the input range holds the text label that describes the data — this is the case in Figure 10-18 — select the Labels check box.

4. **Choose a sampling method.**

   Excel provides two sampling methods for retrieving or identifying items in your data set:

   - *Periodic:* A periodic sampling method grabs every nth item from the data set. For example, if you choose every fifth item, that's periodic sampling. To select or indicate that you want to use periodic sampling, select the Periodic radio button. Then enter the period into its corresponding Period text box.

   - *Random:* To randomly choose items from the data set, select the Random radio button and then enter the number of items that you want in the Number of Samples text box.

5. **Select an output area.**

   Select from the three radio buttons in the Output Options area to select where the sampling result should appear. To put sampling results into an output range in the current worksheet, select the Output Range radio button and then enter the output range into the text box provided. To store the sampling information in a new worksheet or on a new workbook, select either the New Worksheet Ply or the New Workbook radio button.

   Note that Excel grabs item information from the input range. For example, Figure 10-20 shows the information that Excel places on a new worksheet if you use periodic sampling and grab every fifth item. Figure 10-21 shows how Excel identifies the sample if you randomly select five items. Note that the values shown in both Figures 10-20 and 10-21 are the title ID numbers from the input range.

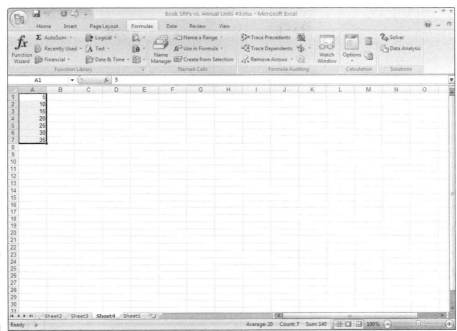

Figure 10-20:
An example
of periodic
sampling.

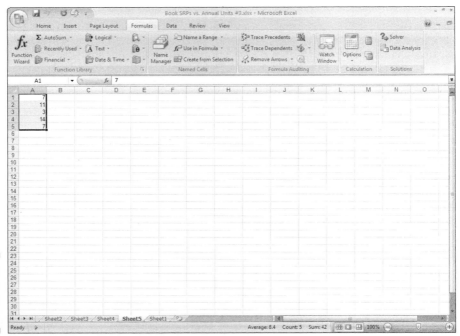

Figure 10-21:
An example
of random
sampling.

Chapter 11

Inferential Statistics

● ●

In This Chapter

▶ Discovering the Data Analysis t-test tools

▶ Performing a z-test

▶ Creating a scatter plot

▶ Using the Regression tool that comes with Data Analysis

▶ Using the Correlation tool that comes with Data Analysis

▶ Implementing the ANOVA data analysis tools

▶ Comparing variances from populations with the f-test Data Analysis tool

▶ Using the Fourier Data Analysis tool

● ●

*1*n this chapter, I talk about the more sophisticated tools provided by the Excel Data Analysis add-in, such as t-test, z-test, scatter plot, regression, correlation, ANOVA, f-test, and Fourier. With these other tools, you can perform inferential statistics, which you use to first look at a set of sample observations drawn from a population and then draw conclusions — or make inferences — about population's characteristics. (To read about the simpler descriptive statistical data analysis tools that Excel supplies through the Data Analysis add-in, skip back to Chapter 10.)

Obviously, you need pretty developed statistical skills in order to use these tools — a good basic statistics course in college or graduate school, and then probably one follow-up course. But with some reasonable knowledge of statistics and a bit of patience, you can use some of these tools to good advantage.

Note: You must install the Data Analysis add-in before you can use it. To install the Data Analysis add-in, choose Office➪Excel Options. When Excel displays the Excel Options dialog box, select the Add-Ins item from the left box that appears along the left edge of the Excel Options dialog box. Excel next displays a list of the possible add-ins — including the Analysis ToolPak add-in. Select the Analysis ToolPak item and click Go. Excel displays the Add-Ins dialog box. Select Analysis ToolPak from this dialog box and click OK. Excel installs the Analysis ToolPak add-in.

The sample workbooks used in the examples in this chapter can be downloaded from the book's companion Web site at www.dummies.com/go/e2007dafd.

Using the t-test Data Analysis Tool

The Excel Data Analysis add-in provides three tools for working with t-values and t-tests, which can be useful when you want to make inferences about very small data sets:

✔ **t-Test: Two-Sample Assuming Equal Variances**

✔ **t-Test: Two-Sample Assuming Unequal Variances**

✔ **t-Test: Paired Two Sample for Means**

Briefly, here's how these three tools work. For sake of illustration, assume that you're working with the values shown in Figure 11-1. The worksheet range A1:A21 contains the first set of values. The worksheet range B1:B21 contains the second set of values.

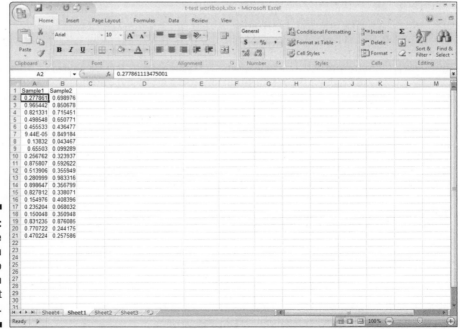

Figure 11-1:
Some fake data you can use to perform t-test calculations.

To perform a t-test calculation, follow these steps:

1. **Choose Data tab's Data Analysis.**

2. **When Excel displays the Data Analysis dialog box, as shown in Figure 11-2, select the appropriate t-test tool from its Analysis Tools list.**

   - *t-Test: Paired Two-Sample For Means:* Choose this tool when you want to perform a paired two-sample t-test.

   - *t-Test: Two-Sample Assuming Equal Variances:* Choose this tool when you want to perform a two-sample test and you have reason to assume the means of both samples equal each other.

   - *t-Test: Two-Sample Assuming Unequal Variances:* Choose this tool when you want to perform a two-sample test but you assume that the two-sample variances are unequal.

Figure 11-2: Select your Data Analysis tool here.

3. **After you select the correct t-test tool, click OK.**

   Excel then displays the appropriate t-test dialog box. Figure 11-3 shows the t-Test: Paired Two Sample for Means dialog box.

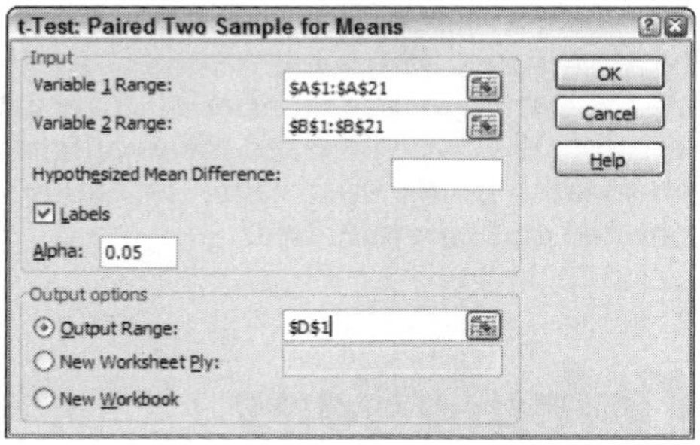

Figure 11-3: The t-Test: Paired Two-Sample for Means dialog box.

The other t-test dialog boxes look very similar.

4. **In the Variable 1 Range and Variable 2 Range input text boxes, identify the sample values by telling Excel in what worksheet ranges you've stored the two samples.**

   You can enter a range address into these text boxes. Or you can click in the text box and then select a range by clicking and dragging. If the first cell in the variable range holds a label and you include the label in your range selection, of course, select the Labels check box.

5. **Use the Hypothesized Mean Difference text box to indicate whether you hypothesize that the means are equal.**

   If you think the means of the samples are equal, enter **0** (zero) into this text box. If you hypothesize that the means are not equal, enter the mean difference.

6. **In the Alpha text box, state the confidence level for your t-test calculation.**

   The confidence level is between 0 and 1. By default, the confidence level is equal to 0.05, which is equivalent to a 5-percent confidence level.

7. **In the Output Options section, indicate where the t-test tool results should be stored.**

   Here, select one of the radio buttons and enter information in the text boxes to specify where Excel should place the results of the t-test analysis. For example, to place the t-test results into a range in the existing worksheet, select the Output Range radio button and then identify the range address in the Output Range text box. If you want to place the t-test results someplace else, select one of the other option radio buttons.

8. **Click OK.**

   Excel calculates the t-test results. Figure 11-4 shows the t-test results for a Paired Two Sample for Means test. The t-test results show the mean for each of the data sets, the variance, the number of observations, the Pearson correlation value, the hypothesized mean difference, the degrees of freedom (abbreviated as *df*), the t-value (or t-stat), and the probability values for one-tail and two-tail tests.

Performing z-test Calculations

If you know the variance or standard deviation of the underlying population, you can calculate z-test values by using the Data Analysis add-in. You might typically work with z-test values to calculate confidence levels and confidence intervals for normally distributed data. To do this, take these steps:

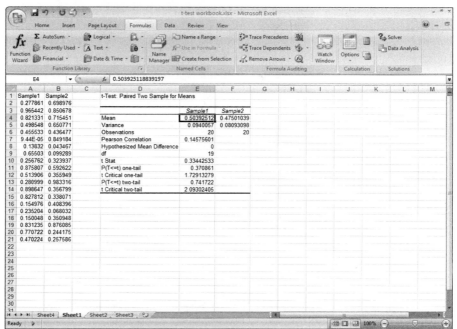

Figure 11-4:
The results
of a t-test.

1. **To select the z-test tool, click the Data tab's Data Analysis command button.**

2. **When Excel displays the Data Analysis dialog box (refer to Figure 11-2), select the z-Test: Two Sample for Means tool and then click OK.**

   Excel then displays the z-Test: Two Sample for Means dialog box, as shown in Figure 11-5.

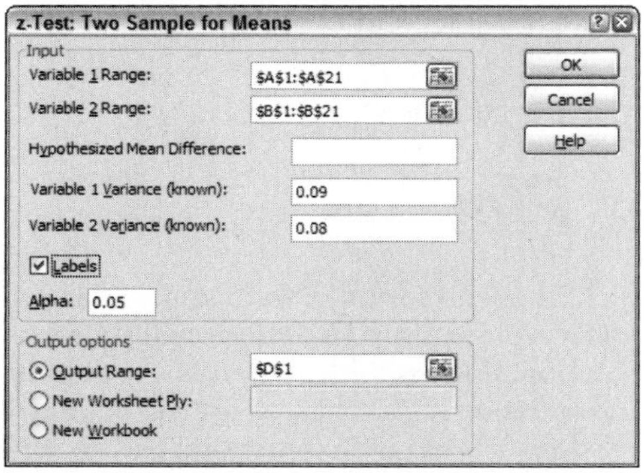

Figure 11-5:
Perform a
z-test from
here.

3. **In the Variable 1 Range and Variable 2 Range text boxes, identify the sample values by telling Excel in what worksheet ranges you've stored the two samples.**

   You can enter a range address into the text boxes here or you can click in the text box and then select a range by clicking and dragging. If the first cell in the variable range holds a label and you include the label in your range selection, select the Labels check box.

4. **Use the Hypothesized Mean Difference text box to indicate whether you hypothesize that the means are equal.**

   If you think that the means of the samples are equal, enter **0** (zero) into this text box or leave the text box empty. If you hypothesize that the means are not equal, enter the difference.

5. **Use the Variable 1 Variance (Known) and Variable 2 Variance (Known) text boxes to provide the population variance for the first and second samples.**

6. **In the Alpha text box, state the confidence level for your z-test calculation.**

   The confidence level is between 0 and 1. By default, the confidence level equals 0.05 (equivalent to a 5-percent confidence level).

7. **In the Output Options section, indicate where the z-test tool results should be stored.**

   To place the z-test results into a range in the existing worksheet, select the Output Range radio button and then identify the range address in the Output Range text box. If you want to place the z-test results some-place else, use one of the other options.

8. **Click OK.**

   Excel calculates the z-test results. Figure 11-6 shows the z-test results for a Two Sample for Means test. The z-test results show the mean for each of the data sets, the variance, the number of observations, the hypothe-sized mean difference, the z-value, and the probability values for one-tail and two-tail tests.

Creating a Scatter Plot

One of the most interesting and useful forms of data analysis is regression analysis. In *regression analysis,* you explore the relationship between two sets of values, looking for association. For example, you can use regression analy-sis to determine whether advertising expenditures are associated with sales, whether cigarette smoking is associated with heart disease, or whether exer-cise is associated with longevity.

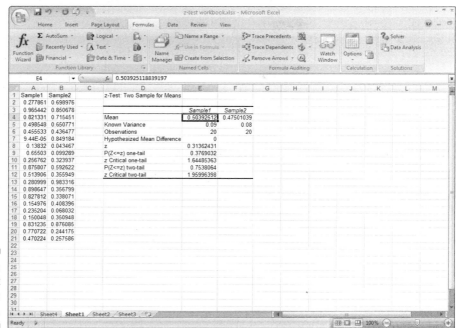

Figure 11-6:
The z-test
calculation
results.

Often your first step in any regression analysis is to create a *scatter plot*, which lets you visually explore association between two sets of values. In Excel, you do this by using an XY (Scatter) chart. For example, suppose that you want to look at or analyze the values shown in the worksheet displayed in Figure 11-7. The worksheet range A1:A11 shows numbers of ads. The worksheet range B1:B11 shows the resulting sales. With this collected data, you can explore the effect of ads on sales — or the lack of an effect.

To create a scatter chart of this information, take the following steps:

1. **Select the worksheet range A1:B11.**

2. **On the Insert tab, click the XY (Scatter) chart command button.**

3. **Select the Chart subtype that doesn't include any lines.**

   Excel displays your data in an XY (scatter) chart, as shown in Figure 11-8.

4. **Confirm the chart data organization.**

   Confirm that Excel has in fact correctly arranged your data by looking at the chart.

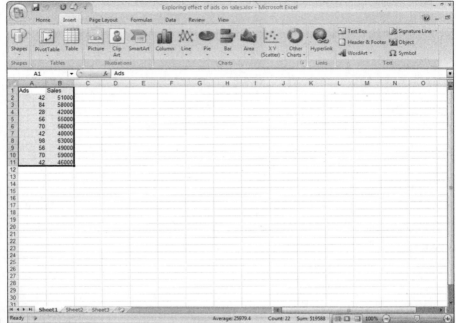

Figure 11-7:
A worksheet with data you might analyze by using regression.

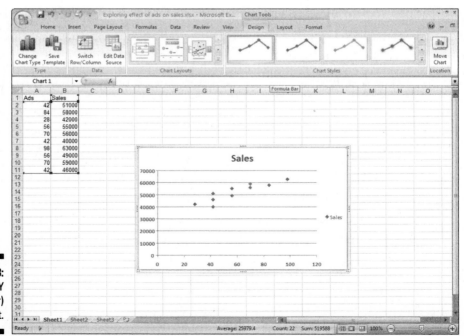

Figure 11-8:
The XY (scatter) chart.

If you aren't happy with the chart's data organization — maybe the data seems backward or flip-flopped — click the Switch Row/Column command button on the Chart Tools Design tab. (You can even experiment with the Switch Row/Column command, so try it if you think it might help.) Note that in Figure 11-10, the data is correctly organized. The chart shows the common-sense result that increased advertising seems to connect with increased sales.

5. **Annotate the chart, if appropriate.**

   Add those little flourishes to your chart that will make it more attractive and readable. For example, you can use the Chart Title and Axis Titles buttons to annotate the chart with a title and with descriptions of the axes used in the chart.

   In Chapter 7, I discuss in detail the mechanics of customizing a chart using the Chart Options dialog box. Refer there if you have questions about how to work with the Titles, Axes, Gridlines, Legend, or Data Labels tabs.

6. **Add a trendline by clicking the Chart Tools Layout tab's Trendline command button.**

   For the Chart Tools tabs to be displayed, you must have either first selected an embedded chart object or displayed a chart sheet.

   Excel displays the Add Trendline menu. Select the type of trendline or regression calculation that you want by clicking one of the trendline options available. For example, to perform simple linear regression, click the Linear button.

7. **Add the Regression Equation to the scatter plot.**

   To show the equation for the trendline that the scatter plot uses, choose the More Trendline Options command from the Add Trendline menu.

   Then select both the Display Equation on Chart and the Display R-Squared Value on Chart check boxes. This tells Excel to add the simple regression analysis information necessary for a trendline to your chart.

   Use the radio buttons and text boxes in the Format Trendline dialog box (shown in Figure 11-9) to control how the regression analysis trendline is calculated. For example, you can use the Set Intercept = check box and text box to force the trendline to intercept the x-axis at a particular point, such as zero. You can also use the Forecast Forward and Backward text boxes to specify that a trendline should be extended backward or forward beyond the existing data or before it.

8. **Click OK.**

   Excel shows the embedded Scatter Plot chart with the line equation and the R-squared value displayed, as shown in Figure 11-10. (In Figure 11-10, I moved the trendline information to the top corner of the chart by dragging.)

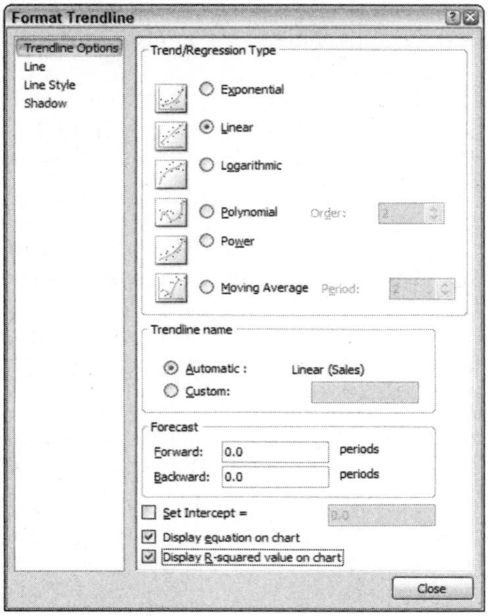

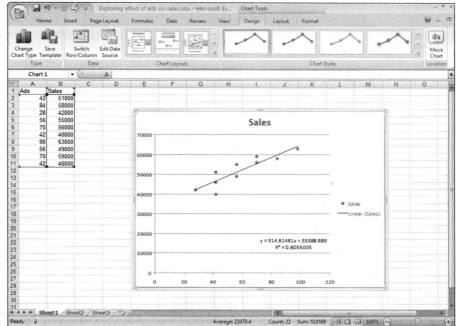

Figure 11-9:
The Format
Trendline
dialog box.

Figure 11-10:
The Scatter
Plot chart
with the
regression
data.

Using the Regression Data Analysis Tool

You can move beyond the visual regression analysis that the scatter plot technique provides. (Read the previous section for more on this technique.) You can use the Regression tool provided by the Data Analysis add-in. For example, say that you used the scatter plotting technique, as I describe earlier, to begin looking at a simple data set. And, after that initial examination, suppose that you want to look more closely at the data by using full blown, take-no-prisoners, regression. To perform regression analysis by using the Data Analysis add-in:

1. **Tell Excel that you want to join the big leagues by clicking the Data Analysis command button on the Data tab.**

2. **When Excel displays the Data Analysis dialog box, select the Regression tool from the Analysis Tools list and then click OK.**

   Excel displays the Regression dialog box, as shown in Figure 11-11.

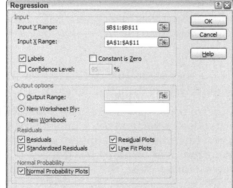

Figure 11-11:
The Regression dialog box.

3. **Identify your Y and X values.**

   Use the Input Y Range text box to identify the worksheet range holding your dependent variables. Then use the Input X Range text box to identify the worksheet range reference holding your independent variables.

   Each of these input ranges must be a single column of values. For example, if you want to use the Regression tool to explore the effect of advertisements on sales (this is the same information shown earlier in the scatter plot discussion in Figure 11-10), you enter **$A$1:$A$11** into the Input X Range text box and **$B$1:$B$11** into the Input Y Range text box. If your input ranges include a label, as is the case of the worksheet shown earlier in Figure 11-10, select the Labels check box.

4. **(Optional) Set the constant to zero.**

   If the regression line should start at zero — in other words, if the dependent value should equal zero when the independent value equals zero — select the Constant Is Zero check box.

5. **(Optional) Calculate a confidence level in your regression analysis.**

   To do this, select the Confidence Level check box and then (in the Confidence Level text box) enter the confidence level you want to use.

6. **Select a location for the regression analysis results.**

   Use the Output Options radio buttons and text boxes to specify where Excel should place the results of the regression analysis. To place the regression results into a range in the existing worksheet, for example, select the Output Range radio button and then identify the range address in the Output Range text box. To place the regression results someplace else, select one of the other option radio buttons.

7. **Identify what data you want returned.**

   Select from the Residuals check boxes to specify what residuals results you want returned as part of the regression analysis.

   Similarly, select the Normal Probability Plots check box to add residuals and normal probability information to the regression analysis results.

8. **Click OK.**

   Excel shows a portion of the regression analysis results for the worksheet shown earlier in Figure 11-7, as depicted in Figure 11-12.

   There is a range that supplies some basic regression statistics, including the R-square value, the standard error, and the number of observations. Below that information, the Regression tool supplies *analysis of variance* (or ANOVA) data, including information about the degrees of freedom, sum-of-squares value, mean square value, the f-value, and the significance of F. Beneath the ANOVA information, the Regression tool supplies information about the regression line calculated from the data, including the coefficient, standard error, t-stat, and probability values for the intercept — as well as the same information for the independent variable, which is the number of ads in the example I discuss here.

Using the Correlation Analysis Tool

The Correlation analysis tool (which is also available through the Data Analysis command) quantifies the relationship between two sets of data. You might use this tool to explore such things as the effect of advertising on sales, for example. To use the Correlation analysis tool, follow these steps:

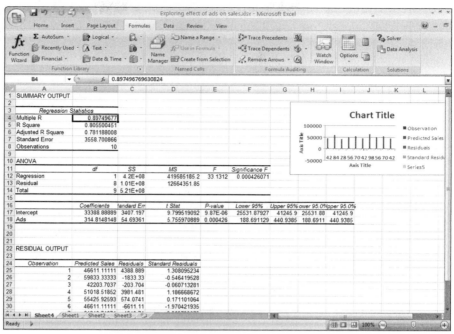

Figure 11-12:
The
regression
analysis
results.

1. **Click Data tabs Data Analysis command button.**

2. **When Excel displays the Data Analysis dialog box, select the Correlation tool from the Analysis Tools list and then click OK.**

   Excel displays the Correlation dialog box, as shown in Figure 11-13.

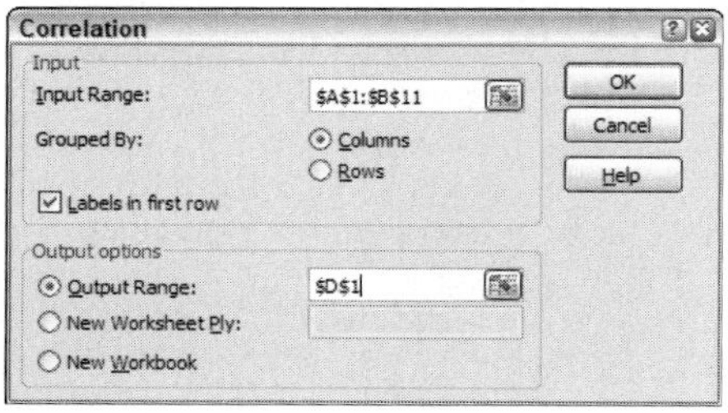

Figure 11-13:
The
Correlation
dialog box.

3. **Identify the range of X and Y values that you want to analyze.**

   For example, if you want to look at the correlation between ads and sales — this is the same data that appears in the worksheet shown in

Figure 11-7 — enter the worksheet range **$A$1:$B$11** into the Input Range text box. If the input range includes labels in the first row, select the Labels in First Row check box. Verify that the Grouped By radio buttons — Columns and Rows — correctly show how you've organized your data.

4. Select an output location.

Use the Output Options radio buttons and text boxes to specify where Excel should place the results of the correlation analysis. To place the correlation results into a range in the existing worksheet, select the Output Range radio button and then identify the range address in the Output Range text box. If you want to place the correlation results some-place else, select one of the other option radio buttons.

5. Click OK.

Excel calculates the correlation coefficient for the data that you identi-fied and places it in the specified location. Figure 11-14 shows the corre-lation results for the ads and sales data. The key value is shown in cell E3. The value 0.897497 suggests that 89 percent of sales can be explained through ads.

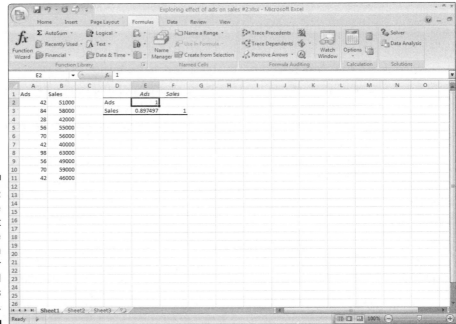

Figure 11-14:
The worksheet showing the correlation results for the ads and sales information.

Using the Covariance Analysis Tool

The Covariance tool, also available through the Data Analysis add-in, quantifies the relationship between two sets of values. The Covariance tool calculates the average of the product of deviations of values from the data set means.

To use this tool, follow these steps:

1. **Click the Data Analysis command button on the Data tab.**

2. **When Excel displays the Data Analysis dialog box, select the Covariance tool from the Analysis Tools list and then click OK.**

   Excel displays the Covariance dialog box, as shown in Figure 11-15.

3. **Identify the range of X and Y values that you want to analyze.**

   To look at the correlation between ads and sales data from the worksheet shown in Figure 11-7, for example, enter the worksheet range $A$1:$B$11 into the Input Range text box.

   Select the Labels in First Row check box if the input range includes labels in the first row.

   Verify that the Grouped By radio buttons — Columns and Rows — correctly show how you've organized your data.

4. **Select an output location.**

   Use the Output Options radio buttons and text boxes to specify where Excel should place the results of the covariance analysis. To place the results into a range in the existing worksheet, select the Output Range radio button and then identify the range address in the Output Range text box. If you want to place the results someplace else, select one of the other Output Options radio buttons.

5. **Click OK after you select the output options.**

   Excel calculates the covariance information for the data that you identified and places it in the specified location. Figure 11-16 shows the covariance results for the ads and sales data.

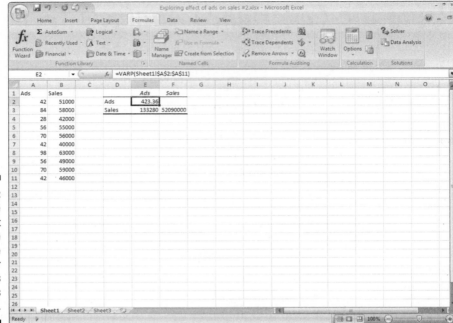

Figure 11-16:
The
worksheet
showing the
covariance
results for
the ads
and sales
information.

Using the ANOVA Data Analysis Tools

The Excel Data Analysis add-in also provides three ANOVA (analysis of variance) tools: ANOVA: Single Factor, ANOVA: Two-Factor With Replication, and ANOVA: Two-Factor Without Replication. With the ANOVA analysis tools, you can compare sets of data by looking at the variance of values in each set.

As an example of how the ANOVA analysis tools work, suppose that you want to use the ANOVA: Single Factor tool. To do so, take these steps:

1. **Click Data tab's Data Analysis command button.**

2. **When Excel displays the Data Analysis Dialog box, choose the appropriate ANOVA analysis tool and then click OK.**

   Excel displays the appropriate ANOVA dialog box. (In this particular example, I chose the Anova: Single Factor tool, as shown in Figure 11-17.)

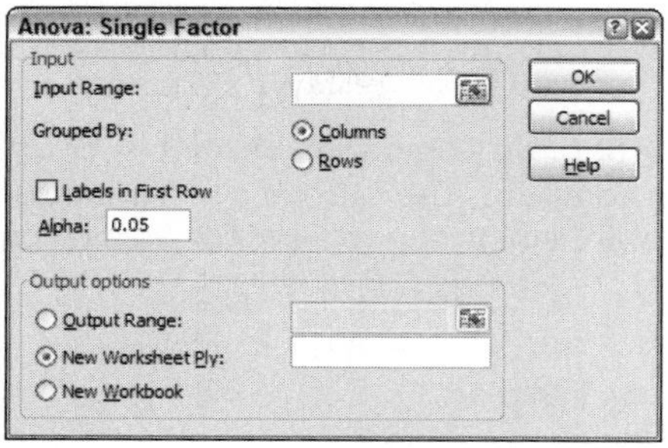

Figure 11-17:
The Anova:
Single
Factor
dialog box.

3. **Describe the data to be analyzed.**

   Use the Input Range text box to identify the worksheet range that holds the data you want to analyze. Select from the Grouped By radio buttons — Columns and Rows — to identify the organization of your data. If the first row in your input range includes labels, select the Labels In First Row check box. Set your confidence level in the Alpha text box.

4. **Describe the location for the ANOVA results.**

   Use the Output Options buttons and boxes to specify where Excel should place the results of the ANOVA analysis. If you want to place the ANOVA results into a range in the existing worksheet, for example, select the Output Range radio button and then identify the range address in the Output Range text box. To place the ANOVA results someplace else, select one of the other Output Options radio buttons.

5. **Click OK.**

   Excel returns the ANOVA calculation results.

Creating an f-test Analysis

The Excel Data Analysis add-in also provides a tool for calculating two-sample f-test calculations. f-test analysis enables you to compare variances from two populations. To use the f-Test Analysis tool, click the Data Analysis command button on the Data tab, select f-Test Two-Sample For Variances from the Data Analysis dialog box that appears, and click OK. When Excel displays the F-Test Two-Sample for Variances dialog box, as shown in Figure 11-18, identify the data the tools should use for the f-test analysis by using the Variable Range text boxes. Then specify where you want the f-test analysis results placed using the Output Options radio buttons and text boxes. Click OK and Excel produces your f-test results.

f-test analysis tests to see whether two population variances equal each other. Essentially, the analysis compares the ratio of two variances. The assumption is that if variances are equal, the ratio of the variances should equal 1.

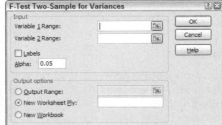

Figure 11-18:
The F-Test Two-Sample for Variances dialog box.

Using Fourier Analysis

The Data Analysis add-in also includes a tool for performing Fourier analysis. To do this, click the Data tab's Data Analysis command button, select Fourier Analysis from the Data Analysis dialog box that appears, and click OK. When Excel displays the Fourier Analysis dialog box, as shown in Figure 11-19, identify the data that Excel should use for the analysis by using the Input Range text box. Then specify where you want the analysis results placed by selecting from the Output Options radio buttons. Click OK; Excel performs your Fourier analysis and places the results at the specified location.

Figure 11-19:
The Fourier Analysis dialog box.

Chapter 12

Optimization Modeling with Solver

. . . .

In This Chapter

▶ Understanding optimization modeling

▶ Setting up a Solver worksheet

▶ Solving an optimization modeling problem

▶ Reviewing the Solver reports

▶ Noodling around with the Solver options

▶ Setting a limit on Solver

▶ Understanding the Solver error messages

. . . .

*I*n the preceding chapters of this book, I discuss how to use Excel tools to analyze data stored in an Excel workbook. However, you can also perform another sort of data analysis. You can perform data analysis that looks not at labels and values stored in cells but rather at formulas that describe business problems. In fact, Excel includes just such a tool for working on these kinds of problems: the Solver.

When you use optimization modeling and the Excel Solver, you aren't problem solving or analyzing based on raw data. You are problem solving and analyzing based on formulaic descriptions of a situation. Nevertheless, although the abstraction takes some getting used to, analyzing situations or problems based on formulaic descriptions of objective functions and constraints can be a powerful tool. And powerful tools can lead to powerful new insights.

In this chapter, I describe the sorts of data analysis problems that Solver helps you figure out. I show you a simple example of how the Solver works in action. Although Solver seems terribly complicated, it's actually an easier tool to use than you might think, so stick with me here.

Understanding Optimization Modeling

Suppose that you're a one-person business. This example is sort of artificial, but I need to take some liberties in order to make optimization modeling and what the Solver does easy to understand.

Optimizing your imaginary profits

In your business, you make money two ways: You write books and you give seminars. Imagine that when you write a book, you make $15,000 for roughly six weeks of work. If you work out the math on that — dividing $15,000 by 240 hours — you see that you make roughly $62.50 an hour by writing a book.

Also assume that you make $20,000 for giving a one-day seminar on some subject on which you're an expert. You make about $830.00 an hour for giving the seminar. I calculate this number by dividing the $20,000 that you make by the 24 hours that presenting the seminar requires you to invest.

In many situations, you might be able to figure out how many books you want to write and how many seminars you want to give simply by looking at the profit that you make in each activity. If you make roughly $62 an hour writing a book and you make roughly $830 an hour giving a seminar, the obvious answer to the question, "How many books should I write and how many seminars should I give?" is, do as many seminars as possible and as few books as possible. You make more money giving seminars, so you should do that more.

Recognizing constraints

In many situations, however, you can't just look at the profit per activity or the cost per activity. You typically need to consider other constraints in your decision making. For example, suppose that you give seminars on the same subject that you write books about. In this case, it might be that in order to be in the seminar business, you need to write at least one book a year. And so that constraint of writing one book a year needs to be considered while you think about what makes most sense about how you maximize your profits.

Commonly, other constraints often apply to a problem like this. For example — and I know this because one of my past jobs was publishing books — book publishers might require that you give a certain number of seminars a year in order to promote your books. So it might also be that in order to write books, you need to give at least four seminars a year. This requirement to give at least four book-promoting seminars a year becomes another constraint.

Consider other constraints, too, when you look at things such as financial resources available and the capacity of the tools that you use to provide your products or services. For example, perhaps you have only $20,000 of working capital to invest in things like writing books or in giving seminars. And if a book requires $500 to be tied up in working capital but a seminar requires $2,500 to be tied up in working capital, you're limited in the number of books that you can write and seminars that you can give by your $20,000 of working capital balance.

Another common type of constraint is a capacity constraint. For example, although there are 2,080 hours in a working year, assume that you want to work only 1,880 hours in a year. This would mean, quite conventionally, that you want to have 10 holidays a year and three weeks of vacation a year. In this case, if a book requires 240 hours and a seminar requires 24 hours, that working-hours limit constrains the number of books and seminars that you can give, too.

This situation is exactly the kind of problem that Solver helps you figure out. What Solver does is find the optimum value of what's called your *objective function*. In this case, the objective function is the profit function of the business. But Solver, in working through the numbers, explicitly recognizes the constraints that you describe.

Setting Up a Solver Worksheet

Figure 12-1 shows an Excel workbook set up to solve an optimization modeling problem for the one-person business that I describe earlier in this chapter. Here I describe the pieces and parts of this workbook. If you've carefully read the earlier discussion in the chapter about what optimization modeling is, you should have no trouble seeing what's going on here.

The Solver workbook is available at the *For Dummies* Web site at the URL address www.dummies.com/go/e2007dafd. You might want to retrieve this workbook before you begin noodling around with the optimization modeling problem that I describe here. Having a workbook set up for you makes things easier, especially if you're working with the Solver for the first time.

If you choose to construct the Solver workbook example yourself (a fine idea), you want to tell Excel to display actual formulas rather than formula results in the workbook. This is what the workbook shown in Figure 12-1 does, by the way. To do this, select the worksheet range in which you want to display the actual formulas rather than the formula results and then simultaneously press the Ctrl and the ` (grave) keys. By pressing Ctrl+`, you tell Excel to display the formula rather than the formula result within the selected range.

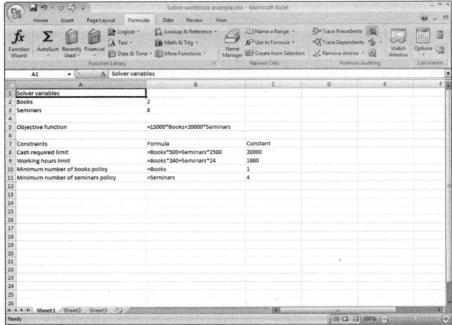

Figure 12-1:
A sample
workbook
set up to
solve an
optimization
modeling
problem for
a one-
person
business.

Setting up a Solver workbook requires three steps:

1. Identify the Solver variables.

First, you want to identify the variables in your optimization modeling problem. In the case of trying to figure out the number of books to write and seminars to give to make the most money in your one-person business, the two Solver variables are *books* and *seminars*.

In Figure 12-1, I enter the labels shown in range A1:A3 and then the starting variable values shown in range B2:B3. This part of the worksheet isn't anything magical. It simply identifies which variables go into the objective function. The objective function is the formula that you want to maximize or minimize. The values stored in the worksheet range B2:B3 are my starting guesses about what the optimal variable values should be. In Figure 12-1, for example, I'm just guessing that the optimal number of books to write is two and that the optimal number of seminars to give is eight. You won't know what the optimal number of books and seminars actually is until you work out the problem.

Although you don't have to name the cells that hold the variable values — in this case, cells B2 and B3 — naming those cells makes your objective function formula and your constraint formulas much easier to understand. So I recommend that you name the cells.

If you set up a workbook like the one shown in Figure 12-1, you can name the variable value cells by selecting the worksheet range A2:B3 and then clicking the Data tab's Create from Selection command button. When Excel displays the Create Names from Selection dialog box, as shown in Figure 12-2, select the Left Column check box and click OK. This tells Excel to use the labels in the left column: This would be the range A2:A3 — to name the range B2:B3. In other words, by following these steps, you name cell B2 Books and you name cell B3 Seminars.

2. **Describe the objective function.**

The objective function, shown in cell B5 in Figure 12-1, gives the formula that you want to optimize. In the case of a profit formula, you want to maximize a function because you want to maximize profits, of course.

I should note and you should remember that not all objective functions should be maximized. Some objective functions should be minimized. For example, if you create an objective function that describes the cost of some advertising program or the risk of some investment program, you can logically choose to minimize your costs or minimize your risks.

To describe the objective function, create a formula that describes the value that you want to optimize. In the case of a profit function for the one-person business that I detail in the earlier section "Recognizing constraints," you make $15,000 for every book that you write and $20,000 for every seminar that you give. You can describe this by entering the formula **=15000*Books+20000*Seminars**. In other words, you can calculate the profits of your one-person business by multiplying the number of books that you write times $15,000 and the number of seminars that you give times $20,000. This is what shows in cell B5.

3. **Identify any objective function constraints.**

In the worksheet range A8:C11, I describe and identify the constraints on the objective function. As I note earlier, four constraints can limit the profits that you can make in your business:

- *Cash required limit:* The first constraint shown in Figure 12-1 (cell A8) quantifies the cash required constraint. In this example, each book requires $500 cash, and each seminar requires $2,500 cash. If you have $20,000 cash to invest (I assume to temporarily invest) in books and seminars, you're limited in the number of books that you can write and the number of seminars that you can give by the cash, up-front investment that you need to make in these activities. The formula in cell B8, =Books*500+Seminars*2500, describes the cash required by your business. The value shown in cell C8, 20000, identifies the actual constraint.

- *Working hours limit:* The working hours limit constraint is quantified by having the formula =Books*240+Seminars*24 in cell B9 and the value 1880 in cell C9. Use these two pieces of information, the formula and the constant value, to describe a working hours limit. In a nutshell, this constraint says that the number of hours that you spent on books and seminars needs to be less than 1880.

- *Minimum number of books policy:* The constraint that you must write at least one book a year is set up in cells B10 and C10. The formula =Books goes into cell B10. The minimum number of books, 1, goes into cell C10.

- *Minimum number of seminars policy:* The constraint that you must give at least four seminars a year is set up in cells B11 and C11. The formula =Seminars goes into cell B11. The minimum number of seminars constant value, 4, goes into cell C11.

After you give the constraint formulas and provide the constants to which the formula results will be compared, you're ready to solve your optimization modeling problem. With the workbook set up (refer to Figure 12-1), solving the function is actually very easy.

Setting up the workbook and defining the problem of objective function and constraint formulas is the hard part.

Solving an Optimization Modeling Problem

After you have your workbook set up, you solve the optimization modeling problem by identifying where you've stored the solver variables, the objective function formula, the constraint formulas, and the constant values to which constraint formulas need to be compared. This is actually very straightforward. Here are the steps that you follow:

1. **Tell Excel to start the Solver by clicking the Data tab's Solver command button.**

   Excel displays the Solver Parameters dialog box, as shown in Figure 12-3.

Figure 12-3:
The Solver
Parameters
dialog box.

If the Tools menu doesn't supply the Solver command, you need to install the Solver add-in. To do this, choose the Microsoft Office button and click Excel Options. When Excel displays the Excel Options dialog box, select the Add-Ins item from the left box that appears along the left edge of the Excel Options dialog box. Excel next displays a list of the possible add-ins — including the Solver add-in. Select the Solver add-in item and click Go. Excel apparently doesn't think you're serious about this Solver Add-in business because it displays another dialog box, called the Add-Ins dialog box. Select the Solver add-in from this dialog box and click OK. Excel installs the Solver add-in. Whew. (***Note:*** Excel will probably prompt you to find and insert the Excel or Office CD.) From this point on, you can use the Solver without trouble.

2. **In the Set Target Cell text box of the Solver Parameters dialog box, identify the cell location of the objective function formula.**

   In the case of the example workbook shown earlier in Figure 12-1, the objective function formula is stored in cell B5. If you were solving an optimization modeling problem using the workbook from Figure 12-1, therefore, you enter $B$5 into the Set Target Cell text box.

3. **Describe what optimization means.**

As I note earlier, not every objective function should be maximized in order to be optimized. In the case of a profit function, because you want to maximize profits — which is the case here — you want to make the objective function formula result as big as possible. But other objective functions might need to be minimized or even set to some specific value.

Select one of the Equal To radio buttons available in the Solver Parameters dialog box to define what optimization means. For example, in the case of a profit function that you want to maximize, select the Max radio button. If instead you're working with a cost function and you want to save costs, you select the Min radio button. In the special case in which optimizing the objective function means getting the function to return a specific value, you can even select the Value Of radio button and then make an entry in the Value Of text box to specify exactly what the objective function formula should return.

4. **In the By Changing Cells text box of the Solver Parameters dialog box, identify the Solver variables.**

   You need to identify the variables that can be adjusted in order to optimize the objective function. In the case of a one-person business in which you're noodling around with the number of books that you should write and the number of seminars that you should give, the Solver variables are *books* and *seminars*.

   To identify the Solver variables, you can enter either the cell addresses into the By Changing cells text box or the cell names. In Figure 12-3, I enter **Books,** a comma, and then **Seminars** into the By Changing Cells text box. Note that these labels refer to cells B2 and B3. I could have also entered **$B$2, $B$3** into the By Changing Cells text box.

5. **Click the Add button in the Solver Parameters dialog box to describe the location of the constraint formulas and the constant values to which the constraint formulas should be compared.**

   Excel displays the Add Constraint dialog box, as shown in Figure 12-4. From the Add Constraint dialog box, you identify the constraint formula and the constant value for each of your constraints. For example, to identify the cash requirements constraint, you need to enter **$B$8** into the Cell Reference text box. Select the less-than or equal-to logical operator from the drop-down list (between the Cell Reference and the Constraint text boxes). Then enter **$C$8** into the Constraint text box. In Figure 12-4, you can see how you indicate that the cash requirements constraint formula is described in cells B8 and C8.

Figure 12-4:
The Add Constraint dialog box.

Note that the logical operator is very important. Excel needs to know how to compare the constraint formula with the constant value.

After you describe the constraint formula, click the Add button. To add another constraint, you click the Add button and follow the same steps. You need to identify each of the constraints.

6. (Optional) Identify any integer constraints.

Sometimes you have implicit integer constraints. In other words, you might need to set the Solver variable value to an integer value. In the example of the one-person business, to get paid for a book, you need to write an entire book. The same thing might be true for a seminar, too. (Or it might not be true for a seminar — perhaps you can do, for example, half of a seminar and have a consulting-buddy do the other half. . . .)

To identify integer constraints, you follow the same steps that you take to identify a regular constraint except that you don't actually need to store integer constraint information in your workbook. What you can do is click the Add button on the Solver Parameters dialog box. In the Add Constraint dialog box that appears, enter the Solver variable name into the Cell Reference box and select int from the drop-down list, as shown in Figure 12-5.

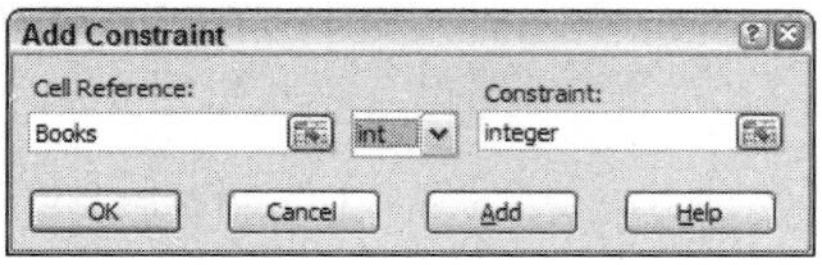

Figure 12-5:
Set up an integer constraint here.

7. (Optional) Define any binary constraints.

In the same manner that you define integer constraints, you can also describe any binary constraints. A *binary constraint* is one in which the solver variable must equal either 0 or 1.

To set up a binary constraint, click the Add button in the Solver Parameters dialog box. When Excel displays the Add Constraint dialog box, enter the Solver variable name into the Cell Reference box. Select Bin from the drop-down list and then click OK.

8. Solve the optimization modeling problem.

After you identify the objective function, identify the Solver variables, and describe the location of the constraint formulas, you're ready to solve the problem. To do this, simply click the Solve button.

Assuming that Excel can solve your optimization problem, it displays the Solver Results dialog box, as shown in Figure 12-6. The Solver

Results dialog box provides two radio buttons. To have Solver retain the optimal solution, select the Keep Solver Solution radio button and then click OK. In the case of the one-person book and seminar business, for example, the optimal number of books to write a year is 7 and the optimal number of seminars to give is 6.6 (shown in cells B2 and B3 in the sample workbook shown in Figure 12-6).

The Solver Parameters dialog box also includes two, presumably self-descriptive command buttons: Change and Delete. To remove a constraint from the optimization model, select the constraint from the Subject to the Constraints list box and then click the Delete button. If you want to change a constraint, select the constraint and then click the Change button. When Excel displays the Change Constraint dialog box, which resembles the Add Constraint dialog box, use the Cell Reference text box, the operator drop-down list, and the Constant text box to make your change.

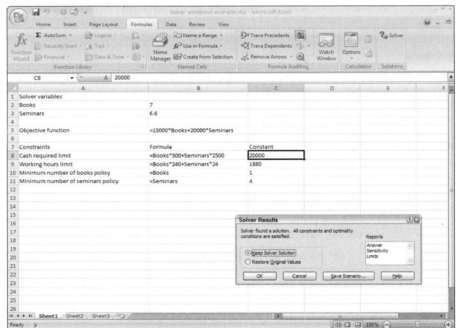

Figure 12-6:
Get Solver results here.

Reviewing the Solver Reports

Refer to the Solver Results dialog box in Figure 12-6 to see the Reports list box. The Reports list box identifies three solver reports you can select: Answer, Sensitivity, and Limits. You might be able to use these to collect more information about your Solver problem.

The Answer Report

Figure 12-7 shows an Answer Report for the one-person business optimization modeling problem. I should tell you that I needed to remove the integer constraints to show all the Solver reports, so some of these values don't jibe perfectly with the Solver results shown in Figure 12-6. Don't worry about that but instead look at the information provided by the Answer Report.

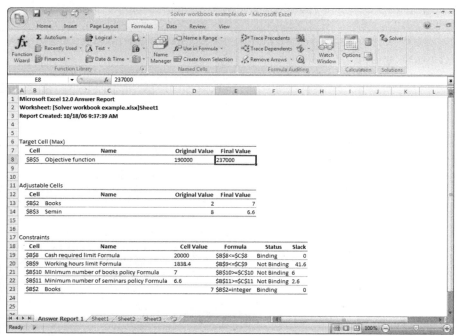

Figure 12-7:
The Answer Report.

The main piece of information provided by the Answer Report is the value of the optimized objective function. This information appears in cell E8 in Figure 12-7. In the case of the one-person book writing and seminar business, for example, the final value, which is the value of the optimized objective function, equals 237000. This tells you that the best mix of book-writing and seminar-giving produces roughly $237,000 of profit.

The Answer Report also shows the original value of the objective function. If you set your original Solver variable values to your first guess or your current configuration, you could compare the original value and the final value to see by what amount Solver improves your objective function value. In this case, such a comparison could show you by what amount Solver helped you increase your profits, which is pretty cool.

The Adjustable Cells area of the Answer Report compares the original value and final values of the solver variables. In the case of the one-person book-writing and seminar-giving business, this area of the worksheet compares the original value for the number of books written (two) with the final value for the number of books written (seven books). The Adjustable Cells area also shows the original value of the number of seminars given (eight) and the final value of the number of seminars given (roughly six and a half seminars).

The Constraints area of the Answer Report is really interesting. The Constraints area shows you what constraint limits the objective function. You might, in the simple case of the one-person business, be able to guess what the limiting factors were intuitively. But in many real-life optimization modeling problems, guessing about what constraint is binding or limiting is more difficult.

In the case of the simple one-person business problem, the Constraints area shows that the first two constraints, cash requirements and working hours, are the ones that limit, or bind, the optimization modeling problem. You can easily see this by looking at the Slack column (shown in cells G19:G23). Slack equals zero for both the cash requirements function and the working hours limit. This means that the objective function value uses up all the cash and all the working hours to produce the final value of $237,000. The other two constraints concerning the minimum number of books written and the minimum number of seminars given aren't limiting because they show slack.

The Sensitivity Report

Figure 12-8 shows the Sensitivity Report. A Sensitivity Report shows reduced gradient values and Lagrange multipliers, which sounds like a whole lot of gobbledygook. But actually these values aren't that hard to understand and can be quite useful.

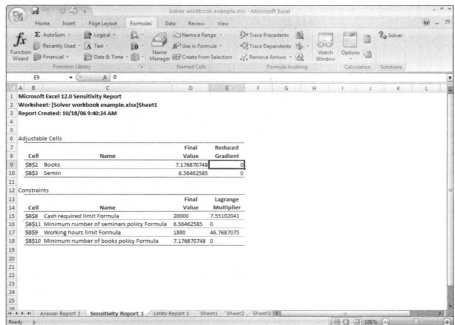

Figure 12-8:
A Sensitivity
Report.

A *reduced gradient value* quantifies the change in the objective function if the variable value increases by one. The *Lagrange multiplier* quantifies how the objective function changes if a constant constraint value increases by one.

In the Sensitivity Report shown in Figure 12-8, the reduced gradient values equal zero. This zero indicates that the variable value can't be increased. For example, the reduced gradient value of zero for books indicates that you can't write more books because of the limiting effect of the constraints. The same thing is true for the reduced gradient value of zero for the seminars variable.

The Lagrange multiplier values sometimes show as zero, too. When the Lagrange multiplier value shows as zero, that means that constraint isn't limiting. For example, in Figure 12-8, the Lagrange multiplier for both the minimum number of books policy formula and the minimum number of seminars policy formula show as zero. As you may recall from the earlier discussion of the Solver results, neither of these two constraints is binding. The Lagrange multiplier value of 7.55102041 in cell E15 shows the amount by which the objective function would increase if the cash requirements constant value increased by one dollar. The Lagrange multiplier value of 46.7687075 in cell E16 shows the amount by which the objective function value would increase if you had one additional hour in which to work.

The Limits Report

The Limits Report, an example of which is shown in Figure 12-9, shows the objective function optimized value, the Solver variable values that reduce the optimized objective function value, and the upper and lower limits possible for the Solver variables. The upper and lower limits show the range of Solver variable values that still produce an optimal function. In many cases, there is predictably no range of possible Solver variable values.

If you take a close look at Figure 12-9, for example, you see that the lower limit for the number of seminars (shown in cell F14) and the upper limit for the number of seminars (shown in cell I14) both equal 6.56462585. In other words, no range of seminar variable values will produce the optimized objective function result $238,946. The lowest value that number of seminars can be set to is roughly 6.56, and the highest value that the number of seminars can be set to is 6.56. In some cases, however, the Solver variable could be set to a range of acceptable, optimal values.

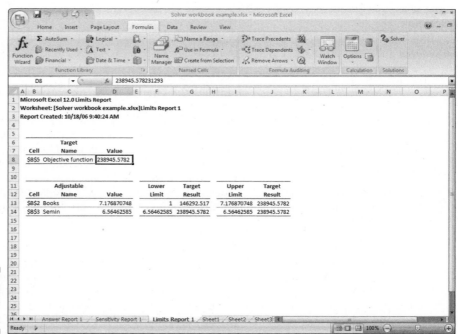

Figure 12-9:
The Limits
Report.

The lower limit and the upper limit for the number of books written does show a range of values. The lower limit shown in cell F13 equals 1. The upper limit shown in cell I13 equals roughly 7.18. I don't think this is correct, however. The target result value shown in cell G13 equals $146,292.517. This is obviously not the optimal objective function result. So you can't really set the number of books to any variable from 1 to 7.18 and still get the optimal function result of roughly $238,946.

To produce a Sensitivity Report or a Limits Report, the solver problem cannot have integer constraints. Accordingly, to produce the reports shown in Figures 12-8 and 12-9, I had to remove the integer constraints on books, which was used in the earlier Answer Report shown in Figure 12-7. Removing this integer constraint changed the objective function optimal value.

Some other notes about Solver reports

You can run the Solver multiple times and get new sets of Answer, Sensitivity, and Limits reports each time that you do. The first set of Solver reports that you get is numbered with a 1 on each sheet tab. The second set, cleverly, is numbered with a 2.

If you want to delete or remove Solver report information, just delete the worksheet on which Excel stores the Solver report. You can delete a report sheet by right-clicking the sheet's tab and then choosing Delete from the shortcut menu that appears.

Working with the Solver Options

If you're an observant reader, you might have noticed that the Solver Parameters dialog box includes an Options button. Click this button, and Excel displays the Solver Options dialog box, as shown in Figure 12-10. You might never need to use this dialog box. But if you want to fine-tune the way that Solver works, you can use the buttons and boxes provided by the Solver Options dialog box to control and customize the way that Solver works. Here I briefly describe how these options work.

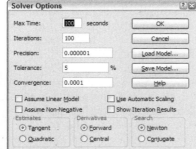

Figure 12-10: The Solver Options dialog box.

Setting a limit on Solver

Use the Max Time and Iterations text boxes to limit the amount of work that Solver does to solve an optimization modeling problem. Now, the simple example that I discuss here doesn't take much time to solve. But real-life problems are often much more complicated. A real-life problem might have many more Solver variables to deal with. The constraints might be more numerous and more complicated. And you might complicate optimization by doing things such as working with lots of integer or binary constraints.

When you work with large, complex, real-life problems, the time that Solver takes to optimize might become very lengthy. In these cases, you can set a maximum time limit that Solver takes by using the Max Time text box. You can also set a maximum number of iterations that Solver makes by using the Iterations text box. Both the Max Time and Iterations text boxes accept a value as large as 32,767, and 32,767 seconds roughly equals 9 hours of calculation.

You can stop the Solver's calculations by pressing Esc.

Deciding how nit-picky to be

Use the Precision and Tolerance text boxes to decide how much nit-picking you want to do about Solver's calculation results.

The Precision text box tells Solver how precise it should be when looking for the optimal value of the objective function. By default, Excel assumes that a precision setting of 0.000001 is okay. Excel interprets that setting to mean that if a constraint formula value is within 0.000001 of the constraint constant, everything is hunky-dory. Excel can consider the constraint met.

You can set the precision box to any value between 0 and 1. To loosen up on your precision, use a larger value. To tighten up on your precision, use a smaller precision value.

In the Tolerance text box, you specify how precise Solver should be in making sure that integer constraints are met. By default, Solver assumes that if an integer constraint is within 5 percent of the integer value, that's okay. If you want to make sure that integer constraints are met more precisely, you can enter a smaller value into the Tolerance text box.

The Tolerance setting comes into play only when you're working with an integer constraint. If you have an optimization modeling problem that doesn't have any integer constraints, the Tolerance text box has no effect.

Predictably, the more precision and less tolerance that you want, the longer and harder that Excel needs to work.

Saying when

Have you ever been to a restaurant where your server wanders around at some point in the meal with a huge peppermill asking whether you want black pepper on your salad? If you have, you know that part of the ritual is that at some point, you tell the server when he or she has ground enough pepper for your green salad.

The Convergence text box provided in the Solver Options dialog box works in roughly the same way. You use the Convergence box to tell Excel *when* it should stop looking for a better solution. The Convergence text box accepts any value between 0 and 1. When the change in the objective function formula result is less then the value shown in the convergence text box, Excel figures that things are getting close enough, so additional iterations aren't necessary.

I should mention that the value that you enter into the Convergence text box applies only to non-linear optimization modeling problems. (For more on this, read the following section.) Oh, another thing that I should mention: With larger convergence values, Excel reaches a reasonable solution more quickly and with less work. And with smaller or very precise convergence values, Excel works harder and takes more time.

When you assume . . .

The Solver Options dialog box includes two check boxes with which you tell Solver what to assume about your modeling: Assume Linear Model and Assume Non-Negative.

Select the Assume Linear Model check box when you're working on a linear programming problem. This just means that the relationships in your optimization modeling program are linear. Simple optimization functions and constraints like those that I demonstrate and describe earlier in this chapter are linear. In general, non-linear optimization modeling uses much more complicated objective function formulas and constraint formulas (presumably formulas that include things like exponents).

Select the Assume Non-Negative check box if your Solver variables must equal or be greater than zero. This is something that you need to do because in some cases, an optimal objective function result can be created by using negative Solver variable values. But obviously, in many situations, negative Solver variable values wouldn't make sense. For example, in the simple example of the one-person book-writing and seminar-giving business, you can't write a negative number of books or give a negative number of seminars.

Using automatic scaling

You can select the Use Automatic Scaling check box when you're working with variables that greatly differ in magnitude. For example, if you're working with interest rates and multimillion dollar account balances, you might want to use the automatic scaling option to tell Excel, "Hey dude, the Solver variable values greatly differ in magnitude, so you ought to automatically scale these babies."

Showing iteration results

If you don't have anything better to do, select the Show Iteration Results check box. When you do this, Excel stops after it calculates each objective function using a new set of Solver variable values and shows you the intermediate calculation results. Most people won't and shouldn't care about seeing intermediate calculation results. But heck, I suppose that in some cases, you might want to see how Solver is working toward the objective function optimal result.

Tangent versus quadratic estimates

Choose either Estimates radio buttons — Tangent or Quadratic — to specify how Excel should come up with its first trial solution to the objective function. If Excel should extrapolate linearly from the tangent vector, you select the Tangent radio button. If Excel should extrapolate quadratically because you're using non-linear formulas, you select the Quadratic radio button. If you don't have a clue and find the two terms *tangent* and *quadratic* befuddling and anxiety producing, don't pay any attention to them.

Forward versus central derivatives

Select from the two Derivatives radio buttons — Forward and Central — to tell Excel how to estimate partial derivatives when it's working with the objective function and constraint formulas. In most cases, everything works just fine if Excel uses forward derivatives. But, in some cases, forward derivatives don't work. And in this situation, you might be able to specify that Excel use central derivatives.

Using central derivatives requires much more work of Excel, but some highly constrained problems can more easily and more practically be solved using central derivatives.

Newton versus conjugate algorithms

Select either of the two Search radio buttons — Newton or Conjugate — to tell Excel what or which algorithm it should use to solve your optimization modeling problem. By default, Excel assumes that, "Hey, dude it's cool," if you use the Newton algorithm. However, the Newton algorithm only practically works if your computer has a lot of memory. If your computer doesn't have a lot of memory, you can use the Conjugate algorithm. The Conjugate algorithm takes more time, but it requires less memory. Typically, by the way, using the Conjugate algorithm is necessary only on very large and very complicated optimization modeling problems.

Saving and reusing model information

The Solver Options dialog box provides two buttons, Save Model and Load Model, with which you save optimization modeling problem information. If you click the Save Model button, for example, Excel displays the Save Model dialog box, as shown in Figure 12-11. To save the current optimization modeling information, you enter a worksheet range address in the Select Model Area text box that Excel can use to save the model information.

To later reuse that model information, click the Load Model command button and then specify the worksheet range that you used to originally store model information.

Figure 12-11: The Save Model dialog box.

Understanding the Solver Error Messages

For simple problems, Solver usually quickly finds the optimal Solver variable values for the objective function. However, in some cases — in fact, maybe quite frequently in the real world — Solver has trouble finding the Solver variable values that optimize the objective function. In these cases, however, Solver typically displays a message or an error message that describes or discusses the trouble that it's having with your problem. Quickly, before I wrap up this chapter, I briefly identify and comment on the messages and error messages that Solver might display as it finishes or gives up on the work that it's doing.

Solver has converged to the current solution

The `Solver has converged to the current solution` message tells you that Excel has found a solution but isn't particularly confident in the solution. In essence, this message alerts you to the possibility that a better solution to your optimization modeling problem might exist. To look for a better solution, adjust the Convergence setting in the Solver Options dialog box so that Excel works at a higher level of precision. I describe how you do this in the earlier section, "Saying when."

Solver cannot improve the current solution

The `Solver cannot improve the current solution` message tells you that, well, Excel has calculated a rough, pretty darn accurate solution, but, again, you might be able to find a better solution. To tell Excel that it should look for a better solution, you need to increase the precision setting that Solver is using. This means, of course, that Excel will take more time. But that extra time might result in it finding a better solution. To adjust the precision, you again use the Solver Options dialog box. Read the earlier section, "Deciding how nit-picky to be."

Stop chosen when maximum time limit was reached

The `Stop chosen when maximum time limit was reached` **message** tells you that Excel ran out of time. You can retry solving the optimization modeling problem with a larger Max Time setting. (Read more about this in the earlier section, "Setting a limit on Solver.") Note, however, that if you do see this message, you should save the work that Excel has already performed as part of the optimization modeling problem solving. Save the work that Excel has already done by clicking the Keep Solver Results button when Excel displays this message. Excel will be closer to the final solution the next time that it starts looking for the optimal solution.

Stop chosen when maximum iteration limit was reached

The `Stop chosen when maximum iteration limit was reached` message tells you that Excel ran out of iterations before it found the optimal solution. You can get around this problem by setting a larger iterations value in the Solver Options dialog box. Read the earlier section, "Showing iteration results."

Set target cell values do not converge

The `Set target cell values do not converge` message tells you that the objective function doesn't have an optimal value. In other words, the objective function keeps getting bigger (or keeps getting smaller) even though the constraint formulas are satisfied. In other words, Excel finds that it keeps getting a better objective function value with every iteration, but it doesn't appear any closer to a final objective function value.

If you encounter this error, you've probably not correctly defined and described your optimization modeling problem. Your objective function might not make a lot of sense or might not be congruent with your constraint formulas. Or maybe one or more of your constraint formulas — or probably several of them — don't really make sense.

Solver could not find a feasible solution

The `Solver could not find a feasible solution` message tells you that your optimization modeling problem doesn't have an answer. As a practical matter, when you see this message, it means that your set of constraints excludes any possible answer.

For example, returning one last time to the one-person business, suppose that it takes 3,000 hours to write a book and that only 2,000 hours for work are available in a year. If you said that you wanted to write at least one book a year, there's no solution to the objective function. A book requires up to 3,000 hours of work, but you only have 2,000 hours in which to complete a 3,000-hour project. That's impossible, obviously. No optimal value for the objective function exists.

Conditions for assume linear model are not satisfied

The `Conditions for assume linear model are not satisfied` message indicates that although you selected the Assume Linear Model check box (in the Solver Options dialog box), Excel has now figured out that your model isn't actually linear. And it's mad as heck. So it shows you this message to indicate that it can't solve the problem if it has to assume that your objective function and constraint formulas are linear. (For more on Assume Linear Model, see the earlier section, "When you assume . . .")

If you do see this message, however, your first response shouldn't necessarily be to clear the Assume Linear Model check box. Rather, first display the Solver Options dialog box and then select the Use Automatic Scaling check box. If you get the same message again after making this change, you need to clear the Assume Linear Model check box. Hopefully, you'll then be able to solve your problem.

Solver encountered an error value in a target or constraint cell

The `Solver encountered an error value in a target or constraint cell` message means that one of your formula results in an error value or that you goofed in describing or defining some constraint. To work around this problem, you need to fix the bogus formula or the goofy constraint.

There is not enough memory available to solve the problem

The `There is not enough memory available to solve the problem` message is self-descriptive. If you see this message, Solver doesn't have enough memory to solve the optimization modeling problem that you're working on. Your only recourse is to attempt to free up memory, perhaps by closing any other open programs and any unneeded documents or workbooks. If that doesn't work, you might also want to add more memory to your computer, especially if you're going to commonly do optimization modeling problems. Memory is cheap.

Part IV
The Part of Tens

In this part . . .

The chapters in this part list useful tidbits, tips, and factoids on using Excel to analyze data. Here I give you the quick lowdown on the basics of statistics, as well as lists of tips for presenting list results and for visually analyzing and presenting your data.

Chapter 13

Almost Ten Things You Ought to Know about Statistics

In This Chapter

▶ Descriptive statistics are straightforward

▶ Averages aren't so simple sometimes

▶ Standard deviations describe dispersion

▶ Probability distribution functions aren't always confusing

▶ Parameters aren't so complicated

▶ Skewness and kurtosis describe a probability distribution's shape

▶ An observation is an observation

▶ A sample is a subset of values

▶ Inferential statistics are cool but complicated

*I*n as much that I discuss how to use Excel for statistical analysis in a number of chapters in this book, I thought it might make sense to cover some of the basics.

Don't worry. I'm not going to launch into some college-level lecture about things like chi-square or covariance calculations. You'll see no Greek symbols in this chapter.

If you've never been exposed to statistics in school or it's been a decade or two since you were, let this chapter to help you use (comfortably) some of the statistical tools that Excel provides.

Descriptive Statistics Are Straightforward

The first thing that you ought to know is that some statistical analysis and some statistical measures are pretty darn straightforward. Descriptive statistics, which include things such as the pivot table cross-tabulations (that I present in Chapters 3 and 4), as well as some of the statistical functions, make sense even to somebody who's not all that quantitative.

For example, if you sum a set of values, you get a sum. Pretty easy, right? And if you find the biggest value or the smallest value in a set of numbers, that's pretty straightforward, too.

I mention this point about descriptive statistics because a lot of times people freak out when they hear the word *statistics.* That's too bad because many of the most useful statistical tools available to you are simple, easy-to-understand descriptive statistics.

Averages Aren't So Simple Sometimes

Here's a weird thing that you might remember if you ever took a statistics class. When someone uses the term *average,* what he or she usually refers to is the most common average measurement, which is a *mean.* But you ought to know that several other commonly accepted average measurements exist, including mode, median, and some special mean measurements such as the geometric mean and harmonic mean.

I want to quickly cover some of these . . . not because you need to know all this stuff, but because understanding that the term *average* is imprecise makes some of the discussions in this book and much of Excel's statistical functionality more comprehensible.

To make this discussion more concrete, assume that you're looking at a small set of values: 1, 2, 3, 4, and 5. As you might know or be able to intuitively guess, the mean in this small set of values is 3. You can calculate the mean by adding together all the numbers in the set (1+2+3+4+5) and then dividing this sum (15) by the total number of values in the set (5).

Two other common average measurements are mode and median. I start with the discussion of the median measurement first because it's easy to understand using the data set that I introduce in the preceding paragraph. The *median value* is the value that separates the largest values from the smallest values. In the data set 1, 2, 3, 4, and 5, the median is 3. The value 3 separates the largest values (4 and 5) from the smallest values (1 and 2). In other words, the median shows the middle point in the data. Half of the data set values are larger than the median value, and half of the data set values are smaller than the median value.

When you have an even number of values in your data set, you calculate the median by averaging the two middle values. For example, the data set 1, 2, 3, and 4 has no middle value. Add the two middle values — 2 and 3 — and then divide by 2. This calculation produces a median value of 2.5. With the median value of 2.5, half of the values in the data set are above the median value, and half of the values in the data set are below the median value.

The mode measurement is a third common average. The *mode* is the most common value in the data set. To show you an example of this, I need to introduce a new data set. With the data set 1, 2, 3, 5, and 5, the mode is 5 because the value *5* occurs twice in the set. Every other value occurs only once.

As I mention earlier, other common statistical measures of the average exist. The mean measurement that I refer to earlier in this discussion is actually an arithmetic mean because the values in the data set get added together arithmetically as part of the calculation. You can, however, combine the values in other ways. Financial analysts and scientists sometimes use a geometric mean, for example. There is also something called a harmonic mean.

You don't need to understand all these other different average measurements, but you should remember that the term *average* is pretty imprecise. And what people usually imply when they refer to an average is the *mean*.

Standard Deviations Describe Dispersion

Have you ever heard the term *standard deviation?* You probably have. Any statistical report usually includes some vague or scary reference to either standard deviation or its close relative, the variance. Although the formula for standard deviation is terrifying to look at — at least if you're not comfortable with the Greek alphabet — intuitively, the formula and the logic are pretty easy to understand.

A *standard deviation* describes how values in a data set vary around the mean. Another way to say this same thing is that a standard deviation describes how far away from the mean the average value is. In fact, you can almost think of a standard deviation as being equal to the average distance from the mean. This isn't quite right, but it's darn close.

Suppose you're working with a data set, and its mean equals 20. If the data set standard deviation is 5, you can sort of think about the average data set value as being 5 units away from the mean of 20. In other words, for values less than the mean of 20, the average is sort of 15. And for values that are larger than the mean, the average value is kind of 25.

The standard deviation isn't really the same thing as the average deviation, but it's pretty darn close in some cases. And thinking about the standard deviation as akin to the average deviation — or average difference from the mean — is a good way to tune into the logic.

The neat thing about all this is that with statistical measures like a mean and a standard deviation, you often gain real insights into the characteristics of the data that you're looking at. Another thing is that with these two bits of data, you can often draw inferences about data by looking at samples.

I should tell you one other thing about the standard deviation. The statistical terms *variance* and *standard deviation* are related. A *standard deviation* equals the square root of a variance. Another way to say this same thing is that a *variance* equals the square of a standard deviation.

It turns out that when you calculate things such as variances and standard deviations, you actually arrive at the variance value first. In other words, you calculate the variance before you calculate the standard deviation. For this reason, you'll often hear people talk about variances rather than standard deviations. Really, however, standard deviations and variances are the same thing. In one case, you're working with a square root. In another case you are working with a square.

It's six of one, half a dozen of the other . . . sort of.

An Observation Is an Observation

Observation is one of the terms that you'll encounter if you read anything about statistics in this book or in the Excel online Help. An observation is just an observation. That sounds circular, but bear with me. Suppose that you're constructing a data set that shows daily high temperatures in your neighborhood. When you go out and observe that the temperature some fine July afternoon is 87° F, that measurement (87°) is your first observation. If you go out and observe that the high temperature the next day is 88° F, that measurement is your second observation.

Another way to define the term observation is like this: Whenever you actually assign a value to one of your random variables, you create an observation. For example, if you're building a data set of daily high temperatures in your neighborhood, every time that you go out and assign a new temperature value (87° one day, 88° the next day, and so on) you're creating an observation.

A Sample Is a Subset of Values

A *sample* is a collection of observations from a population. For example, if you create a data set that records the daily high temperature in your neighborhood, your little collection of observations is a sample.

In comparison, a sample is not a population. A *population* includes all the possible observations. In the case of collecting your neighborhood's high temperatures, the population includes all the daily high temperatures — since the beginning of the neighborhood's existence.

Inferential Statistics Are Cool but Complicated

As I note earlier in this chapter, some statistics are pretty simple. Finding the biggest value in a set of numbers is a *statistical measurement*. But it's really pretty simple. Those simple descriptive statistical measures are called, cleverly, *descriptive statistics*.

Another more complicated but equally useful branch of statistics is *inferential statistics*. Inferential statistics are based on this very useful, intuitively obvious idea. If you look at a sample of values from a population and the sample is representative and large enough, you can draw conclusions about the population based on characteristics of the sample.

For example, for every presidential election in the United States, the major television networks (usually contrary to their earlier promises) predict the winner after only a relatively small number of votes have been calculated or counted. How do they do this? Well, they sample the population. Specifically, they stand outside polling places and ask exiting voters how they voted. If you ask a large sample of voters whether they voted for the one guy or the other guy, you can make an inference about how all the voters voted. And then you can predict who has won the election.

Inferential statistics, although very powerful, possess two qualities that I need to mention:

- ✔ **Accuracy issues:** When you make a statistical inference, you can never be 100 percent sure that your inference is correct. The possibility always exists that your sample isn't representative or that your sample doesn't return enough precision to estimate the population value.

  This is partly what happened with the 2000 presidential election in the United States. Initially, some of the major news networks predicted that Al Gore had won based on exit polls. Then based on other exit polls, they predicted that George W. Bush had won. Then, perhaps finally realizing that maybe their statistics weren't good enough given the closeness of the race . . . or perhaps just based on their own embarrassment about bobbling the ball . . . they stopped predicting the race. In retrospect, it's not surprising that they had trouble with calling the race because the number of votes for the two candidates was *extremely* close.

- ✔ **Steep learning curve:** Inferential statistics quickly gets pretty complicated. When you work with inferential statistics, you immediately start encountering terms such as *probability distribution functions,* all sorts of crazy (in some cases) parameters, and lots of Greek symbols.

As a practical matter, if you haven't at least taken a statistics class — and probably more than one statistics class — you'll find it very hard to move into inferential statistics in a big way. You probably can, with a single statistics class and perhaps the information in this book, work with inferential statistics based on normal distributions and uniform distributions. However, working with inferential statistics and applying those inferential statistics to other probability distributions becomes very tricky. At least, that's my observation.

Probability Distribution Functions Aren't Always Confusing

One of the statistical terms that you'll encounter a little bit in this book — and a whole bunch if you dig into the Excel Help file — is *probability distribution function.* This phrase sounds pretty tricky; in some cases, granted, maybe it is. But you can actually understand intuitively what a probability distribution function is with a couple of useful examples.

One common distribution that you hear about in statistics classes, for example, is a T distribution. A *T distribution* is essentially a normal distribution except with heavier, fatter tails. There are also distributions that are skewed (have the hump tilted) one way or the other. Each of these probability distributions, however, has a probability distribution function that describes the probability distribution chart.

Here are two probability distribution functions that you probably already understand: uniform distribution and normal distribution.

Uniform distribution

One common probability distribution function is a uniform distribution. In a *uniform distribution,* every event has the same probability of occurrence. As a simple example, suppose that you roll a six-sided die. Assuming that the die is fair, you have an equal chance of rolling any of the values: 1, 2, 3, 4, 5, or 6. If you roll the die 60,000 times, what you would expect to see (given the large number of observations) is that you'll probably roll a 1 about 10,000 times. Similarly, you'll probably also roll a 2, 3, 4, 5, or 6 about 10,000 times each. Oh sure, you can count on some variance between what you expect (10,000 occurrences of each side of the six-sided die) and what you actually experience. But your actual observations would pretty well map to your expectations.

The unique thing about this distribution is that everything is pretty darn level. You could say that the probability or the chance of rolling any one of the six sides of the die is even, or *uniform.* This is how uniform distribution gets its name. Every event has the same probability of occurrence. Figure 13-1 shows a uniform distribution function.

Normal distribution

Another common type of probability distribution function is the *normal distribution,* also known as a *bell curve* or a *Gaussian distribution.*

A normal distribution occurs naturally in many situations. For example, intelligence quotients (IQs) are distributed normally. If you take a large set of people, test their IQs, and then plot those IQs on a chart, you get a normal distribution. One characteristic of a normal distribution is that most of the values in the population are centered around the mean. Another characteristic of a normal distribution is that the mean, the mode, and the median all equal each other.

Do you kind of see now where this probability distribution function business is going? A probability distribution function just describes a chart that, in essence, plots probabilities. Figure 13-2 shows a normal distribution function.

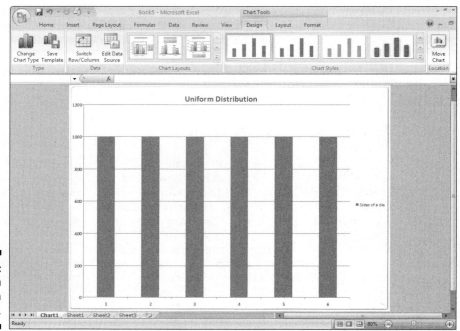

Figure 13-1:
A uniform
distribution
function.

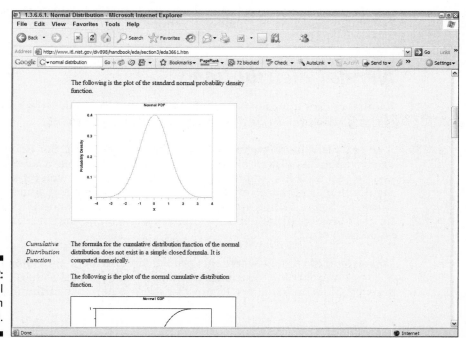

Figure 13-2:
A normal
distribution
function.

A probability distribution function is just a function, or equation, that describes the line of the distribution. As you might guess, not every probability distribution looks like a normal distribution or a uniform distribution.

Parameters Aren't So Complicated

After you grasp the concept that a probability distribution function is essentially an equation or formula that describes the line in a probability distribution chart, it's pretty easy to understand that a *parameter* is an input to the probability distribution function. In other words, the formula or function or equation that describes a probability distribution curve needs inputs. In statistics, those inputs are called parameters.

Refer to Figure 13-2 to see its probability function. Most of those crazy Greek symbols refer to parameters.

Some probability distribution functions need only a single simple parameter. For example, to work with a uniform distribution, all you really need is the number of values in the data set. A six-sided die, for example, has only six possibilities. Because you know that only six possibilities exist, you can pretty easily calculate that there's a 1-in-6 chance that any possibility will occur.

A normal distribution uses two parameters: the mean and the standard deviation.

Other probability distribution functions use other parameters.

Skewness and Kurtosis Describe a Probability Distribution's Shape

A couple of other useful statistical terms to know are skewness and kurtosis. *Skewness* quantifies the lack of symmetry in a probability distribution. In a perfectly symmetrical distribution, like the normal distribution (refer to Figure 13-2), the skewness equals zero. If a probability distribution leans to the right or the left, however, the skewness equals some value other than zero, and the value quantifies the lack of symmetry.

Kurtosis quantifies the heaviness of the tails in a distribution. In a normal distribution, kurtosis equals zero. In other words, zero is the measurement for a tail that looks like a tail in a normal distribution. The *tail* is the thing that reaches out to the left or right. However, if a tail in a distribution is heavier than a normal distribution, the kurtosis is a positive number. If the tails in a distribution are skinnier than in a normal distribution, the kurtosis is a negative number.

Chapter 14

Almost Ten Tips for Presenting Table Results and Analyzing Data

- -

In This Chapter

▶ Working hard to import data

▶ Designing information systems to produce rich data

▶ Remembering to forget about third-party sources

▶ Always exploring descriptive statistics

▶ Watching for trends

▶ Cross-tabulating and re-cross-tabulation

▶ Charting it, baby

▶ Being aware of inferential statistics

- -

Throughout the pages of this book, here and there I scatter tips on analyzing data with Excel. In this chapter, however, I want to take a step back from the details of data analysis and offer a handful of general tips. Mostly, these tips summarize and generalize the things that I discuss in the preceding chapters of this book.

Work Hard to Import Data

Working to import good, rich data into Excel workbooks really is worthwhile. I know that sometimes importing data can be problematic. Headaches and heartbreaks can happen when trying to grab data from other management information systems and when trying to work with a database administrator to get the right data into a format that provides for useful data analysis with Excel.

But in spite of the hassles of obtaining the data, you will find — I promise — that importing good data into Excel is well worth the effort. Traditionally, people make decisions by using very standard information sources . . . like the accounting system, or some third-party report, or newsletter, or publication. And those traditional sources produce traditional insights, which is great. But when you can work with a richer, deeper data set of raw information, you often glean insights that simply don't appear in the traditional sources.

Design Information Systems to Produce Rich Data

More than 20 years ago now, as a young systems consultant with Arthur Andersen (yes, *that* Arthur Andersen), I designed accounting systems and financial information systems for large companies. In those days, we concentrated on creating systems that produced the reports that managers and decision makers wanted and that produced forms (such as invoices and checks and purchase orders) that businesses required to operate.

Those items are still obviously key things to think about while you design and install and manage information systems, such as an accounting system. But I think that you also need to recognize that there will probably be unplanned, unorthodox, unusual but still very valuable ways in which the data that is collected by these management information systems can be analyzed. And so, if you work with or design or participate in implementing information systems, you should realize that raw data from the system can and should be passed to data analysis tools like Excel.

A simple example of this will show you what I mean. It applies even to the smallest businesses. The QuickBooks accounting system, which I discuss a little bit in earlier chapters in this book, is an extremely popular accounting tool for small businesses. Hundreds of thousands of small businesses use QuickBooks for their accounting, for example. And the one thing that I would say about QuickBooks users in general is that they often want to use the QuickBooks system simply for accounting. They want to use it as a tool for producing things like checks and invoices and for creating documents that report on profits or estimate cash flow information.

And that's good. If you're a business owner or manager, you definitely want that information. But even with a simple system like QuickBooks, businesses should collect richer sets of data . . . very detailed information about the products or services a firm sells, for example. By doing this, even if you don't want to report on this information within QuickBooks, you create a very rich data set that you can later analyze for good effect with Excel.

Having rich, detailed records of the products or services that a firm sells enables that firm to see trends in sales by product or service. Additionally, it allows a firm to create cross-tabulations that show how certain customers choose and use certain products and services.

The bottom line, I submit, is that organizations need to design information systems so that they also collect good, rich, raw data. Later on, this data can easily be exported to Excel, where simple data analysis — such as the types that I describe in the earlier chapters of this book — can lead to rich insights into a firm's operation, its opportunities, and possible threats.

Don't Forget about Third-Party Sources

One quick point: Recognize that many third-party sources of data exist. For example, vendors and customers might have very interesting data available in a format accessible to Excel that you can use to analyze their market or your industry.

Earlier in the book, for example, I mention that the slowdown in computer book sales and in computer book publishing first became apparent to me based on an Excel workbook supplied by one of the major book distributors in North America. Without this third-party data source, I would have continued to find myself bewildered about what was happening in the industry in which I work.

A quick final comment about third-party data sources is this: the Web Query tool available in Excel (and as I describe in Chapter 3) makes extracting information from tables stored on Web pages very easy.

Just Add It

You might think that powerful data analysis requires powerful data analysis techniques. Chi-squares. Inferential statistics. Regression analysis.

But I don't think so. Some of the most powerful data analysis that you can do involves simply adding up numbers. If you add numbers and get sums that other people don't even know about — and if those sums are important or show trends — you can gain important insights and collect valuable information through the simplest data analysis techniques.

Again, in echoing earlier tips in this chapter, the key thing is collecting really good information in the first place and then having that information stored in a container, such as an Excel workbook, so that you can arithmetically manipulate and analyze the data.

Always Explore Descriptive Statistics

The descriptive statistical tools that Excel provides — including measurements such as a sum, an average, a median, a standard deviation, and so forth — are really powerful tools. Don't feel as if these tools are beyond your skill set, even if this book is your first introduction to these tools.

Descriptive statistics simply describe the data you have in some Excel worksheet. They're not magical, and you don't need any special statistical training to use them or to share them with the people to whom you present your data analysis results.

Note, too, that some of the simplest descriptive statistical measures are often the most useful. For example, knowing the smallest value in a data set or the largest value can be very useful. Knowing the mean, median, or mode in a data set is also very interesting and handy. And even seemingly complicated sophisticated measures such as a standard deviation (which just measures dispersion about the mean) are really quite useful tools. You don't need to understand anything more than this book describes to use or share this information.

Watch for Trends

Peter Drucker, perhaps the best-known and most insightful observer of modern management practices, noted in several of his last books that one of the most significant things data analysis can do is spot a change in trends. I want to echo this here, pointing out that trends are almost the most significant thing you can see. If your industry's combined revenues grow, that's significant. If they haven't been growing or if they start shrinking, that's probably even more significant.

In your own data analysis, be sure to construct your worksheets and collect your data in a way that helps you identify trends and, ideally, identify changes in trends.

Slicing and Dicing: Cross-Tabulation

The PivotTable command, which I describe in Chapter 4, is a wonderful tool. Cross-tabulations are extremely useful ways to slice and dice data. And as I note in Chapter 4, the neat thing about the PivotTable tool is that you can easily re-cross-tabulate and then re-cross-tabulate again.

I go into a lot of detail in Chapter 4 about why cross-tabulation is so cool, so I don't repeat myself here. But I do think that if you have good rich data sources and you're not regularly cross-tabulating your data, you're probably missing absolute treasures of information. There's gold in them thar hills.

Chart It, Baby

In Chapter 15, I provide a list of tips that you might find useful to graphically or visually analyze data. In a nutshell, though, I think that an important component of good data analysis is presenting and examining your data visually.

By looking at a line chart of some important statistic or by creating a column chart of some set of data, you often see things that aren't apparent in a tabular presentation of the same information. Basically, charting is often a wonderful way to discover things that you won't otherwise see.

Be Aware of Inferential Statistics

To varying degrees in Chapters 9, 10, and 11, I introduce and discuss some of the inferential statistics tools that Excel provides. Inferential statistics enable you to collect a sample and then make inferences about the population from which the sample is drawn based on the characteristics of the sample.

In the right hands, inferential statistics are extremely powerful and useful tools. With good skills in inferential statistics, you can analyze all sorts of things to gain all sorts of insights into data that mere common folk never get. However, quite frankly, if your only exposure to inferential statistical techniques is this book, you probably don't possess enough raw statistical knowledge to fairly perform inferential statistical analysis.

Chapter 15

Ten Tips for Visually Analyzing and Presenting Data

This isn't one of those essays about how a picture is worth a thousand words. In this chapter, I just want to provide some concrete suggestions about how you can more successfully use charts as data analysis tools and how you can use charts to more effectively communicate the results of the data analysis that you do.

Using the Right Chart Type

What many people don't realize is that you can make only five data comparisons in Excel charts. And if you want to be picky, there are only four practical data comparisons that Excel charts let you make. Table 15-1 summarizes the five data comparisons.

Table 15-1	The Five Possible Data Comparisons in a Chart	
Comparison	**Description**	**Example**
Part-to-whole	Compares individual values with the sum of those values.	Comparing the sales generated by individual products with the total sales enjoyed by a firm.
Whole-to-whole	Compares individual data values and sets of data values (or what Excel calls *data series*) to each other.	Comparing sales revenues of different firms in your industry.
Time-series	Shows how values change over time.	A chart showing sales revenues over the last 5 years or profits over the last 12 months.
Correlation	Looks at different data series in an attempt to explore correlation, or association, between the data series.	Comparing information about the numbers of school-age children with sales of toys.
Geographic	Looks at data values using a geographic map.	Examining sales by country using a map of the world.

If you decide or can figure out which data comparison you want to make, choosing the right chart type is very easy:

- ✔ **Pie, doughnut, or area:** If you want to make a *part-to-whole* data comparison, choose a pie chart (if you're working with a single data series) or a doughnut chart or an area chart (if you're working with more than one data series).

- ✔ **Bar, cylinder, cone, or pyramid:** If you want to make a *whole-to-whole* data comparison, you probably want to use a chart that uses horizontal data markers. Bar charts use horizontal data markers, for example, and so do cylinder, cone, and pyramid charts. (You can also use a doughnut chart or radar chart to make whole-to-whole data comparisons.)

- ✔ **Line or column:** To make a *time-series* data comparison, you want to use a chart type that has a horizontal category axis. By convention, western societies (Europe, North America, and South America) use a horizontal axis moving from left to right to denote the passage of time. Because of this culturally programmed convention, you want to show time-series data comparisons by using a horizontal category axis. This means you probably want to use either a line chart or column chart.

- ✔ **Scatter or bubble:** If you want to make a *correlation* data comparison in Excel, you have only two choices. If you have two data series for which you're exploring correlation, you want to use an XY (Scatter) chart. If you have three data series, you can use either an XY (Scatter) chart or a bubble chart.

- ✔ **Surface:** If you want to make a *geographic* data comparison, you're very limited in what you can do in Excel. You might be able to make a geographic data comparison by using a surface chart. But, more likely, you need to use another data mapping tool such as MapPoint from Microsoft.

The data comparison that you want to make largely determines what chart type you need to use. You want to use a chart type that supports the data comparison that you want to make.

Using Your Chart Message as the Chart Title

Chart titles are commonly used to identify the organization that you're presenting information to or perhaps to identify the key data series that you're applying in a chart. A better and more effective way to use the chart title, however, is to make it into a brief summary of the message that you want your chart to communicate. For example, if you create a chart that shows that sales and profits are increasing, maybe your chart title should look like the one shown in Figure 15-1.

Using your chart message as the chart title immediately communicates to your audience what you're trying to show in the chart. This technique also helps people looking at your chart to focus on the information that you want them to understand.

Beware of Pie Charts

You really want to avoid pie charts. Oh, I know, pie charts are great tools to teach elementary school children about charts and plotting data. And you see them commonly in newspapers and magazines. But the reality is that pie charts are very inferior tools for visually understanding data and for visually communicating quantitative information.

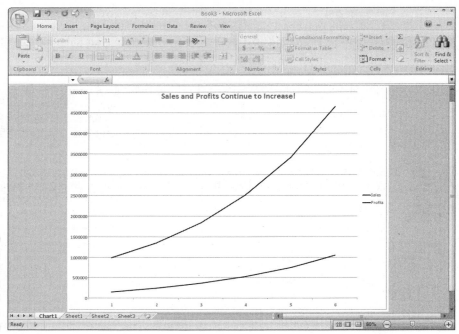

Figure 15-1:
Use a
chart's chart
message as
its title.

Almost always, information that appears in a pie chart would be better displayed in a simple table.

Pie charts possess several debilitating weaknesses:

- **You're limited to working with a very small set of numbers.**

  This makes sense, right? You can't slice the pie into very small pieces or into very many pieces without your chart becoming illegible.

- **Pie charts aren't visually precise.**

  Readers or viewers are asked to visually compare the slices of pie, but that's so imprecise as to be almost useless. This same information can be shown much better by just providing a simple list or table of plotted values.

- **With pie charts, you're limited to a single data series.**

  For example, you can plot a pie chart that shows sales of different products that your firm sells. But almost always, people will find it more interesting to also know profits by product line. Or maybe they also want to know sales per sales person or geographic area. You see the problem. Because they're limited to a single data series, pie charts very much limit the information that you can display.

Consider Using Pivot Charts for Small Data Sets

Although using pivot tables is often the best way to cross-tabulate data and to present cross-tabulated data, remember that for small data sets, pivot charts can also work very well. The key thing to remember is that a pivot chart, practically speaking, enables you to plot only a few rows of data. Often your cross-tabulations will show many rows of data.

However, if you create a cross-tabulation that shows only a few rows of data, try a pivot chart. Figure 15-2 shows a cross-tabulation in a pivot *table* form; Figure 15-3 shows a cross-tabulation in a pivot *chart* form. I wager that for many people, the graphical presentation shown in Figure 15-3 shows the trends in the underlying data more quickly, more conveniently, and more effectively.

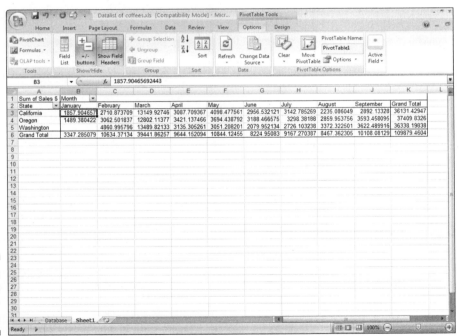

Figure 15-2:
A pivot table cross-tabulation.

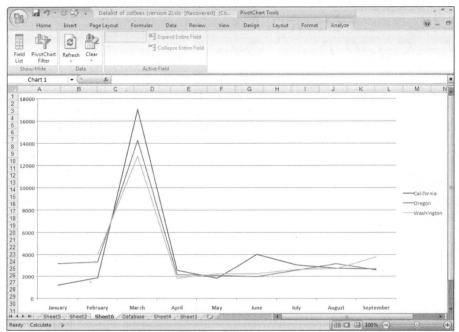

Figure 15-3:
A pivot chart cross-tabulation.

Avoiding 3-D Charts

In general, and perhaps contrary to the wishes of the Microsoft marketing people, you really want to avoid three-dimensional charts.

The problem with 3-D charts isn't that they don't look pretty: They do. The problem is that the extra dimension, or illusion, of depth reduces the visual precision of the chart. With a 3-D chart, you can't as easily or precisely measure or assess the plotted data.

Figure 15-4 shows a simple column chart. Figure 15-5 shows the same information in a 3-D column chart. If you look closely at these two charts, you can see that it's much more difficult to precisely compare the two data series and to really see what underlying data values are being plotted.

Now, I'll admit that some people — those people who really like 3-D charts — say that you can deal with the imprecision of a 3-D chart by annotating the chart with data values and data labels. Figure 15-6 shows the way a 3-D column chart would look with this added information. I don't think that's a good solution because charts often too easily become cluttered with extraneous and confusing information. Adding all sorts of annotation to a chart to compensate for the fundamental weakness in the chart type doesn't make a lot of sense to me.

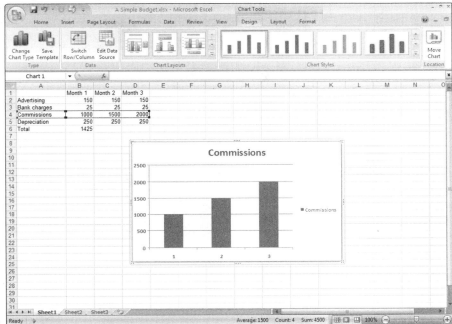

Figure 15-4:
A 2-D
column
chart.

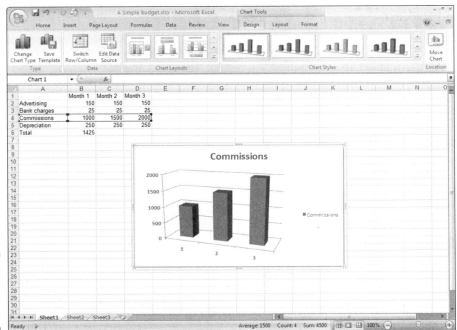

Figure 15-5:
A 3-D
column
chart.

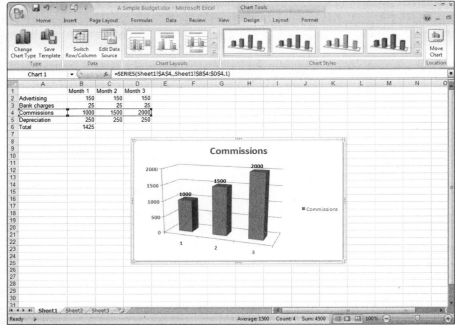

Figure 15-6:
Adding too
much detail
to 3-D
charts can
make them
hard to
read.

Never Use 3-D Pie Charts

Hey, here's a quick, one-question quiz: What do you get if you combine a pie chart and three-dimensionality? Answer: A mess!

Pie charts are really weak tools for visualizing, analyzing, and visually communicating information. Adding a third dimension to a chart really reduces its precision and usefulness. When you combine the weakness of a pie chart with the inaccuracy and imprecision of three-dimensionality, you get something that really isn't very good. And, in fact, what you often get is a chart that is very misleading.

Figure 15-7 shows the cardinal sin of graphically presenting information in a chart. The pie chart in Figure 15-7 uses three-dimensionality to exaggerate the size of the slice of the pie in the foreground. Newspapers and magazines often use this trick to exaggerate a story's theme.

You never want to make a pie chart 3-D.

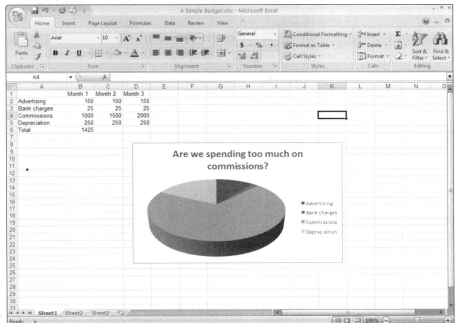

Be Aware of the Phantom Data Markers

One other dishonesty that you sometimes see in charts — okay, maybe sometimes it's not dishonesty but just sloppiness — is phantom data markers.

A *phantom data marker* is some extra visual element on a chart that exaggerates or misleads the chart viewer. Figure 15-8 shows a silly little column chart that I created to plot apple production in the state of Washington. Notice that the chart legend, which appears off to the right of the plot area, looks like another data marker. It's essentially a phantom data marker. And what this phantom data marker does is exaggerate the trend in apple production.

Use Logarithmic Scaling

I don't remember much about logarithms, although I think I studied them in both high school and college. Therefore, I can understand if you hear the word *logarithms* and find yourself feeling a little queasy. Nevertheless, logarithms and logarithmic scaling are tools that you want to use in your charts because they enable you to do something very powerful.

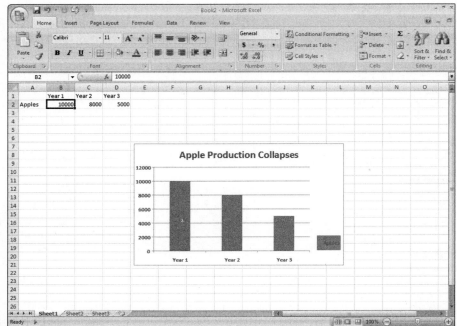

Figure 15-8:
Phantom
data
markers can
exaggerate
data.

With logarithmic scaling of your value axis, you can compare the relative change (not the absolute change) in data series values. For example, say that you want to compare the sales of a large company that's growing solidly but slowly (10 percent annually) with the sales of a smaller firm that's growing very quickly (50 percent annually). Because a typical line chart compares absolute data values, if you plot the sales for these two firms in the same line chart, you completely miss out on the fact that one firm is growing much more quickly than the other firm. Figure 15-9 shows a traditional simple line chart. This line chart doesn't use logarithmic scaling of the value axis.

Now, take a look at the line chart shown in Figure 15-10. This is the same information in the same chart type and subtype, but I changed the scaling of the value axis to use logarithmic scaling. With the logarithmic scaling, the growth rates are shown rather than the absolute values. And when you plot the growth rates, the much quicker growth rate of the small company becomes clear. In fact, you can actually extrapolate the growth rate of the two companies and guess how long it will take for the small company to catch up with the big company. (Just extend the lines.)

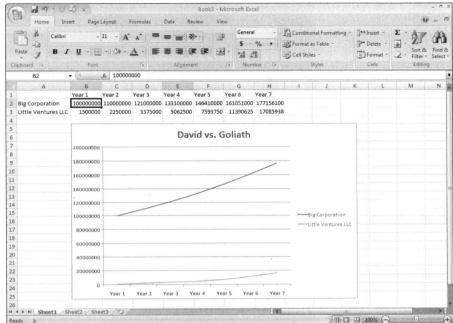

Figure 15-9:
A line chart that plots two competitors' sales but without logarithmic scaling.

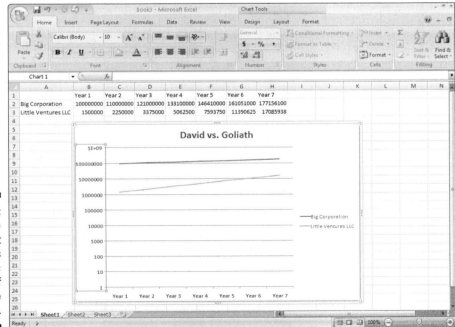

Figure 15-10:
A simple line chart that uses logarithmic scaling of the value axis.

To tell Excel that you want to use logarithmic scaling of the value access, follow these steps:

1. **Right-click the value (Y) axis and then choose the Format Axis command from the shortcut menu that appears.**

2. **When the Format Axis dialog box appears, select the Axis Options entry from the list box.**

3. **To tell Excel to use logarithmic scaling of the value (Y) axis, simply select the Logarithmic Scale check box and then click OK.**

   Excel re-scales the value axis of your chart to use logarithmic scaling. Note that initially Excel uses base 10 logarithmic scaling. But you can change the scaling by entering some other value into the Logarithmic Scale Base box.

Don't Forget to Experiment

All the tips in this chapter are, in some ways, sort of restrictive. They suggest that you do this or don't do that. These suggestions — which are tips that I've collected from writers and data analysts over the years — are really good guidelines to use. But you ought to experiment with your visual presentations of data. Sometimes by looking at data in some funky, wacky, visual way, you gain insights that you would otherwise miss.

There's no harm in, just for the fun of it, looking at some data set with a pie chart. (Even if you don't want to let anyone know you're doing this!) Just fool around with a data set to see what something looks like in an XY (Scatter) chart.

In other words, just get crazy once in a while.

Get Tufte

I want to leave you with one last thought about visually analyzing and visually presenting information. I recommend that you get and read one of Edward R. Tufte's books. Tufte has written seven books, and these three are favorites of mine: *The Visual Display of Quantitative Information*, 2nd Edition, *Visual Explanations: Images and Quantities, Evidence and Narrative*, and *Envisioning Information*.

These books aren't cheap; they cost between $40 and $50. But if you regularly use charts and graphs to analyze information or if you regularly present such information to others in your organization, reading one or more of these books will greatly benefit you.

By the way, Tufte's books are often hard to get. However, you can buy them from major online bookstores. You can also order Tufte's books directly from his Web site: www.edwardtufte.com. If you're befuddled about which of Tufte's books to order first, I recommend *The Visual Display of Quantitative Information*.

Part V
Appendix

By Rich Tennant

"No, that's not the icon for Excel, it's the icon for Excuse, the database of reasons why you haven't learned the other programs in Office."

In this part . . .

In this part is a glossary that you can refer to whenever you need to shed light on the meanings of some less-than-apparent statistics terms. Ever been baffled by binomial distributions? Puzzled by *p*-values? Wonder no more . . . .

Appendix

Glossary of Data Analysis and Excel Terms

· ·

3-D pie charts: Perhaps the very worst way to share the results of your data analysis — and often inexcusable.

absolute reference: A cell address used in a formula that Excel doesn't adjust if you copy the formula to some new location. To create an absolute cell reference, you precede the column letter and row number with a dollar sign ($).

Access: A database program developed and sold by Microsoft. Use Access to build and work with large, sophisticated, relational databases; you can easily export information from Access databases to Excel. Just choose the Access Microsoft Office menu's Export command.

arithmetic operators: The standard operators that you use in Excel formulas. To add numbers, use the addition (+) operator. To subtract numbers, use the subtraction (–) operator. To multiply numbers, use the multiplication (*) operator. To divide numbers, use the division (/) operator. You can also perform exponential operations by using the exponential operator (^). *See also operator precedence.*

ascending order: A sorting option that alphabetizes labels and arranges values in smallest-value-to-largest-value order. *See also chronological order; descending order.*

ASCII text file: A type of text file that in essence is just straight text and nothing else. *See also delimited text file; importing.*

AutoFilter: An Excel tool (available from the Data tab's Filter command) that helps you produce a new table that's a subset of your original table. For example, in the case of a grocery list table, you could use AutoFilter to create a subset that shows only those items that you'll purchase at a particular store, in specified quantities, or that exceed a certain price.

average: Typically, the arithmetic mean for a set of values. Excel supplies several averaging functions. *See also median; mode.*

binomial distributions: Used to calculate probabilities in situations in which you have a limited number of independent trials, or tests, which can either succeed or fail. Success or failure of any one trial is independent of other trials.

Boolean expressions: Also known as *logical expressions,* these expressions describe a comparison that you want to make. For example, to compare fields with the value 1,000,000, you use a Boolean expression. To construct a Boolean expression, you use a comparison operator and then a value used in the comparison.

calculated field: Used to insert a new row or column into a pivot table and then fill the new row or column with a formula.

calculated item: An amount shown in a pivot table that you create by calculating a formula. Frankly, adding a calculated item usually doesn't make any sense. But, hey, strange things happen all the time, right?

cells: In Excel, the intersections of rows and columns. A cell location is described using the column letter and row number. For example, the cell in the upper-left corner of the workbook is labeled *A1.*

chart data labels: Annotate data markers with pivot table information or list information.

chart legend: Identifies the data series that you plot in your chart.

chart titles: Text that you use to label the parts of a chart.

chart type: Includes column, bar, line, pie, XY, surface, and so on. In Excel, you can create 14 different types of charts.

Chi-square: Used to compare observed values with expected values, returning the level of significance, or probability (also called a p-value). That p-value lets you assess whether differences between the observed and expected values represent chance.

chronological order: A sorting option that arranges labels or values in chronological order such as Monday, Tuesday, Wednesday, and so on. ***See also*** *ascending order; descending order.*

comparison operator: A mathematical operator used in a Boolean expression. For example, the > comparison operator makes *greater than* comparisons. The = operator makes *equal to* comparisons. The <= operator makes *less than or equal to* comparisons. Cool, huh? ***See also*** *Boolean expressions.*

counting: Used for useful statistical functions for counting cells within a worksheet or list. Excel provides four counting functions: COUNT, COUNTA, COUNTBLANK, and COUNTIF. Excel also provides two useful functions for counting permutations and combinations: PERMUT and COMBIN.

cross-tabulation: An analysis technique that summarizes data in two or more ways. For example, if you run a business and summarize sales information both by customer and by product, that's a cross-tabulation because you tabulate the information in two ways. *See also pivot table.*

custom calculations: Used to add many semi-standard calculations to a pivot table. By using Custom Calculations, for example, you can calculate the difference between two pivot table cells, percentages, and percentage differences. *See also pivot table.*

Data Analysis: An Excel add-in with which you perform statistical analysis.

data category: Organizes the values in a data series. That sounds complicated; however, in many charts, identifying the data category is easy. In any chart (including a pivot chart) that shows how some value changes over time, the data category is *time. See also data series.*

data list: Another name for an Excel table.

data series: Oh geez, this is another one of those situations where somebody's taken a ten-cent idea and labeled it with a five-dollar word. Charts show data series. And a chart legend names the data series that a chart shows. For example, if you want to plot sales of coffee products, those coffee products are your data series. *See also data category.*

data validation: An Excel command with which you describe what information can be entered into a cell. The command also enables you to supply messages that give data input information and error messages to help users correct data entry errors.

database functions: A special set of functions for simple statistical analysis of information that you store in Excel tables.

delimited text file: A type of text file. Delimited text files use special characters, called *delimiters,* to separate fields of information in the report. For example, such files commonly use the Tab character to delimit. *See also ASCII text file; importing.*

descending order: A sorting order that arranges labels in reverse alphabetical order and values in largest-value-to-smallest-value order. *See also ascending order; chronological order.*

descriptive statistics: Describe the values in a set. For example, if you sum a set of values, that sum is a descriptive statistic. If you find the largest value or the smallest value in a set of numbers, that's also a descriptive statistic.

exponential smoothing: Calculates the moving average but weights the values included in the moving average calculations so that more recent values have a bigger effect. *See also moving average.*

exporting: In the context of databases, moving information to another application. If you tell your accounting system to export a list of vendors that Excel can later read, for example, you're exporting. Many business applications, by the way, do easily export data to Excel. *See also importing.*

F distributions: Compare the ratio in variances of samples drawn from different populations and draw a conclusion about whether the variances in the underlying populations resemble each other.

field: In a database, stores the same sort of information. In a database that stores people's names and addresses, for example, you'll probably find a Street Address field. In Excel, by the way, each column shows a particular sort of information and therefore represents a field.

field settings: Determine what Excel does with a field when it's cross-tabulated in the pivot table. *See also cross-tabulation; pivot table.*

formulas: Calculation instructions entered into worksheet cells. Essentially, this business about formulas going into workbook cells is the heart of Excel. Even if an Excel workbook did nothing else, it would still be an extremely valuable tool. In fact, the first spreadsheet programs did little more than calculate cell formulas. *See also text labels; value.*

function: A pre-built formula that you can use to more simply calculate some amount, such as an average or standard deviation.

function arguments: Needed in most functions; also called *inputs*. All database functions need arguments, which you include inside parentheses. If a function needs more than one argument, you separate arguments by using commas. *See also database functions.*

header row: A top row of field names in your table range selection that names the fields.

histogram: A chart that shows a frequency distribution.

importing: In the context of databases, grabbing information from some other application. Excel rather easily imports information from popular databases (such as Microsoft Access), other spreadsheets (such as Lotus 1-2-3), and from text files. *See also* exporting.

inferential statistics: Based on a very useful, intuitively obvious idea that if you look at a sample of values from a population and if the sample is representative and large enough, you can draw conclusions about the population based on characteristics of the sample.

kurtosis: A measure of the tails in a distribution of values. *See also* skewness.

list: Another name for *table*, a list is, well, a list. This definition sounds circular, I guess, but if you make a list (sorry) of the things that you want to buy at the grocery store, that's a list. Excel lists, or tables, usually store more information than just names of items. Usually, Excel tables also store values. In the case of a grocery list, the Excel table might include prices and quantities of the items that you're shopping for.

logarithmic scale: Used in a chart to view rates of change, rather than absolute changes, in your plotted data.

median: The middle value in a set of values. Half the values fall below the median, and half the values fall above the median. *See also* average; mode.

Microsoft Access: *See* Access.

Microsoft Query: *See* Query.

mode: The most common value in a set. *See also* average; median.

moving average: An average that's calculated by using only a specified set of values, such as an average based on just the last three values. *See also* exponential smoothing.

normal distribution: The infamous bell curve. Also known as a *Gaussian distribution*.

objective function: The formula that you want to optimize when performing optimization modeling. In the case of a profit formula, for example, you want to maximize a function. But some objective functions should be minimized. For example, if you create an objective function that describes the cost of some advertising program or the risk of some investment program, you may logically choose to minimize your costs or risks. *See also* optimization modeling.

observation: Suppose that you're constructing a data set that shows daily high temperatures in your neighborhood. When you go out and *observe* that the temperature some fine July afternoon is 87°, that measurement is your observation.

operator precedence: Standard rules that determine the order of arithmetic operations in a formula. For example, exponential operations are performed first. Multiplication and division operations are performed second. Addition and subtraction operations are performed third. To override these standard rules, use parentheses. *See also formulas.*

optimization modeling: A problem-solving technique in which you look for the optimum value of an objective function while explicitly recognizing constraints. *See also objective function.*

parameter: An input to a probability distribution function.

phantom data marker: Some extra visual element on a chart that exaggerates the chart message or misleads the chart viewer. Usually, phantom data markers are embellishments that someone has added (hopefully, not you!) that sort of resemble the chart's real data markers — especially to the eyes of casual chart viewers.

pivot chart: A cross-tabulation that appears in a chart. *See also cross-tabulation.*

pivot table: Perhaps the most powerful analytical tool that Excel provides. Use the PivotTable command to cross-tabulate data stored in Excel lists. *See also cross-tabulation.*

pivoting and **Re-pivoting:** The thing that gives the pivot table its name. You can continue cross-tabulating the data in the pivot table. You can pivot, and re-pivot, and re-pivot again. . . .

primary key: In sorting, the field first used to sort records. *See also secondary key; sort;* and if you're really interested, *tertiary key.*

probability distribution: A chart that plots probabilities. *See also normal distribution; uniform distribution.*

probability distribution function: An equation that describes the line of the probability distribution. *See also probability distribution.*

p-value: The level of significance, or probability.

Query: A program that comes with Excel. Use Query to extract information from a database and then place the results into an Excel workbook.

QuickBooks: The world's most popular small business accounting program — and one of the many business applications that easily, happily, and without complaint exports information to Excel. In QuickBooks, for example, you simply click a button cleverly labeled *Excel*.

range: In terms of Excel data analysis, refers to two different items. A range can be a reference to a rectangle of cells in a worksheet, or a range can show the difference between the largest and smallest values in the data set.

record: A collection of related fields in a table. In Excel, each record goes into a separate row.

refreshing pivot data: Updating the information shown in a pivot table or pivot chart to reflect changes in the underlying data. You can click the Refresh data tool provided by the PivotTable toolbar button to refresh.

regression analysis: Plotting pairs of independent and dependent variables in an XY chart and then finding a linear or exponential equation that best describes the plotted data.

relational database: Essentially, a collection of tables or lists. *See also* *table; list.*

relative reference: A cell reference used in a formula that Excel adjusts if you copy the formula to a new cell location. *See also* *absolute reference.*

scatter plot: An XY chart that visually compares pairs of values. A scatter plot is often a good first step when you want to perform regression analysis. *See also* *regression analysis.*

secondary key: In sorting, the second field used to sort records. The secondary key comes into play only when the primary keys of records have the same value. *See also* *primary key; sort.*

skewness: A measure of the symmetry of a distribution of values. *See also* *kurtosis.*

solve order: The order in which calculated item formulas should be solved. *See also* *calculated item.*

solver: An Excel add-in with which you perform optimization modeling. *See also* *optimization modeling.*

solver variables: The variables in an optimization modeling problem. *See optimization modeling.*

sort: To arrange list records in some particular order, such as alphabetically by last name. Excel includes easy-to-use tools for doing this, by the way.

standard deviation: Describes dispersion about the data set's mean. You can think of a standard deviation as an average deviation from the mean. *See also* average; variance.

table: In relational databases and also in Excel 2007, where information is stored. Tables are essentially spreadsheets, or lists, that store database information.

tertiary key: In sorting, the third field used to sort records. The tertiary key comes into play only when the primary and secondary keys of records have the same value. *See also* primary key; secondary key; sort.

text file: A file that's all text. Many programs export text files, by the way, because other programs (including Excel) often easily import text files.

text functions: Used to manipulate text strings in ways that enable you to easily rearrange and manipulate the data that you import into an Excel workbook. Typically, these babies are extremely useful tools for scrubbing or cleaning the data that you want to later analyze.

text labels: Includes letters and numbers that you enter into worksheet cells but that you don't want to use in calculations. For example, your name, a budget expense description, and a telephone number are all examples of text labels. None of these pieces of information get used in calculations.

time-series chart: Shows how values change over time. A chart that shows sales revenues over the last 5 years or profits over the last 12 months, for example, is a time-series chart.

Tufte, Edward: The author of a series of wonderful books about visually analyzing and visually presenting information. I recommend that you read at least one of Tufte's books.

t-value: Sort of like a poor-man's z-value. When you're working with small samples — fewer than 30 or 40 items — you can use what's called a *student t-value* to calculate probabilities rather than the usual z-value, which is what you work with in the case of normal distributions. Not coincidentally, Excel provides three T distribution functions. *See also* z-value.

uniform distribution: Having the same probability of occurrence in every event. One common probability distribution function is a uniform distribution.

value: Some bit of data that you enter into a workbook cell and may want to later use in a calculation. For example, the actual amount that you budget for some expense would always be a number or value. ***See also*** *formulas; text labels; workbook.*

variance: Describes dispersion about the data set's mean. The variance is the square of the standard deviation. Conversely, the standard deviation is the square root of the variance. ***See also*** *average; standard deviation.*

Web query: Grabbing data from a table that's stored in a Web page. Excel provides a very slick tool for doing this, by the way.

workbook: An Excel spreadsheet document or file. A spreadsheet comprises numbered rows and lettered columns. ***See also*** *cells.*

x-values: The independent values in a regression analysis.

y-values: The dependent values in a regression analysis.

z-value: In statistics, describes the distance between a value and the mean in terms of standard deviations. (How often does one get to include a legitimate Z entry in a glossary! Not often, but here I do.) ***See also*** *average; standard deviation.*

Index

• *B* •

• *R* •

Notes

Custom Auto Filter   pg 24
Advanced Filtering   pg 28
Importing Text Files   pg 37

Notes

Notes

Notes

SINESS, CAREERS & PERSONAL FINANCE

Fundraising FOR DUMMIES

0-7645-9847-3

Investing FOR DUMMIES

0-7645-2431-3

Also available:

Business Plans Kit For Dummies
0-7645-9794-9

Economics For Dummies
0-7645-5726-2

Grant Writing For Dummies
0-7645-8416-2

Home Buying For Dummies
0-7645-5331-3

Managing For Dummies
0-7645-1771-6

Marketing For Dummies
0-7645-5600-2

Personal Finance For Dummies
0-7645-2590-5*

Resumes For Dummies
0-7645-5471-9

Selling For Dummies
0-7645-5363-1

Six Sigma For Dummies
0-7645-6798-5

Small Business Kit For Dummies
0-7645-5984-2

Starting an eBay Business For Dummies
0-7645-6924-4

Your Dream Career For Dummies
0-7645-9795-7

OME & BUSINESS COMPUTER BASICS

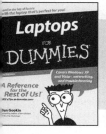

Laptops FOR DUMMIES

0-470-05432-8

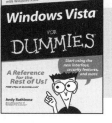

Windows Vista FOR DUMMIES

0-471-75421-8

Also available:

Cleaning Windows Vista For Dummies
0-471-78293-9

Excel 2007 For Dummies
0-470-03737-7

Mac OS X Tiger For Dummies
0-7645-7675-5

MacBook For Dummies
0-470-04859-X

Macs For Dummies
0-470-04849-2

Office 2007 For Dummies
0-470-00923-3

Outlook 2007 For Dummies
0-470-03830-6

PCs For Dummies
0-7645-8958-X

Salesforce.com For Dummies
0-470-04893-X

Upgrading & Fixing Laptops For Dummies
0-7645-8959-8

Word 2007 For Dummies
0-470-03658-3

Quicken 2007 For Dummies
0-470-04600-7

OD, HOME, GARDEN, HOBBIES, MUSIC & PETS

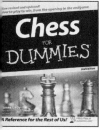

Chess FOR DUMMIES

0-7645-8404-9

Guitar FOR DUMMIES

0-7645-9904-6

Also available:

Candy Making For Dummies
0-7645-9734-5

Card Games For Dummies
0-7645-9910-0

Crocheting For Dummies
0-7645-4151-X

Dog Training For Dummies
0-7645-8418-9

Healthy Carb Cookbook For Dummies
0-7645-8476-6

Home Maintenance For Dummies
0-7645-5215-5

Horses For Dummies
0-7645-9797-3

Jewelry Making & Beading For Dummies
0-7645-2571-9

Orchids For Dummies
0-7645-6759-4

Puppies For Dummies
0-7645-5255-4

Rock Guitar For Dummies
0-7645-5356-9

Sewing For Dummies
0-7645-6847-7

Singing For Dummies
0-7645-2475-5

TERNET & DIGITAL MEDIA

eBay FOR DUMMIES

0-470-04529-9

iPod & iTunes FOR DUMMIES

0-470-04894-8

Also available:

Blogging For Dummies
0-471-77084-1

Digital Photography For Dummies
0-7645-9802-3

Digital Photography All-in-One Desk Reference For Dummies
0-470-03743-1

Digital SLR Cameras and Photography For Dummies
0-7645-9803-1

eBay Business All-in-One Desk Reference For Dummies
0-7645-8438-3

HDTV For Dummies
0-470-09673-X

Home Entertainment PCs For Dummies
0-470-05523-5

MySpace For Dummies
0-470-09529-6

Search Engine Optimization For Dummies
0-471-97998-8

Skype For Dummies
0-470-04891-3

The Internet For Dummies
0-7645-8996-2

Wiring Your Digital Home For Dummies
0-471-91830-X

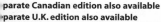

SPORTS, FITNESS, PARENTING, RELIGION & SPIRITUALITY

0-471-76871-5

0-7645-7841-3

Also available:
- Catholicism For Dummies
  0-7645-5391-7
- Exercise Balls For Dummies
  0-7645-5623-1
- Fitness For Dummies
  0-7645-7851-0
- Football For Dummies
  0-7645-3936-1
- Judaism For Dummies
  0-7645-5299-6
- Potty Training For Dummies
  0-7645-5417-4
- Buddhism For Dummies
  0-7645-5359-3

- Pregnancy For Dummies
  0-7645-4483-7 †
- Ten Minute Tone-Ups For Dummies
  0-7645-7207-5
- NASCAR For Dummies
  0-7645-7681-X
- Religion For Dummies
  0-7645-5264-3
- Soccer For Dummies
  0-7645-5229-5
- Women in the Bible For Dummies
  0-7645-8475-8

TRAVEL

0-7645-7749-2

0-7645-6945-7

Also available:
- Alaska For Dummies
  0-7645-7746-8
- Cruise Vacations For Dummies
  0-7645-6941-4
- England For Dummies
  0-7645-4276-1
- Europe For Dummies
  0-7645-7529-5
- Germany For Dummies
  0-7645-7823-5
- Hawaii For Dummies
  0-7645-7402-7

- Italy For Dummies
  0-7645-7386-1
- Las Vegas For Dummies
  0-7645-7382-9
- London For Dummies
  0-7645-4277-X
- Paris For Dummies
  0-7645-7630-5
- RV Vacations For Dummies
  0-7645-4442-X
- Walt Disney World & Orlando
  For Dummies
  0-7645-9660-8

GRAPHICS, DESIGN & WEB DEVELOPMENT

0-7645-8815-X

0-7645-9571-7

Also available:
- 3D Game Animation For Dummies
  0-7645-8789-7
- AutoCAD 2006 For Dummies
  0-7645-8925-3
- Building a Web Site For Dummies
  0-7645-7144-3
- Creating Web Pages For Dummies
  0-470-08030-2
- Creating Web Pages All-in-One Desk
  Reference For Dummies
  0-7645-4345-8
- Dreamweaver 8 For Dummies
  0-7645-9649-7

- InDesign CS2 For Dummies
  0-7645-9572-5
- Macromedia Flash 8 For Dummies
  0-7645-9691-8
- Photoshop CS2 and Digital
  Photography For Dummies
  0-7645-9580-6
- Photoshop Elements 4 For Dummies
  0-471-77483-9
- Syndicating Web Sites with RSS Feeds
  For Dummies
  0-7645-8848-6
- Yahoo! SiteBuilder For Dummies
  0-7645-9800-7

NETWORKING, SECURITY, PROGRAMMING & DATABASES

0-7645-7728-X

0-471-74940-0

Also available:
- Access 2007 For Dummies
  0-470-04612-0
- ASP.NET 2 For Dummies
  0-7645-7907-X
- C# 2005 For Dummies
  0-7645-9704-3
- Hacking For Dummies
  0-470-05235-X
- Hacking Wireless Networks
  For Dummies
  0-7645-9730-2
- Java For Dummies
  0-470-08716-1

- Microsoft SQL Server 2005 For Dummies
  0-7645-7755-7
- Networking All-in-One Desk Reference
  For Dummies
  0-7645-9939-9
- Preventing Identity Theft For Dummies
  0-7645-7336-5
- Telecom For Dummies
  0-471-77085-X
- Visual Studio 2005 All-in-One Desk
  Reference For Dummies
  0-7645-9775-2
- XML For Dummies
  0-7645-8845-1

HEALTH & SELF-HELP

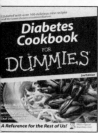

0-7645-8450-2

0-7645-4149-8

Also available:

- Bipolar Disorder For Dummies
  0-7645-8451-0
- Chemotherapy and Radiation
  For Dummies
  0-7645-7832-4
- Controlling Cholesterol For Dummies
  0-7645-5440-9
- Diabetes For Dummies
  0-7645-6820-5* †
- Divorce For Dummies
  0-7645-8417-0 †

- Fibromyalgia For Dummies
  0-7645-5441-7
- Low-Calorie Dieting For Dummies
  0-7645-9905-4
- Meditation For Dummies
  0-471-77774-9
- Osteoporosis For Dummies
  0-7645-7621-6
- Overcoming Anxiety For Dummies
  0-7645-5447-6
- Reiki For Dummies
  0-7645-9907-0
- Stress Management For Dummies
  0-7645-5144-2

EDUCATION, HISTORY, REFERENCE & TEST PREPARATION

0-7645-8381-6

0-7645-9554-7

Also available:

- The ACT For Dummies
  0-7645-9652-7
- Algebra For Dummies
  0-7645-5325-9
- Algebra Workbook For Dummies
  0-7645-8467-7
- Astronomy For Dummies
  0-7645-8465-0
- Calculus For Dummies
  0-7645-2498-4
- Chemistry For Dummies
  0-7645-5430-1
- Forensics For Dummies
  0-7645-5580-4

- Freemasons For Dummies
  0-7645-9796-5
- French For Dummies
  0-7645-5193-0
- Geometry For Dummies
  0-7645-5324-0
- Organic Chemistry I For Dummies
  0-7645-6902-3
- The SAT I For Dummies
  0-7645-7193-1
- Spanish For Dummies
  0-7645-5194-9
- Statistics For Dummies
  0-7645-5423-9

Get smart @ dummies.com®

- **Find a full list of Dummies titles**
- **Look into loads of FREE on-site articles**
- **Sign up for FREE eTips e-mailed to you weekly**
- **See what other products carry the Dummies name**
- **Shop directly from the Dummies bookstore**
- **Enter to win new prizes every month!**